UNCRITICAL THEORY
Postmodernism, Intellectuals and the Gulf War

Christopher Norris

UNCRITICAL THEORY

Postmodernism, Intellectuals and the Gulf War

Lawrence & Wishart

LONDON

Lawrence & Wishart Limited
144a Old South Lambeth Road
London SW8 1XX

First published 1992 by Lawrence and Wishart

Photoset in North Wales by
Derek Doyle & Associates, Mold, Clwyd
Printed and bound in Great Britain by
Dotesios, Trowbridge

Only the absolute lie now has any freedom to speak the truth. The confounding of truth and lies, making it almost impossible to maintain the distinction, and a labour of Sisyphus to hold on to the simplest piece of knowledge, marks the victory in the field of logical organization of the principle that lies crushed on that of battle. The conversion of all questions of truth into questions of power, a process that truth itself cannot escape if it is not to be annihilated by power, not only suppresses truth as in earlier despotic regimes, but has attacked the very heart of the distinction between true and false, which the hirelings of logic were in any case diligently working to abolish. So Hitler, of whom no-one can say whether he died or escaped, survives.

Among today's adept practitioners, the lie has long since lost its honest function of misrepresenting reality. Nobody believes anybody, everyone is in the know. Lies are told only to convey to someone that one has no need either of him or his good opinion. The lie, once a liberal means of communication, has today become one of the techniques of insolence enabling each individual to spread around him the glacial atmosphere in whose shelter he can thrive.

Theodor W. Adorno, *Minima Moralia:*
Reflections from a damaged life

CONTENTS

ACKNOWLEDGMENTS

This book was written during a period (January to June 1991) when world events and the political climate in this country were hardly conducive to sustained intellectual effort. I am therefore much indebted to various individuals – in Cardiff and elsewhere – for helping to focus the relevant issues and providing me with occasions on which to elaborate its argument, revise points of detail, and respond to some highly constructive criticism. One such opportunity was a splendid Lancaster conference on Postmodernism and Politics, organized by Alison Easson and Tony Pinkney; another the Critical Realism event at Sussex University, to which I received a timely invitation from Roy Bhaskar and Andrew Sayers. There were also lectures and seminars in Manchester (thanks to Antony Easthope), in Oxford, Treforest, Lisbon, Lund, Gothenberg, Stockholm, Uppsala and Oslo, each of which offered some welcome stimulus at various stages of the work-in-progress. Most of all I am grateful to my friends, students and colleagues in Cardiff for their help in locating relevant source material, their willingness to read and criticize draft versions, and – more than anything – their comradeship in bad times. Let me thank in particular John Abraham, Taieb Belghazi, Andrew Belsey, Mercedes Bengoechea, Carol Bretman, Clive Cazeaux, Ray Davies, Roy Evans, Terry Hawkes, Bernard Jones, Kathy Kerr, Wendy Lewis, Nigel Mapp, Lyn Meredith, Kevin Mills, Scott Newton, Lynne Reynolds, David Roden, Peter Sedgwick, David Skilton, Beattie Smith, Shiva Srinavasan, and Zouher Zoughbi. I am especially indebted to Kathy for numerous helpful ideas and improvements of detail; also to Sally Davison of Lawrence and Wishart who edited the typescript with exemplary thoroughness and tact. The Red Choir (Côr Cochion) Cardiff was a constant source of inspiration and a lesson in the politics of cultural resistance that leaves most theorizing far behind. As always I received great support (and forgiveness) from Alison, Clare and Jenny, to whom this book is offered as recompense of kinds.

August 1991

NOTE

Parts of this book will have appeared in modified form in the journals *New Formations*, *Works and Days*, *Southern Review*, *Southern Humanities Review* and *Philosophy and Social Criticism*. I am grateful to the editors and publishers for permission to reprint this material.

1
BAUDRILLARD AND THE WAR
THAT NEVER HAPPENED

THE REALITY GULF

How far wrong can a thinker go and still lay claim to serious attention? One useful test-case is Jean Baudrillard, a cult figure on the current 'postmodernist' scene, and purveyor of some of the silliest ideas yet to gain a hearing among disciples of French intellectual fashion.

Just a couple of days before war broke out in the Gulf, one could find Baudrillard regaling readers of *The Guardian* newspaper with an article which declared that this war would never happen, existing as it did only as a figment of mass-media simulation, war-games rhetoric or imaginary scenarios which exceeded all the limits of real-world, factual possibility.[1] Deterrence had 'worked' for the past forty years in the sense that war had become strictly unthinkable except as a rhetorical phenomenon, an exchange of ever-escalating threats and counter-threats whose 'exorbitant' character was enough to guarantee that no such event would ever take place. What remained was a kind of endless charade, a phoney war in which the stakes had to do with the management of so-called 'public opinion', itself nothing more than a reflex response to the images, the rhetoric and PR machinery which create the illusion of consensus support by supplying all the right answers and attitudes in advance. There would be no war, Baudrillard solemnly opined, because talk of war had now become a substitute for the event, the occurrence or moment of outbreak which the term 'war' had once signified. Quite simply, we had lost all sense of the difference – or the point of transition – between a war of words, a mass-media simulation conducted (supposedly) by way of preparing us for 'the real thing', and the thing itself which would likewise 'take place' only in the minds and imaginations of a captive TV audience, bombarded with the same sorts of video-game imagery that had filled their screens during the build-up campaign. After all, wouldn't it be the case – if and when 'war' occurred – that *everyone* would have to rely on a second-hand or simulated knowledge of events, from prime-time viewers to presidents, politicians, 'front-line' generals, Pentagon strategists and so forth? In this situation – so Baudrillard argues – we might as well drop all the self-deluding talk of 'real' *versus* 'phoney' wars, and acknowledge that reality is no longer what it used to be, the (real or imaginary) truth behind appearances.

So Baudrillard is not to be caught out in the event – the unlikely event, as he still sees it – that 'the Gulf War' should actually materialize to the point where bellicose words give way to belligerent deeds. For even then there will be nobody in a position to know that what they are seeing, reading or hearing is not some fictive 'simulacrum' of the real, conjured up by the ubiquitous propaganda-machine or the various techniques of media disinformation. Indeed, it is culpably naive to carry on thinking in those terms, as if there remained any operative difference between truth and falsehood, veridical knowledge and its semblance as created by the feedback mechanisms of media reporting, opinion-polls, 'parliamentary debate' and so forth. For those effects are just as 'real' – just as capable of influencing the day-to-day course of events – as anything that might (for all that we can know) have actually happened, or be happening now, beyond reach of the saturation TV coverage. In short, there is no point lamenting the lack of factual, objective or unbiassed information when we simply don't possess any yardstick – any grounds for comparison – that could enable even the most expert observer to achieve such a critical perspective. 'Our strategic site is the television screen, from which we are daily bombarded.'

And this applies not only to the viewing millions but also to those figures of authority and power whom we might suspect – wrongly, it seems – of being 'in the know' on matters concealed from the mass of bewildered citizens. For their situation is pretty much the same as ours, plugged in as they are – like everyone else – to a system whose workings they are thought to 'control', in some notional executive sense, but which in fact feeds them with a constant stream of simulated images and pre-packaged news-bites. After all, don't we have it from 'reliable' sources like CNN that even the apparent protagonists in this affair – George Bush, John Major, the Pentagon strategists and so forth – are picking up some crucial battleground 'facts' from those same television channels, subject (of course) to the need for security and on-the-spot censorship of everything reaching their screens? But however unreal their perception of events it is still plainly the case that decisions arrived at or words uttered on the strength of such impressions will henceforth have a genuine impact not only on 'public opinion' but also on the conduct of 'real-world' war-fighting strategy. All of which proves – if proof were needed – that we have entered a phase of terminal indifference where the passage to war is a non-event, something that either won't happen – as Baudrillard inclines to believe – or whose happening will in any case not be noticed, since we have long since lost any means of distinguishing 'reality' from its simulated counterpart. 'First safe sex, now safe war. A Gulf War would not even register two or three on the Richter Scale this way. It is unreal, war without the symptoms of war, a form of war which means never needing to face up to war, which enables war to be "perceived" from deep within a darkroom.'

In short, the whole campaign is a media benefit, an extension of video war games technology by alternative means, a 'hyperreal' scenario (Baudrillard's phrase) where truth is defined solely in performative or rhetorical terms, i.e. as what presently counts as such according to the latest feedback consensus. Nor can we complain, in the time-honoured fashion, that 'truth is always the first casualty of war', and that the government is withholding information – or exploiting mendacious propaganda techniques – so as to marginalize dissident voices and prevent any properly informed public debate. For this would just show that we hadn't caught up with the 'postmodern' rules of the game, the fact that nowadays things have moved on to the point where there is no last ground of appeal to those old, self-deluding 'enlightenment' values that once possessed authority (or the semblance thereof), at least in some quarters. Anyone who continues to invoke such standards is plainly in the grip of a nostalgic desire for some ultimate truth-telling discourse – whether Platonist, Kantian, Marxist or whatever – that would offer a delusory refuge from the knowledge that we are nowadays utterly without resources in the matter of distinguishing truth from falsehood. Least of all will it be possible to say at any stage – on the 'evidence' currently to hand – that war in the Gulf has actually started, as opposed to its various fictive enactments, imaginary scenarios, mass-media representations and so forth. For any such claim would still be banking on a realist ontology that clung to some variant of the truth/falsehood or fact/fiction dichotomy. And in Baudrillard's view it would therefore be played off the field by these omnipresent signs of a postmodern 'hyperreality' whose effect is to cancel or level the distinction between truth and what is currently – for all practical purposes – 'good in the way of belief'.

So perhaps it would be missing the point to observe that Baudrillard's predictions were flat wrong, that the Gulf War *did* break out as a matter of all too definite fact, and that his arguments should thus be viewed as decidedly suspect. For he could still bounce back by asking what could possibly count as *evidence* for these or similar claims, given that our 'knowledge' of the events in question is a pseudo-knowledge utterly dependent on the various forms of superinduced media illusion. At any rate this seems to be his fall-back line against the obvious rejoinder in light of subsequent events. Moreover, he offers a brief account of the stages through which we have rapidly passed on the way to this current 'reality gulf', this condition of existing in a permanent hiatus, a twilight zone between war-game illusions and the unthinkable event itself. 'We dreamed of a pure war', Baudrillard writes, 'a strategic orbital war purged of local and political details.' Such was the stage of transition from one lunatic scenario ('deterrence' or 'Mutually Assured Destruction') to the yet more extravagant surrealist fantasy of Reagan's Star Wars initiative. But we have now lived through and beyond that stage, so Baudrillard thinks, into a kind of steady-state terminal exhaustion, a mood of collective indifference or apathy where 'war' is just a word, a floating signifier, devoid of any referential bearing or real-world operative force. 'We ought to have been on our guard', he writes, 'because of the disappearance of the declaration of war. There can be no real war without a declaration – it is the moment of passing from the word to the deed.' And in the absence of any such overt declaration – so his argument runs – we are simply unable to know for sure whether war has in fact broken out, or whether (more likely) we are witnessing the continued simulation of a war-games charade whose 'reality' consists solely in its power to conjure up the requisite kinds of mass-media response.

To those familiar with his previous writings this argument will perhaps have come as no surprise.[2] For it is Baudrillard's contention that we now inhabit a realm of purely fictive or illusory appearances; that truth has gone the way of enlightened reason and suchlike obsolete ideas; that 'reality' is nowadays defined through and through by the play of multiplied 'simulacra' or reality-effects; that there is no point criticizing 'false' appearances (whether on epistemological or socio-political grounds) since those appearances are all that we have, like it or not; and that henceforth we had better make peace with this so-called 'postmodern condition', rather than cling to an outworn paradigm whose truth-claims no longer possess the least degree of operative (i.e. suasive or rhetorical) force. During a long period – more than two millenia – the idea prevailed among philosophers, moralists, social theorists and others that truth could indeed be arrived at through an effort of disciplined critical thought, a process that would finally enable the thinker to distinguish veridical propositions (or authentic values) from the various kinds of illusion, false consciousness, ideological misrecognition and so forth. From Plato to Kant, Hegel, Marx and beyond this conviction held firm despite all the manifold paradigm shifts that have characterized the history of Western thought. But it has now become obsolete, Baudrillard thinks, in so far as we have lost all sense of the difference – the ontological or epistemological difference – between truth and the various true-seeming images, analogues and fantasy-substitutes which currently claim that title. So the Gulf War figures as one more example in Baudrillard's extensive and varied catalogue of postmodern 'hyperreality'. It is a conflict waged – for all that we can know – entirely at this level of strategic simulation, a mode of vicarious spectator-involvement that extends all the way from fictive war-games to saturation coverage of the 'real-world' event, and which thus leaves us perfectly incapable of distinguishing the one from the other.

GETTING DERRIDA WRONG

That this is all sheer nonsense – a postmodern update on well-worn sophistical themes – should be obvious to anyone not wholly given over to the vagaries of current intellectual fashion. I have written at length elsewhere about Baudrillard's philosophical muddles, so this is not the place for a detailed explanation of just what is wrong with his arguments.[3] But I had better repeat the basic points over again if we are to understand first why the Gulf War piece should have appeared at such a time and given rise to a good deal of earnest debate, and second how it has come about that Baudrillard – and the whole postmodern tendency for which he speaks – could ever have achieved such prominence on the present-day cultural scene. For there is, to say the least, something deeply disturbing in the fact that The Guardian should have picked up his article as somehow representative of 'advanced' opinion among (presumably) a significant proportion of its readership with an interest in such matters. Besides, there is plenty of evidence elsewhere – for instance, in the pages of *Marxism Today, New Left Review* and other prestigious journals – that Baudrillard's ideas have attained wide currency and are taken seriously (if not endorsed) by a good many well-placed theorists and commentators. In short, he is undoubtedly a thinker to be reckoned with, even if – as I shall argue – his present high standing and influence are merely the most visible symptoms of a widespread cultural malaise for which 'postmodernism' is a useful diagnostic term.

The main confusion in Baudrillard's thought is his habit of equating what is currently, contingently 'good in the way of belief' with the limits of what can possibly be known from a critical or truth-seeking standpoint. Of course this goes along with the wider fashion for pragmatist, anti-foundationalist or consensus-based theories of knowledge, theories which take it pretty much for granted that 'truth' in any given situation can only be a matter of the values and beliefs that happen to prevail among members of some existing 'interpretive community'. Such ideas have enjoyed a considerable vogue among post-analytical philosophers like Richard Rorty, literary critics of a kindred persuasion like Stanley Fish, and others who seek to cut philosophy (or 'theory') down to size by arguing that its truth-claims are wholly redundant, that its concepts and categories are so many sublimated metaphors or items of surplus metaphysical baggage, and that therefore we might as well junk this whole tradition of misguided philosophical endeavour, together with its various latter-day offshoots in sociology, jurisprudence, literary criticism, and the 'human sciences' at large.[4] Then again, post-structuralism has promoted the idea that 'reality' is a purely discursive phenomenon, a product of the various codes, conventions, language games or signifying systems which provide the only means of interpreting experience from some given socio-cultural perspective.[5] This anticognitivist outlook has been further reinforced by Foucault's Nietzschean 'genealogies' of power/knowledge, by the New Historicism with its constant talk of history as a force-field of contending ideological discourses, and also by a prevalent misreading of Derrida's work which takes him to be arguing – in solipsist fashion – that there is, quite simply, 'nothing outside the text'.[6] Put all these fashionable doctrines together (along with the so-called 'linguistic turn' across various related disciplines) and you begin to understand how Baudrillard has been able to swing such a sizable readership behind him in advancing a range of extravagant propositions which would otherwise merit nothing more than a footnote in some future anatomy of the nonsense of the times.

However, the fact remains that his arguments *are* taken seriously, to the point where Baudrillard can deliver his ludicrous theses on the Gulf War without fear of subsequent exposure as a charlatan or of finding those theses resoundingly disconfirmed by the course of real-world events. Now it may well be said – and with some justification – that Baudrillard is by no means a 'representative' figure; that he pushes the argument to lengths far beyond what others would deem acceptable; and that therefore his absurdities shouldn't be treated as a standing indictment of the whole enterprise. Nor would I wish to deny this point, having spent much time over the past few years in an effort to disentangle the strands of broadly post-structuralist thinking, and to show how (for instance) Derridean deconstruction sustains the impulse of enlightenment critique even while subjecting that tradition to a radical re-assessment of its grounding concepts and categories.[7] Any adequate account of these differences would need to focus on ethical as well as epistemological issues, since in both respects Derrida has been at some pains to dissociate his project from the kind of irrationalist or nihilist outlook which takes it for granted – in Baudrillard's manner – that truth and reason are obsolete values, overtaken by the advent of postmodern 'hyperreality'.

Thus one could cite many passages from Derrida's work where he asserts that deconstruction is *not*, as his opponents would have it, a discourse with no further use for criteria of reference, validity, or truth; that it squarely repudiates the 'anything goes' school of postmodern hermeneutic thought; and that to deconstruct naive or commonsense ideas of how language hooks up with reality is not to suggest that it should henceforth be seen as a realm of open-ended textual 'freeplay' or floating signifiers devoid of referential content.[8] In ethical terms likewise, it is a gross misunderstanding to suppose that deconstruction ignores or suspends the question of interpretive responsibility, the requirement that texts should be read – or utterances construed – with a due respect for those other-regarding maxims (of good faith, fidelity, attentiveness to detail etc) which prevent it from becoming just a super-subtle game, a licence for all kinds of readerly extravagance. On the contrary: this attitude of 'recognition and respect' is described by Derrida in *Of Grammatology* as an 'indispensable guardrail', a necessary starting-point for any interpretation that would not 'risk developing in any direction at all and authorize itself to say almost anything'.[9] And if he then goes on to complicate this argument by claiming that the appeal to authorial intention 'has always only *protected*, it has never *opened* a reading', we should still be wrong to interpret these words as surreptitiously retracting the original point. For it is among the greatest virtues of Derrida's work – and again I must refer readers to what I have written on this topic elsewhere – that it raises issues of ethical accountability (along with epistemological questions) which are rendered invisible by the straightforward appeal to reference, intentions, textual authority, right reading, authorial warrant and so forth.[10] What hostile commentators regularly fail to grasp is the fact that Derrida conserves these standards – maintains them, in his own carefully chosen words, as an 'indispensable guardrail' – even while showing that they cannot (or should not) set absolute limits on the exercise of critical thought.

So there is clearly no question of Derrida's falling into that facile strain of postmodernist rhetoric that cheerfully pronounces an end to the regime of reality, truth, and enlightenment critique. The point is made with increasing emphasis in his recent responses to critics like Habermas and Searle, assuming as they do – on the basis of a minimal acquaintance with his work – that deconstruction is nothing more than a textualist variant on some well-worn sophistical themes out of school.[11] It seems to me that Derrida carries the argument by sheer force of reasoning and meticulous attention to the blind-spots in his opponents' discourse, as well as through his quite extraordinary skill in turning their charges back against themselves in a *tour de force* of sustained *tu quoque* polemics. At any rate it shouldn't any longer be possible for opponents – or, for that matter, ill-informed disciples – to treat deconstruction as one more offshoot of the current postmodernist or counter-enlightenment trend. All the same one has to recognize that this is the way deconstruction has been perceived by many who lack the time or interest to examine the relevant texts at first hand, or to read them with anything like an adequate sense of their complex philosophical prehistory, their implicit axiomatics, specialized modes of argument, etc. And a further source of misunderstanding is the fact that these texts have been taken up with most enthusiasm by the members of a different 'interpretive community' – US and British literary theorists – who approach them with a quite different set of motivating interests and priorities.

This is not – or not simply – a large-scale instance of the usual distorting mechanism, the kind of collective misreading or *deformation professionel* that occurs when some specific project or activity of thought is translated into the language of another discipline with its own purposes in view. Indeed, Derrida has made a point of denying that 'his' practice of deconstruction should in any way stand as a model or paradigm, or again, that other versions of that same nominal enterprise – as for instance in US literary theory or the current fashion for 'deconstructive theology' – should therefore be seen as somehow deviant, parasitic or based on a misappropriation of his texts. But this doesn't prevent him from objecting (very rightly) when opponents like Searle and Habermas resort to the litany of pseudo-deconstructionist *idées recues* rather than addressing his arguments at the level of informed philosophical debate. And they are able to do so mainly on account of the widespread belief – promulgated not only by literary critics but also by 'post-analytical' philosophers like Richard Rorty – that deconstruction is of interest *precisely in so far as* it breaks with those old delusory values of truth, reason, and enlightened critique.[12] Thus Searle and Rorty are pretty much agreed in their reading of Derrida as a latter-day sophist, a skilled rhetorician whose only real talent is for scoring points off the mainstream tradition of serious, constructive or problem-solving thought. The difference between them is simply that Searle thinks this a perverse and wrongheaded attitude, while Rorty – in line with his pragmatist beliefs – considers it a thoroughly welcome development, a sign of philosophy's having at last given up its grandiose pretensions and assumed a more modest participant role in the 'cultural conversation of mankind'.

I think it is unfortunate – all the more so in light of Baudrillard's latest pronouncements – that Derrida has not come out firmly against this postmodernist takeover bid, this attempt to annex deconstruction on behalf of a thoroughgoing relativist creed. For the effect of such thinking, especially when joined to the current ascendance of literary theory as a paradigm 'discourse' for other areas of study, is to promote the idea that 'reality' is constructed entirely in and through language or the structures of this or that localized signifying practice; that there is no possible access to truth or matters of historical record except by way of those same discursive representations; and therefore – as Baudrillard triumphantly concludes – that we inhabit a realm of unanchored free-floating language-games (or modes of persuasive utterance) where rhetoric quite simply goes all the way down, and where nothing could count as an argument against what the media or the government information-machine would presently have us believe.

The main problem here is that the reasons for *not* going along with this view of deconstruction are reasons that involve not only a detailed knowledge of Derrida's work but also a grasp of some fairly technical issues in the province of epistemology, philosophy of language, truth-conditional semantics etc; issues which figure hardly at all among the interests of most students of literature or, indeed, professional literary theorists. Hence the extraordinary ease with which Derrida's texts have been assimilated to a postmodern-pragmatist trend whose slogans would collapse into manifest nonsense if subjected to the kind of analytical scrutiny that he regularly brings to bear upon the writings of philosophers from Plato to Kant, Hegel, Husserl and Austin. A representative sampling of these slogans – apart from those already mentioned – would include the following choice specimens: that all reading is misreading, all interpretation misinterpretation, etc; that 'theory' is a pointless and misguided endeavour, since it cannot make the least difference to our in-place habits of thought and belief; that concepts are merely sublimated metaphors, rhetorical figures whose bringing-to-light is enough to discredit the entire enterprise of Western 'logocentric' reason; and finally – the pay-off for literary theorists – that, given all this, we had better play by the current (postmodern) rules of the game, since reality and truth have now been 'deconstructed' to the point where every discipline has to acknowledge its own inescapably textual predicament. One could take these propositions one by one and demonstrate their falsity – or their utter lack of argumentative scruple and rigour – when set against the relevant passages in Derrida's work.[13] But again, this would require the kind of critical reading, allied to a knowledge of developments outside the charmed circle of post-structuralist debate, which literary theorists are rarely willing to provide. A situation has thus arisen in which a thinker like Baudrillard – along with other figures on the postmodern scene – can reckon on gaining a large and receptive readership for arguments whose blatant illogicality would leap off the page were it not for this lamentable down-turn in the standards of informed intellectual exchange.

Worst of all is the placid assumption, pretty much *de rigueur* among many 'advanced' thinkers in the present-day human sciences, that because every text can be shown to involve some kind of narrative or story-telling interest, *therefore* we can be in no position to distinguish factual, historical or documentary writings on the one hand from fictive, imaginary or simulated episodes on the other. Baudrillard is just the most extreme instance of a tendency that is also manifest in post-structuralist, neo-pragmatist, and New Historicist thinking, as well as in Foucault's Nietzschean genealogies of power-knowledge and Hayden White's treatment of historical discourse under the rubric of a generalized tropology – or study of the modes of narrative emplotment – indifferent to issues of factual or veridical warrant.[14] What unites these thinkers across otherwise considerable differences of view is the idea that every discipline should henceforth be instructed in the modes of rhetorical or textual exegesis – along with the rejection of 'naive' realist ontologies – that have characterized *avant-garde* literary theory over the past three decades.

The result, as Tony Bennett remarks, is to redefine 'history' in textualist terms as a realm of purely discursive operations, a notional referent to which we have access only through a process of perpetual transcoding or narrative reinvention. 'Historical in principle and in the abstract', Bennett writes,

> post-structuralism has had relatively little impact on the terms in which historical debates are conducted. Nor is it likely to do so: mainly because, at root, its conception of history is a literary one. Transferring the properties of the literary text to the past – understood, in this light, as an unfathomable text, unreadable as such yet also infinitely rewritable – post-structuralism is unable to offer any positive knowledge of the past that is capable of surfacing and having effects within the disciplined procedures of historical scholarship. Instead, history becomes an occasion for extending the sphere of application of literary techniques of reading as the past, redefined as a literary object, is constituted as the site for an unconstrained, diachronized word-play.[15]

I should want to take issue with this admirably clear-headed passage only as concerns Bennett's claim that post-structuralism has had 'little impact' on the currency of recent historical debate. For in fact there are signs – as I have suggested elsewhere – that such arguments have found a receptive audience among the emergent school of right-wing revisionist historians, those for whom it clearly comes as good news that past events can only be interpreted according to present-day consensus values, or ideas of what currently and contingently counts as 'good in the way of belief'.[16]

TEXTUALITY RULES

I hope that many readers with an interest in 'theory' will have shared my reaction to Baudrillard's *Guardian* piece: that it amounted to a grand exposure of postmodernist thinking from the inside. Up to then it had been possible to regard such ideas as a depressing but fairly harmless symptom of the way that theory was liable to go when exploited by writers with a flair for publicity or the knack of avoiding peer-group review. After all, it is no great cause for concern – at least outside the specialized enclaves of cultural criticism – when these notions are applied (as in much of Baudrillard's previous writing) to a range of trivial phenomena like Disneyland, TV commercials, soap-operas, phone-in chatshows and so forth, items whose manifest 'hyperreality' indeed calls out for such debunking treatment. In fact it is only fair to say that, at his best, Baudrillard is a sharp-eyed diagnostician with a keen sense for the absurdity of these and kindred signs of the times. But his own arguments take on a similar absurdity when he pushes beyond this level of diagnostic commentary to claim that we have arrived at a stage of terminal indifference with regard to issues of truth and falsehood; that ontological distinctions no longer hold up in an epoch of all-pervasive media 'simulation'; and that we might as well abandon talk of matters such as 'truth' and 'reality' and adapt to living in a postmodern world of proliferating language-games, signs without referents, and illusions that we could never recognise as such. In which case clearly an 'event' like the Gulf War must be seen as a kind of mass-induced media fantasy, a product of the various suasive techniques which create the semblance of informed public debate while placing it beyond hope of attainment.

In one sense Baudrillard is undoubtedly right: that is to say, in his argument that public opinion (or what counts as such) can be swung so far that it completely loses touch with any knowledge of real-world issues and events. To the extent that we are reliant on the 'textual' evidence – on the TV coverage and newspaper reporting – it is hard to escape his cynical conclusion that nobody can possibly claim any knowledge beyond what is offered by the official machinery of state-sponsored censorship and disinformation. On the one hand we are bombarded with a ceaseless stream of images, statistics, 'front-line' dispatches, Pentagon briefings and so forth, all of which serve to create the illusion that this is the first war in history to be covered in such detail and communicated 'live' to a world-wide community of highly informed viewers, listeners and readers. On the other it becomes increasingly apparent – at least to anyone who sifts and compares the 'evidence' – that this whole relentless barrage of media coverage is designed to overload our receptive and cognitive faculties to the point where the line between fact and fiction (or, in Baudrillard's terms, the 'real' and the 'hyperreal') seems well-nigh impossible to draw. But from this, Baudrillard draws the absurd – yet on his own terms seductively plausible – conclusion that we *just cannot know* whether war has indeed 'broken out', as opposed to the simulated images of war that both preceded the 'event' and continued thereafter as our only source of news and information. Such is the 'reality gulf' that has opened up between war and its postmodern fantasy-substitute. It no longer makes sense to think in terms which imply that there must be some truth behind appearances, some means of ultimately *telling the difference* between what we are presently given to believe through the news reports, government statements, official casualty figures etc, and what will at last turn out to have been the case when all the relevant facts come in. On the contrary, Baudrillard argues: if there is one lesson to be learned from this war (or this hyperreal 'simulacrum' of war) it is the irrelevance of half-way pragmatist doctrines like 'truth at the end of enquiry', and the need to make terms with a new situation where nothing – no appeal to historical realities or the putative facts of the case – could warrant the use of terms like 'propaganda', 'indoctrination', 'media bias' and so forth, words that still trade on the same old range of hopelessly outmoded epistemic or ontological distinctions.

It is not surprising that Baudrillard's ideas have been taken up with such relish by US readers, even when he offers them what might be thought some rather unpalatable home truths, as for instance that America is a realm of unlimited substitute-gratification, of depthless surfaces and 'hyperreal', self-parodic life styles which exceed all the bounds of rational comprehension.[17] For these remarks are often taken – and apparently intended – as the highest compliment that could possibly be paid by a postmodern intellectual guru who finds all his arguments so strikingly borne out by the evidence to hand. And if further confirmation were needed then US responses to the Gulf conflict would provide quite a mass of socio-documentary (or psycho-pathological) support. Judith Williamson captured the mood well enough in a *Guardian* piece written from San Diego during the third week of hostilities.

> It is the unreality of anywhere outside the US, in the eyes of its citizens, which must frighten any foreigner. Like an infant who has yet to learn there are other centres of self, this culture sees others merely as fodder for its dreams and nightmares . . . The hyped-up concern over US children's fears ('Will Saddam kill me Mommy?') is obscene when you consider that American bombs are right now killing Iraqi children. It isn't that Americans don't *care* (God knows they care) but that for most of them, other lands and people cannot be imagined as real. If Mattel brought out a doe-eyed doll called Iraqi Baby, it could be guaranteed to evoke pity. Meanwhile on the national news, shots of birds caught in 'Saddam's oil slick' have been presented more poignantly than the human victims of our bombing.[18]

Probably Williamson faxed her article before it was revealed – or somebody caught on – that those birds couldn't have been victims of 'Saddam's oil-slick', since the slick was drifting several miles out to sea while the birds were filmed making painful efforts to drag themselves onto dry land. Of course we cannot *know*, as Baudrillard would be quick to point out, that some alternative explanation was the *truthful* account, or that – as seemed very likely – the spillage in question had been caused by US bombing of inshore installations. But this episode was just one instance of the numerous contradictions, cross-purpose statements, non-sequiturs, and manifest untruths that came to light during the first few weeks of the so-called 'Allied' propaganda campaign. Even so, as Williamson suggests in her article, such revelations could have had little impact on the state of US 'public opinion', given over as it was to a kind of collective hysteria, a media-induced climate of paranoid delusion, and an utter refusal to contemplate the effects – the real-world human effects – of what was being done to civilian populations in the name of freedom, democracy and a 'new world order'. In which case one might be tempted to conclude that this is indeed a decisive confirmation of Baudrillard's postmodernist claims, an instance of the henceforth unbridgeable 'reality gulf'. What price truth in an age when mass-media simulation determines the agenda, the admissible viewpoints, or the very 'horizon of intelligibility' in matters of factual, moral and political concern?

But this conclusion only follows if one accepts the postmodern-textualist premise: that reality *just is* whatever we make of it according to this or that predominant language-game, discourse, or mode of signifying practice. Once reject that premise – as most people would unless drilled into accepting it by prolonged exposure to the fads and fashions of cultural theory – and the whole line of argument simply collapses.[19] The export of ideas from the realm of *avant garde* literary theory to adjacent disciplines such as historiography, as commented on by Bennett in the passage cited earlier, has had the effect of promoting an extreme anti-cognitivist and relativist doctrine. In this sense one could justifiably argue that Baudrillard was waiting at the end of the road that structuralism and post-structuralism had been travelling for the past three decades and more. The movement started out, in Perry Anderson's phrase, as an 'abusive extrapolation' from the specialized methodology of Saussure; it took certain strictly heuristic precepts from the realm of structuralist language-study and made them the basis for a full-scale assault on the concepts of truth, reality, and representation.[20] It has finished by promoting a postmodern-pragmatist worldview, which blithely deconstructs the 'notional' difference between 'war' as a simulated pseudo-event – a fictive 'referent' conjured up by the opinion-polls, TV images, rhetorical sabre-rattling – and war as a real-world state of affairs in which countless thousands of Iraqi civilian men, women and children were daily being killed in an aerial bombardment of unprecedented scale and ferocity. Small wonder, as I say, that Baudrillard's ideas have achieved such a cult following at a time and in a context – that of the current US drive for renewed world hegemony – when few intellectuals seem able or willing to resist these pressures of ideological recruitment.

TWO REASONS FOR NOT IGNORING BAUDRILLARD

Of course it might be felt – and I acknowledge the force of this argument – that one had best simply ignore Baudrillard's piece, since even to engage him on the topic of the Gulf War is to trivialize the issue by bringing it down to the level of a debate between partisans of this or that current intellectual fad. But there are two main points that I should wish to make here, having registered this moral objection.

One is the fact – brought home with appalling vividness by events in the Gulf and their media representation – that this is indeed in some sense a 'postmodern' war, an exercise in mass-manipulative rhetoric and 'hyperreal' suasive techniques, which does undoubtedly confirm some of Baudrillard's more canny diagnostic observations. How else could one explain the extraordinary inverse relationship between extent of coverage and level of informed public grasp; the profusion of meaningless statistical data served up to create an illusory sense of objective, factual reporting; the absurd claims about 'precision bombing' and 'pinpoint accuracy', designed to convince us that civilian casualties were almost non-existent, despite all the graphic counter-evidence provided by the images of urban mass destruction; the headlong readiness of European governments, 'opposition' parties, newspapers, TV commentators, religious leaders and the rest to fall in with whatever propaganda line the White House or the Pentagon was currently promoting; the marginalization of dissident opinion to the point of near invisibility; and, worst of all perhaps, the brutalizing effect of those standard military euphemisms – 'collateral damage', 'softening-up missions', 'surgical strikes' etc – which rapidly managed to infiltrate the discourse of pro-war and anti-war factions alike. And one could also instance the prevailing sense of 'hyperreality', the mood of collective indifference to issues of factual or documentary truth that enabled such a mass of false information to circulate largely unchallenged from day to day. Often enough there would be a subsequent press release 'correcting' the earlier statement, but apparently this did very little to dent public confidence in the ongoing media charade. And along with all this goes a kind of large-scale historical amnesia, a blank refusal – on the part of most commentators – to consider the various striking parallels between past and present events. Hence the widespread failure to draw any relevant lessons concerning the record of previous US and British military interventions, or to examine the geo-political complexities of the region; similarly there was little attempt to expose such time-worn myths as the confinement of bombing to non-civilian targets. And there was the nonsense of imagining – after Korea, Vietnam, Grenada and similar 'wars of liberation' – that this was a genuine moral crusade, an uncoerced alliance of nations under UN auspices launched in defence of freedom and democracy, without the least taint of economic self-interest or neo-imperialist designs on the part of its US sponsors. In light of all this – amounting, one could argue, to a wholesale collapse of the 'public sphere' of informed critical debate – it can scarcely be denied that Baudrillard's theses have a certain diagnostic value.

So there is reason to take those propositions seriously in so far as they reflect certain aspects – albeit degraded and debilitating aspects – of our present cultural and socio-political condition. But the second (and I think more urgent) reason for engaging postmodernism in terms of the Gulf War 'debate' is one that demands a much greater degree of argued critical resist...ce. That is to say, it brings home with particular force the depth of ideological *complicity* that exists between such forms of extreme anti-realist or irrationalist doctrine and the crisis of moral and political nerve among those whose voices should have been raised against the actions committed in their name.

On Baudrillard's reckoning it is the merest of illusions – just a washed-up relic of the old 'Enlightenment' myth – to suppose that such arguments could possibly make any difference, or that public opinion might have been turned around if a sufficient number of people could be brought to perceive the extent of mass-media disinformation, the propaganda lies, statistical enormities, grossly under-estimated casualty figures and so forth. Perhaps there was a time (say two centuries back, or during subsequent periods of pre-revolutionary ferment) when oppositional discourses possessed at least a measure of rhetorical or 'performative' force, and when it still made sense for progressive intellectuals to adopt a standard-bearing role, as critics of consensus belief or purveyors of a truth hitherto concealed through the workings of ideological illusion. But that time has now passed, Baudrillard argues, since we are living in an epoch of depthless 'simulacra' or signs without referential content, a realm of performative reality-effects where such truth-claims lack any semblance of critical force. In which case the Gulf War would surely figure as the ultimate postmodern or hyperreal event.

The apparent inability of much of what currently passes for critical theory to take any principled oppositional stand on issues of local or world politics must surely be cause for concern. It therefore seems to me that it is time for a thorough-going critique of the whole line of thought which discovers its inaugural moment in Saussure and then runs down to the various schools of present-day post-structuralist, neo-pragmatist or textualist fashion. The main problem with all these movements is their uncritical acceptance of Saussure's basic precepts – in particular the bracketting of referential functions and the treatment of language as a network of differential elements 'without positive terms' – as if such doctrines could be simply transferred from the specialized field of structural-synchronic linguistics to other disciplines like literary theory, cultural criticism, historiography or the analysis of media representation.[21] And along with this levelling pan-textualist view of the relation between different 'discourses' goes a widespread ignorance of other developments in the realm of modern analytical and linguistic philosophy, an ignorance sustained – one is tempted to conclude – by the entrenched dogmatism of current post-structuralist theory and its sheer unwillingness to entertain arguments that would constitute a challenge to its own grounding suppositions.

There is room here only for the briefest indication of the paths not taken by the arbiters of recent (post-1960) Francophile theoretical debate. They would include – for instance – Frege's account of the sense/reference distinction, an account altogether more cogent and precise than the standard post-structuralist wisdom;[22] the work of philosophers like Saul Kripke, Hilary Putnam and Ian Hacking, adopting a variety of positions on the issue of language, meaning and representation, but doing so at a level of informed and rigorous argument far removed from the modish *idées recues* of recent textualist theory;[23] the debate around issues of historical knowledge in relation to the structures of narrative understanding carried on by thinkers in the broadly 'analytical' camp, but with relevant lessons for literary theorists over-impressed by the sceptical conclusions of Foucault, Hayden White or the New Historicists;[24] the sophisticated defence of a realist outlook in the philosophy and history of science advanced by Roy Bhaskar;[25] the tradition of German (mainly Frankfurt) Critical Theory, drawing upon the work of thinkers like Adorno and Habermas, and confronting post-structuralism not only with a full-scale genealogy of its own formative – though unacknowledged – prehistory, but also with a full-scale argued critique of its various demonstrable errors and confusions;[26] and even from within the post-structuralist camp, according to current perceptions, those numerous cautionary passages in Derrida's work where he comes out explicitly *against* any form of the wholesale 'textualist' persuasion, or any such pseudo-deconstructive approach that would treat, for example, poetry, philosophy and history as so many optional 'discourses' or 'kinds of writing', indistinguishable in point of truth, method, or protocols of valid reasoning.[27] That it has displayed such a steadfast indifference to these and other such (by its own lights) irrelevant or obsolete modes of thought may help to explain why post-structuralism has drifted into a largely uncontested *entente cordiale* with Baudrillard's stance of last-ditch cognitive scepticism.

One could start to clear away some of the sources of confusion by pointing out that post-structuralism rests on highly questionable premises; that there exist alternative, more cogent ways of treating the same basic issues;[28] and that Baudrillard's theses cannot hold up when subjected to any kind of reasoned critical scrutiny. Of course I am not suggesting that the best thing to do in these present bad times is to sit around endlessly debating such specialized matters of truth, language and representation. Much better leave off these discussions for now and devote all one's time and energy to protesting the massive injustice of a war whose causes were inextricably tied up with the history of US and British regional policy; whose high-sounding justificatory rhetoric was a cover for crude economic self-interest; whose conduct involved unprecedented levels of coercive propaganda and mass-media distortion; and whose cost in terms of civilian casualties and environmental impact will most likely never be known, since any details coming back are subject to the tightest 'security' restrictions.

In such circumstances it might seem frivolous or worse to make the Gulf War into a pretext for yet further arcane disputes about the 'politics of theory' or the wider implications of current post-structuralist thought. But the connection will perhaps not seem so remote to anyone who has carried on teaching over these past few months and attempted to convince students of the 'relevance' of theory in matters of real-world moral and political conscience, or the idea that such theories should provide at least a starting-point for argued and principled anti-war protest. After all, these latest notions fall in very readily with a 'postmodern' mood of widespread cynical acquiescence, a feeling that the war was indeed so utterly *unreal* – so completely removed from our competence to judge as informed readers, viewers or members of a specialized 'interpretive community' – that nothing we could possibly think or do would have any worthwhile impact as a means of contesting the official (media-sponsored) version of events. One is forced to entertain the suspicion that much of what is currently taught in the name of 'radical' literary and cultural theory is in fact little more than a pedagogic line of least resistance, a self-deceiving ruse that comes up with all manner of alibis, pretexts and sophistical arguments for avoiding any knowledge of its own involvement in the work of ideological mystification.

Of course I am not suggesting – absurdly – that this *trahison des clercs* is a direct result of over-exposure to post-structuralist ideas, or that a better understanding of the philosophic issues would automatically produce the desired change of attitude. Still, it should be cause for some rueful reflection on the part of left-wing intellectuals that 'theory' (or so much of what nowadays passes for advanced theoretical wisdom) has shown itself not only ill-equipped to mount any kind of effective critical resistance, but also quite capable of lending support to neo-pragmatist or consensus-based doctrines which would render such resistance strictly unthinkable. Nor is this in any way surprising, given its pervasive anti-realist drift, its rejection of truth-claims or validity conditions of whatever kind, and its attitude of thoroughgoing Nietzschean contempt for the values of 'liberal-humanist' thought. Merely to use concepts such as conscience, good faith, responsibility, or ethical judgment in the presence of right-thinking orthodox post-structuralists is to find oneself treated with pitying fondness as a relic of that old 'Enlightenment' discourse. For if – as their argument standardly goes – the autonomous subject has now been dispersed into a range of plural, polymorphous 'subject-positions' inscribed within language or existing solely as figments of this or that constitutive discourse, then of course there is no question of those values surviving as anything but a species of chronic self-delusion, a form of 'imaginary' specular investment whose claims have long since been deconstructed through the insights of psychoanalysis, structural linguistics, Foucauldian discourse-theory etc.[29] Thus the so-called 'postmodern condition' applies just as much to issues of ethics and politics as to matters of an epistemological import. That is to say, there is no getting outside the 'discourse' – or the existing range of discursive subject-positions – whose limits are inescapably (in Wittgenstein's phrase) 'the limits of our world', and which therefore set the terms for any meaningful debate about truth, reality, or ethical values. Least of all can we hang on to the Enlightenment (more specifically, the Kantian) project of adjudicating questions in these various domains by appealing to a critical 'doctrine of the faculties', one that would seek to establish the legitimate reach of cognitive (theoretical) understanding on the one hand, and practical (ethical) reason on the other. For this would appear nothing more than an instance of retrograde wishful thinking, an attempt to restore the flagging self-esteem of those old-style 'universal intellectuals' whose representative role – or whose entitlement to speak on behalf of other, less enlightened individuals – was always (as Foucault maintains) a self-aggrandizing myth of their own invention.[30]

Of course there are important distinctions to be marked along this path toward the current fashion for attacking Enlightenment reason and all its works. I should not wish to deny that, in Foucault's case, the scaled-down role of 'specific intellectual' went along with a genuine practical commitment to various projects of social and political reform, notably in the fields of psychiatric medicine, penal institutions, and the structures of oppressive power/knowledge bound up with issues of gender-role identity. And the same applies to thinkers of a kindred persuasion – Edward Said pre-eminent among them – who have argued convincingly for a 'micro-politics' of localized engagement and resistance, a practice based on the close reading of textual or archival sources, and the critique of those deep-laid racial and cultural stereotypes that constitute the discourse of Western Orientalism.[31] Clearly it would be wrong to lump these thinkers together with Baudrillard. But it is a different matter when such arguments are recycled in pre-packaged form by theorists who possess nothing like the same degree of scholarly or ethico-political commitment. For what often results is a half-baked mixture of ideas picked up from the latest fashionable sources, or a series of slogans to the general effect that 'truth' and 'reality' are obsolete ideas, that knowledge is always and everywhere a function of the epistemic will-to-power, and that history is nothing but a fictive construct out of the various 'discourses' that jostle for supremacy from one period to the next. And so it has come about that a thinker like Baudrillard can proffer his ridiculous 'theses' on the Gulf War with every confidence that they will gain wide attention among watchers of the postmodern cultural scene.

2

DECONSTRUCTION *VERSUS* POSTMODERNISM

RORTY ON DERRIDA

At this point it seems appropriate to state a few truths which would hardly need asserting (which would 'stand to reason', if one dares adopt such an old-fashioned phrase) were it not for the extent to which postmodernist ideas have taken hold in many quarters of 'advanced' intellectual debate. First: it is simply wrong – as well as a misreading of Derrida – to think that textuality goes 'all the way down', or that we cannot know anything save what is given in the form of textual (written) representation. To be sure, there is a sense in which Derrida's work invites such misreading through its recourse to an overtly inscriptionalist idiom – a language of 'writing', *archi-écriture*, 'trace', 'graphematics' and so forth – in order to emphasise the culturally produced (as opposed to the natural) character of thought and perception, and the non-availability of any such thing as a direct, unmediated knowledge of the world. But this is not to say that Derrida is some kind of transcendental solipsist, or that deconstruction is a discourse that celebrates the infinitized 'freeplay' of a writing cut off from all the irksome constraints of truth, reference or valid demonstrative argument. On the contrary: what gives deconstruction its critical edge is its address to issues in those three main areas – epistemology, ethics, and aesthetic judgment – which have occupied the central ground of philosophical enquiry at least in that tradition that runs from Kant to the various schools of present-day analytic thought.[1]

This is, I should acknowledge, a reading of Derrida that has been disputed by other commentators, and which certainly requires a lot more in the way of detailed supportive exegesis than I am able to offer here.[2] But the point needs making with particular emphasis at a time like the present when so many forces – intellectual, cultural and

32

socio-political – are conspiring to create a crisis of confidence in the values of enlightened truth-seeking thought. Deconstruction may indeed subject those values to a process of questioning that goes well beyond the stipulative limits that Kant laid down for the exercise of reason in its pure and practical domains. Moreover, it clearly involves the application of textual or rhetorical strategies of reading which tend to undercut – or to render intensely problematic – any confident appeal to those Kantian categories (*a priori* concepts, grounding intuitions, ideas of reason and so forth) which would seem so basic to the whole enterprise that nothing could remain after deconstruction save a series of slogans and watchwords devoid of all cognitive or ethical content. Rorty,[3] for instance, would argue that philosophers such as Derrida (or even Kant) are simply participants in an ongoing 'cultural conversation of mankind', one that takes its bearings from the current consensus of agreed-upon topics for debate, that enables them to tell an interesting story about previous episodes in the same conversation, but which has no use for the idea – Hegel's great error – that there must exist a standpoint of Absolute Reason (or truth at the end of enquiry) from which to adjudicate in matters of ultimate concern.[4] For Rorty, there is a 'bad' side of Derrida that continues to trade on Kantian or 'constructive' notions of truth, validity, argumentative rigour and so forth, and a 'good' side on which his writing can be seen as just a brilliant debunking enterprise, a collection of jokes, intertextual allusions, fantasy interludes, stylistic parodies, pseudo-philosophical arguments, etc, all of them designed to cut the discipline down to size by stressing its kinship with those 'literary' arts – mimesis, feigning, dissimulation – which philosophers since Plato had striven so hard to discredit or conceal from view.[5] And, of course this reading has possessed great appeal for literary critics with a vested interest in claiming Derrida as one of their own party in that 'ancient quarrel' between literature and philosophy which Plato was the first to articulate, and which still rumbles on at the level of faculty or inter-departmental politics.

If this were a correct or even half-way plausible reading of Derrida then there would be little point in protesting, as I have, that deconstruction is *not* just a variant – or a vaguely 'philosophical' offshoot – of that widespread postmodern-irrationalist drift of which Baudrillard stands as the prime representative. But one could cite many passages from Derrida's work which would demonstrate beyond doubt that this reading is mistaken and that, far from renouncing the

Enlightenment project along with its critical, epistemological and ethical resources, he has sought to 'reinscribe' them in contexts of socio-political debate that would fully maintain philosophy's commitment to a *reasoned and responsible* critique of existing forms of institutionalized power/knowledge. Once again I must crave the reader's indulgence in resorting to a summary account rather than arguing the case in adequate detail. But it strikes me that nobody who has read Derrida's work (especially his essays of the past decade) without very fixed preconceptions could possibly have failed to register *both* the continued concern with epistemological issues – i.e. questions in the realm of truth, reality and representation – *and* the insistence that such issues entail an irreducibly ethical dimension, an address to the question of what interests are served (or what other-regarding values and priorities ruled out of court) by the truth-claims of this or that 'enlightened' rational consensus.[6]

Undoubtedly Derrida has done much to problematize that mainstream version of Enlightenment thought which extends from Kant – or a certain orthodox reading of Kant – to Habermas and his claims for an 'ideal speech-situation' exempt from all the errors, the 'misfires' or duplicities of everyday communicative utterance. But, as comes out very clearly in Derrida's exchange with John Searle, his interest in these 'deviant' or 'marginal' cases is also an interest in the real-world effects – the social, political and ethical consequences – that can flow from such breakdowns in the 'normal' machinery of speech-act implicature, social convention, or self-assured communicative grasp.[7] And this applies above all to those essays (like 'The Principle of Reason') where Derrida undoubtedly sets out to 'deconstruct' the discourse of Enlightenment critique, but always with a scrupulous respect for the protocols of reasoned argument and an ethics of open dialogical exchange.[8] This is not to say that deconstruction is best viewed as a latterday variant of Kantian or Marxist *Ideologiekritik*, a discourse that goes more elaborate (rhetorical) ways around to arrive at much the same conclusions. But it does serve to emphasize the crucial difference between Derrida's project and those forms of postmodern-textualist thought whose avowed aim (as with Baudrillard) is to junk the whole tradition of enlightened critical thought.

Let me quote just a few relevant passages from Derrida's 'Afterword: toward an ethic of discussion' (1989), passages that address precisely this issue, and which cannot be accused – like certain formulations in his earlier work – of adopting an ambivalent or evasive strategy of argument. The first has to do with the oft-repeated charge (duly taken up by Habermas and Searle) that deconstruction is a mere rhetorical bag of tricks, a technique for levelling the genre-distinction between philosophy on the one hand and poetry, fiction or literary criticism on the other. On the contrary, says Derrida: 'the value of truth (and all those values associated with it) is never contested or destroyed in my writing, but only reinscribed in more powerful, larger, more stratified contexts'.[9] Those contexts extend – for Derrida as for Kant – from 'technical' issues in the realm of epistemological enquiry to questions of an ethical, socio-political and institutional import. In each case, whatever the problems or aporias brought to light by a deconstructive reading, it should always be possible – so Derrida asserts – 'to invoke rules of competence, criteria of discussion and of consensus, good faith, lucidity, rigour, criticism, and pedagogy'.[10] Moreover, deconstruction is none the less 'ethical' – none the less committed to those same values of enlightened reciprocal exchange – for the fact that it treats them as in principle open to question, or as not enjoying the status of absolute, transcendent, self-validating truths. Thus it may always happen that,

> while analyzing a certain ethicity inscribed in language – and this ethicity is a metaphysics (there is nothing pejorative in defining it as such) – they reproduce, under the guise of describing it in its ideal purity, the given ethical condition of a *given* ethics. They exclude, ignore, relegate to the margins other conditions no less essential to ethics in general, whether of *this given* ethics or of *another*, or of a law that would not answer to Western concepts of ethics, right, or politics.[11]

In other words it is wrong – a definite misreading of Derrida's work – to regard deconstruction as having broken altogether with the discourse of 'enlightened' critique, or (in Habermas's diagnostic terms) as representing just another, deplorable symptom of the current postmodernist malaise, the failure to keep faith with what he calls the 'unfinished project of modernity'. On the contrary, Derrida is sustaining that project by continuing to question its foundational concepts and values, and by doing so – moreover – in a spirit quite accordant with its own critical imperatives.

Why have I always hesitated to characterize it [i.e. deconstruction] in

Kantian terms, for example, or more generally in ethical or political terms, when that would have been so easy and would have enabled me to avoid so much criticism, itself all too facile as well? Because such characterizations seemed to me essentially associated with philosophemes that themselves call for deconstructive questions. Through these difficulties, another language and other thoughts seek to make their way. This language and these thoughts, which are also new responsibilities, arouse in me a respect which, whatever the cost, I neither can nor will compromise.[12]

And the ethical question is always (as in Kant) related *at a certain highly specific remove* to issues in the realm of epistemology and cognitive enquiry, issues which cannot be allowed to bear directly on the exercise of practical reason – since that way determinism lies – but which none the less require the utmost vigilance in determining their proper scope and limits if philosophy is to make good its claims as a discourse of enlightened, emancipatory thought. Hence Derrida's reiterated point: that deconstruction has nothing whatsoever in common with those forms of extreme anti-cognitivist doctrine that would claim to have come out 'beyond' all distinctions between truth and falsehood, reason and rhetoric, fact and fiction etc, and which would also – by the same token – sever any possible link between truth-seeking interests and issues of ethical accountability.

These statements go clean against the prevalent idea of deconstruction as a species of geared-up sophistical wordplay devoted to establishing the unknowability of a world 'outside' the limitless domain of textual representation. And if there is – as Habermas contends[13] – something 'conservative' about Derrida's writings, then this is not a matter of his having regressed (along with other Nietzschean apostles of unreason like Baudrillard) to a pre-Enlightenment discourse indifferent to values of truth and falsehood, but rather of thinking those values through with the utmost regard for their structural genealogy and modes of textual articulation. 'I am for safeguards, for memory – the jealous conservation – of numerous traditions, for example, but not only in the university and scientific, philosophical and literary theory. I am actively committed to such safeguards.'[14] Equally mistaken is the widespread notion – among opponents and camp-followers alike – that deconstruction somehow collapses the difference between truth-seeking discourses of various kinds (philosophy, history, political science) and discourses of a fictive or poetic character where truth is not directly or primarily in question, though these also belong (*vide* Derrida's essay 'White Mythology') to the single 'great chain' of ontological determinations which descends from Aristotle to the present.[15] 'Not that I assimilate the different regimes of fiction, not that I consider laws, constitutions, the declaration of the rights of man, grammar, or the penal code to be the same as novels. I only want to recall that they are not "natural realities", and that they depend on the same structural power that allows novelesque fictions or mendacious inventions and the like to take place.'[16]

Finally – lest any doubt remain on this score – let me cite one further passage where Derrida explicitly rejects the reading of his work put about by hostile critics and postmodernizing commentators alike. 'I have never', he writes,

> 'put such concepts as truth, reference, and the stability of interpretive contexts radically into question' if 'putting radically into question' means contesting that there *are* and that there *should be* truth, reference, and stable contexts of interpretation. I have – but this is something entirely different – posed questions that I hope are radical concerning the possibility of these things, of these values, of these norms, of this stability (which of its essence is always provisional and finite). This discourse and the questioning attuned to its possibility . . . evidently no longer belong simply, or homogeneously, to the order of truth, of reference, of contextuality. But they do not destroy it or contradict it . . . Their 'truth' is not of the same order as the truth they question, but in pragmatically determined situations in which this truth is set forth they must submit . . . to the norms of the context that requires one to prove, to demonstrate, to proceed directly, to conform to the rules of language and to a great number of other social, ethical, political-institutional rules, etc.[17]

I have cited this and other passages at length because they put up maximal resistance to that strain of facile pseudo-deconstructive thought which so easily joins onto Baudrillard's variety of postmodern-textualist rhetoric. At the moment there are many commentators – ranged on both sides, 'for' and 'against' – who take it for granted that deconstruction is indeed just a product, symptom or specialized offshoot of the wider 'postmodern condition', and that the only possible end-point on the road now travelled by 'advanced' literary theorists is one that brings them out on this heady terrain of thoroughgoing cognitive and ethical scepticism. Fortunately Derrida gives reasons enough to reject this view of deconstruction, or at any rate to treat it as a massive simplification of some few passages in his early work that appear to invite such a reading. But the question remains – especially in light of the Gulf War and Baudrillard's 'response' to it – whether we shouldn't after all push the argument back several stages and regard the entire post-structuralist enterprise as a chronic misdirection of critical theory brought about by reliance on a paradigm 'discourse' (that of Saussurean linguistics) whose extrapolation into other disciplines has been the cause of much error and confusion. In which case deconstruction could scarcely be exempted, deriving as it does – at least in large part – from a kindred range of intellectual sources and a similar acceptance of the 'linguistic turn' that is taken to characterize our present cultural predicament.

DECONSTRUCTION AND THE NUCLEAR REFERENT

These issues receive an admirably vigorous and clear-headed treatment in J. Fisher Solomon's book *Discourse and Reference in the Nuclear Age* (1988).[18] In general Solomon takes a sturdy realist stand against what he sees – justifiably enough – as the drift toward positions of extreme cognitive scepticism visible in many quarters of current theoretical debate. More particularly, he takes issue with Derrida's argument (developed in an essay on the topic of 'nuclear criticism') that we have now lived on into an epoch of threatened mass-destruction when the stakes are so inconceivably high – nothing less than the extinction of all life on earth, together with the entire human 'archive' of historical memory, technological achievement, scholarly source-material and so forth – that it no longer makes sense to envisage the arms-race (or its probable outcome) in real-world practical terms.[19]

According to Derrida nuclear war is a 'fabulous' or 'fictive' referent: firstly in the obvious sense that it has *not yet happened* (Hiroshima and Nagasaki, to be sure, but not a two-sided or all-out nuclear exchange) and can therefore be subject to no kind of cognitive, empirical or documented knowledge; and secondly in the sense that its occurrence would entail the complete annihilation of all such categories, the passage to a world in which the 'archive' was erased, or where nobody survived to consult it. And again: if there is a 'logic' of nuclear deterrence or war-fighting capability, then it is (Derrida argues) a pseudo-logic of sheer rhetorical escalation, a strategy waged through the endless exchange of threats and counter-threats, bluffs and counter-bluffs, simulated war-game scenarios etc. This is a game that necessarily exceeds all the limits of rational calculation – since its discourse is riddled with uncertainties, aporias, or downright performative contradictions – but which none the less comes to exert a whole range of 'real-world' practical effects, from the design and stockpiling of weapons to the disposition of military forces, the massive investment in war-related research programmes, the resultant shifts in the balance of geo-political power, and (not least) the material likelihood of an actual war breaking out. Or rather – and here he seems close to Baudrillard's position – we lack any criteria for making such judgments (i.e. the distinction between 'actual' and 'simulated' war) in an epoch when the only 'reality' that counts is the current stage of rhetorical-strategic escalation. At this point, where 'the limit itself is suspended', where 'crisis, decision, and choice are being subtracted from us', there is no falling back on those old forms of ontological security. What we have to address now is an entirely different range of issues, such as can scarcely be comprehended under existing paradigms of knowledge and truth. These include not only the logistics of war, its technological, political and military aspects, but also 'the relations between knowing and acting, between constative speech-acts and performative speech-acts, between the invention that finds what was already there and the one that produces new mechanisms or new spaces'.

In this situation, as Derrida reads it, we no longer possess any means of distinguishing the 'reality' of the arms-race – or the 'nuclear referent' – from those various fictive or fantasy substitutes that currently dictate the terms of so-called strategic thinking. And if this is the case then the question arises as to who can claim the *competence* – the relevant kinds of knowledge or special expertise – to pronounce on such matters. Certainly not those (the military planners, technicians, Pentagon spokesmen, old hands in the diplomatic game, etc) who have up to now sought to monopolize this discourse from a standpoint of accredited expertise. For they are no more competent than anyone else when it comes to assessing the 'real' implications of a shift in strategic posture – or a new move in the rhetorical game – whose potential effects so far outrun the capacities of rational-predictive thought. 'All of them, that is, very few, are in the position of inventing, inaugurating, improvising procedures and giving orders where no model . . . can help them at all.'[20] In which case one could argue (with Derrida) that the nuclear debate should henceforth be open to those whose 'competence' – or whose primary interest – is in fields like semiotics, literary theory, rhetoric, or deconstruction; disciplines that might seem utterly marginal according to the current division of intellectual labour, but which take on a crucial relevance in light of this latest paradigm-shift. 'We can therefore consider ourselves competent', Derrida writes, 'because the sophistication of the nuclear strategy can never do without a sophistry of belief and the rhetorical simulation of a text.'[21] And again, in a passage that could easily (though wrongly) be read as an endorsement of Baudrillard's postmodernist theses:

> the dividing line between *doxa* and *episteme* [i.e., 'mere opinion' and 'genuine knowledge'] begins to blur as soon as there is no longer any such thing as an absolutely legitimizable competence for a phenomenon which is no longer strictly techno-scientific but techno-militaro-politico-diplomatic through and through, and which brings into play the *doxa* or incompetence even in its calculations.[22]

All of which might lead one to conclude that deconstruction is indeed what opponents like Habermas and Searle would make of it: a mode of irresponsible word-spinning sophistry that can turn anything (nuclear war included) into grist for the well-oiled 'textualist' mill.

Solomon doesn't altogether go along with this reading, though he does view Derrida's essay as largely symptomatic of the prevailing anti-realist bias among present-day literary theorists. He offers in its place (and by way of critique) a form of 'potentialist realism' based on the argument (deriving from Aristotle) that we can in fact have knowledge of real-world objects, processes and events by grasping the inherent *probabilities* that exist in any given situation, that is to say, the determinate likelihood that things will turn out – or events unfold – in keeping with hitherto perceived regularities of a causal, purposive or rational-inductive character. There is no room here for an adequate summary of the arguments that Solomon brings up in defence of this far from fashionable view. Sufficient to say that he works his way through the whole range of opposing theoretical positions, from deconstruction to Foucauldian discourse-analysis, neo-pragmatism, reader-response theory, and analytical philosophy (or the versions thereof that end up, like Quine, by asserting some form of 'ontological relativity').[23] Such ideas have gained credence, Solomon argues, mainly on account of the obvious problems with a classical realist epistemology – a theory of knowledge and representation – which rests its claims on the presumed possibility of attaining an accurate, one-to-one match between concepts and the 'facts' of experience, or of somehow checking those concepts against the evidence of real-world objective reality. Of course this presumption founders on the argument that 'facts' exist only in the form of articulate truth-claims, assertions that possess no veridical status apart from the language – or the framework of validating assumptions – which assigns them that privileged role. Thus it simply doesn't make sense to suppose that we could ever achieve a more adequate fit – an improved 'correspondence' between language and the world – by somehow *comparing* our beliefs with the facts, these latter conceived as existing 'out there', or as belonging to a realm of pre-given objective truths against which to test our various propositions, world-hypotheses, ontological commitments, structures of linguistic representation or whatever. For again this ignores the obvious point that 'facts' depend wholly on forms of predicative judgment or assertion, truth-claims that cannot be prised apart from language and then used – as naive realists would have it – to expose the mismatch between things-as-they seem and things-as-they-actually-are.

Solomon comes out very strongly against these varieties of modish neo-pragmatist or textualist thought. That is to say, he accepts the standard case against naive realism – the circularity involved in any appeal to 'the facts' as a measure of real-world, objective truth – but denies that this argument necessarily entails the adoption of a wholesale anti-realist outlook, or an attitude of downright scepticism with regard to truth-claims of whatever kind. For such doctrines rest on the fallacious idea that we could only gain knowledge (genuine, reliable knowledge) through a first-hand acquaintance with the way things are independent of any mediating concepts, categories or structures of representation. And since clearly such knowledge is impossible – since 'facts' are constituted in and through language – therefore (q.e.d.) the realist case collapses, along with all attempts to revive it by appealing to various, equally circular arguments based on the same delusory idea of truth-as-correspondence, or of language as providing an accurate, one-to-one-match between concepts and real-world states of affairs. This is exactly the kind of straw-man position that post-structuralists, postmodernists, neo-pragmatists and others are so expert at knocking down. What they fail to perceive – or, in Rorty's case, what they reject on confused and inadequate grounds – is the argument (familiar at least since Kant, and taken up in different ways by a range of modern analytical schools) that truth-claims in philosophy *don't* stand or fall on the issue of direct, unmediated access to the world; that one *can* defend a critical-realist position on principles that involve no such naive ontological commitment; and that thoroughgoing scepticism of the kind much in vogue among present-day literary theorists is merely a result of the 'linguistic turn' pursued to a point where reality becomes an exclusively textual phenomenon.[24] Among post-structuralists and thinkers of a kindred dogmatic persuasion, any line of counter-argument – any reasoned defence of truth-claims in philosophy or critical theory – is rejected out of hand as a hopeless appeal to obsolete 'Enlightenment' habits of thought. After all, who could possibly *want* to hang on to such notions (or, worse still, imagine they had grounds – philosophical grounds – for so doing) once they had read the relevant passages of Saussure, Barthes, Derrida, Baudrillard etc? Unthinkable that post-structuralism might itself show up as just a species of self-promoting orthodox belief whose success among literary and cultural theorists over the past two decades has depended not so much on its intellectual merits as on its near-total isolation from the sphere of informed philosophical debate or competent peer-group review.

Solomon is much too polite to put it like this but his arguments clearly point in a similar direction. They also have the signal advantage, for present purposes, of raising these issues squarely in the context of discussing war as an object of possible knowledge, rather than treating it as a 'fabulous' or 'hyperreal' pseudo-referent exceeding all the limits of human cognitive grasp. Solomon's argument is intricate in its details but obvious enough in general outline to anyone whose mind has not been captured entirely by the sophistries of current intellectual fashion. 'I am suggesting that our apprehension . . . of the nuclear referent is determined not only by our archival imagination but also by our knowledge of an extra-archival world that is as real in its dispositional potentialities as in its actuated formalities.'[25] That is to say, we can judge and reason in such matters on the basis of a knowledge that may go beyond any straightforward appeal to the facts of the case – any notion of a direct correspondence (*adaequatio*) between language and the world – but which does, none the less, lay claim to a measure of cognitive or truth-telling warrant. As Solomon puts it:

> the reality to which the nuclear referent refers . . . is, in Aristotelian terms, a *potential* reality as well as an actual one. The nuclear referent, in other words, refers to an actual situational configuration of political

and technological conditions that bear within themselves their own concrete potentialities for future development. The futurity of the nuclear referent is bound to the present not only by a tie of logical possibility but also by one of empirical potentiality as well, a potentiality that *can* be calculated through the calculus of probability.[26]

This is not to suggest that Solomon takes the whole Aristotelian doctrine on board, along with its deep-laid teleological assumptions and other commitments that would clearly run counter to his own critical-realist position. What he does wish to rescue – and defend as wholly valid from a present-day perspective – is Aristotle's argument that the unpredictability of future events need not be taken as any cause for scepticism with regard to our knowledge of present realities and their *possible or likely* outcome. Thus he cites the well-known passage from *De Interpretatione* where Aristotle makes this point by way of distinguishing matters of logical necessity from matters of real-world predictive consequence. ' "A sea-fight" [or, we might add, a nuclear war] must either take place tomorrow or not", Aristotle explains, but "it is not necessary that it should take place tomorrow, neither is it necessary that it should not take place." '[27] But it is wrong to conclude from this that reason is powerless in face of such uncertainties, or that we are simply in no position to extrapolate from present evidence to future events on the basis of observed regularities, rational conjectures, the weighing of probable outcomes etc. For the absence of any strictly logical (i.e. deductive) order of necessity does nothing to disqualify these other forms of valid inferential reasoning.

Two further passages from Solomon's book may help to clarify the point. On the one hand, 'the future, Aristotle believes, must establish the propositional truth of our predictions, but those predictions themselves, our words, cannot determine the truth from within, cannot cross over from the word to the act, cannot reduce to indifference the difference between the conformations of our knowledge and the reality that we seek to know'.[28] In which case it might seem that the sceptics are right and that we have no grounds – no possible warrant – for predicting future eventualities on the basis of present observations. More than that: one could press Aristotle's reasoning yet further and argue, in postmodern-textualist fashion, that this scepticism must apply not only to future occurrences but also to existing states of real-world affairs, since here likewise there is no guarantee that the 'conformations of our knowledge' (or the 'facts' as represented in some given language-game) necessarily correspond at any point to 'the reality we seek to know'. But this is simply wrong, as Solomon points out, since the absence of strictly *logical* grounds for predicting future events (or for claiming knowledge of the truth behind present appearances) gives absolutely no reason for doubting our capacity to interpret events and arrive at a better understanding on the basis of evidence and inferential reasoning of a probabilistic kind. 'This . . . is the real challenge that the nuclear referent offers to criticism, a challenge to analyze the ways in which the word relates to the world, how our knowledge actuates the potentiality of a world that is real, that subsists outside our discourse, and that referentially grounds it.'[29]

My one reservation about Solomon's book is that he counts Derrida among the chief exponents of that same anti-Enlightenment creed, whereas – for reasons given above – I would place him as a thinker who resists its more pernicious or nihilistic conclusions, while also (undeniably) adopting a stance of principled scepticism with regard to the truth-claims of 'classical' Enlightenment thought. Solomon states his own position most clearly in the following passage, setting out the case for a 'potentialist metaphysics' (or a form of 'potentialist realism'), as against what he takes to be Derrida's espousal of a wholesale anti-realist or textualist doctrine. 'Such a metaphysics', Solomon writes,

> would not be the same as classical realism, for a potentiality is not a transcendentally universal, static identity. It is dynamic. It is indeed in play. But this play is not an unlimited 'free play'. It is situationally delimited, and its dynamics can be defined only within specified circumstances. In a sense, the ontological reality of a potentiality lies somewhere between identity and differance, between a universal determinism and the unrestricted play of *differance*, appearing to us in the form of empirical propensities, behavioral regularities that can be calculated, and thus grounding our distinctions between beliefs rather than suspending our decision.[30]

Up to a point this is doubtless fair comment, since Derrida's essay does make play with a certain fashionable rhetoric of crisis, an 'apocalyptic tone' (to adopt his own phrase, itself taken up from Kant) which can easily lean over into the kind of nihilist posturing that disfigures so much of the recent debate on so-called 'nuclear criticism'. One also has to recognise that Derrida leaves himself open to such a charge when he writes about the nuclear arms-race as a 'fabulously textual' phenomenon, one that so far exceeds the limits of real-world experience (or rational calculability) that it can only be figured under the aspect of the Kantian sublime, of a nameless 'catastrophe' that threatens every form of knowledge and representation. This is why, as Derrida remarks, 'the "reality" of the nuclear age and the fable of nuclear war are perhaps distinct, but they are not two separate things . . . It is the war (in other words the fable) that triggers this fabulous war effort, this senseless capitalization of sophisticated weaponry, this speed race in search of speed'.[31] And there are other passages in his essay that can likewise be read as falling in with the postmodern-textualist line, that is to say, the idea that we lack any resources – any conceptual, critical, or ethical means – for distinguishing 'reality' from its various orders of fictive or fantasy substitute.

To this extent Solomon is justified in his argument that deconstruction effectively 'suspends' both the truth/falsehood distinction and the ethical issue that arises in relation to matters of truth-telling warrant. In fact Derrida goes further and asserts that deconstruction 'belongs to the nuclear age . . . and to the age of literature' in so far as it partakes of the massive *undecidability* that attaches to all truth-claims in an epoch when the very survival of the 'archive' – of knowledge, culture, literate tradition, science and the human life-world – is threatened by a war that would totally obliterate the record of civilization to date. From which he deduces – by an odd (not to say absurd) twist of argument – that the 'nuclear referent' must therefore be *textual* through and through, produced at the point of a terminal crisis where 'reality' is subject to the kind of radical suspension that occurs in the deconstructive reading of literary texts. If 'literature' is the name we give to those writings 'whose existence, possibility, and significance are the most radically threatened, for the first and last time, by the nuclear catastrophe', then – according to Derrida – this thought allows us to grasp 'the essence of literature, its radical precariousness, and the radical form of its historicity'.[32] In short, we can best come to terms with the unthinkable aporias of nuclear discourse – its utter 'lack of measure' in relation to our powers of cognitive and rational judgment – by reading it as one more symptomatic instance of the present-day crisis of knowledge and representation, a crisis that has long been foreshadowed in the writing of *avant-garde* poets, novelists and critics. Thus 'we may henceforth assert', in Derrida's words,

that the historicity of literature is contemporaneous through and through, or rather structurally indissociable, from something like a nuclear *epoch* (by nuclear 'epoch', I also mean the *epochē* suspending judgment before the ultimate decision). The nuclear age is not *an* epoch, it is the absolute *epochē*; it is not absolute knowledge and the end of history, it is the *epochē* of absolute knowledge.[33]

In which case clearly deconstruction would figure as the one mode of discourse 'competent' to handle these perplexities of rational thought, these symptoms of a generalized crisis in the order of logic, language, and representation. And it would do so, moreover, precisely to the extent that it relinquished all notions of veridical knowledge or ethical accountability, and showed itself capable of 'suspending' such issues in the name of a textual or rhetorical predicament surpassing the bounds of mere 'enlightened' critical reason.

As I say, there are passages in Derrida's essay that positively invite such a reading. They are – not surprisingly – the passages that possess most appeal for literary theorists venturing into this field of 'nuclear criticism', treating everything (war, mass-destruction and the arms-race included) as just another 'kind of writing', a textual 'archive' that opens up marvellous new prospects for rhetorical deconstruction.[34] Solomon is right to cast a cold eye on these textualist antics. And if this were indeed the sole or predominant aspect of Derrida's text then it would scarcely rate a moment's serious attention. But there is, as I have suggested, another reading of his essay that would stress not so much these passages of high-textualist rhetoric as the structure of an argument that runs strongly counter to any such interpretation, and which insists on the absolute necessity of maintaining the highest standards of philosophical rigour and truth, even in the face of a nuclear predicament that would seem – on the first reading – to render those standards wholly obsolete. On this account Derrida has radicalized (but not abandoned) the discourse of Kantian enlightened critique, questioning its 'unthought axiomatics' – that is to say, its aporias and blind-spots of unwarranted presupposition – while none the less continuing to respect its critical and truth-seeking imperatives.

Thus: 'who is more faithful to reason's call, who hears it with a keener ear . . . the one who offers questions in return and tries to think through the possibility of that summons, or the one who does not want to hear any question about the principle of reason?'[35] Of course this is itself a rhetorical question, and one that must to some extent be read ironically, given what Derrida says elsewhere about the crisis now affecting all the forms and modalities of rational thought. Such would be the *épochē* that Derrida describes, the state of radically suspended judgment – or the absence of any relevant norms, criteria, or decision-procedures – brought about by the advent of this threat without measure or precedent. But one should also recall his comment elsewhere that ' "nuclear criticism", like Kantian criticism, is thought about the limits of experience as a thought of finitude'.[36] And again, in a somewhat different but related context: 'even the principle of uncertainty (and ... a certain interpretation of undecidability) continues to operate within the problematics of representation and of the subject-object relation'.[37] Taken together, these statements clearly imply a continuing critical engagement with the truth-claims and ethical values of Enlightenment thought, whatever the degree of conceptual strain – or the mounting pressures of irrational belief – to which those values are subject in an epoch given over to the pseudo-logic of nuclear-strategic escalation.

KANT, DERRIDA, LYOTARD

Purist deconstructors will no doubt object that this amounts to a double-aspect reading of Derrida's work, a reading that vainly strives to separate the valid or substantive arguments from the passages of merely 'textualist' rhetoric, and which thus falls back into the most naive of undeconstructed philosophical assumptions. So I had better grasp the nettle and acknowledge that this is indeed where my arguments have been heading, not only in this book but in everything I have written about deconstruction over the past few years. On the one hand there is that aspect of Derrida's thinking – undeniably prominent in the 'nuclear criticism' piece – which exploits all the well-worn rhetorical *topoi* of current postmodernist fashion to the point where deconstruction seems to offer nothing more than ingenious variations on the standard theme. It is this line of thought that leads him to announce – apparently in all seriousness – that the 'nuclear epoch' is also the age when literature ('its radical precariousness and the radical form of its historicity') becomes the only means of representing a 'reality' beyond all the powers of rational comprehension or adequate conceptual grasp. It also gives rise to a series of related (and equally extravagant) non-sequiturs, for instance the idea that since literature cannot outlive 'the archive', and since nuclear war threatens to obliterate that archive without trace, *therefore* literature is henceforth synonymous with the 'nuclear referent', itself a fictive or fabulous pseudo-concept beyond all the reckonings of real-world calculability. In which case there is ultimately nothing to distinguish 'good' from 'bad' arguments on the nuclear issue. Since truth-claims are no longer in question – since it is henceforth wholly a matter of simulated war-game strategies, rhetorical gambits, threats without reason or measure, etc – therefore we should give up thinking in terms that adhere to an obsolete paradigm of knowledge.

Derrida makes this point with regard to the notion (first floated by Caspar Weinberger, and briefly entertained by strategists in the Reagan administration) that the US might actually *prevail* in a so-called 'limited' nuclear conflict, and could somehow still rely on 'deterrence' to prevent the 'limited' war from escalating into an all-out exchange. An absurd notion, to be sure, since as Derrida reminds us 'if there are wars and a nuclear threat, it is because "deterrence" has neither "original meaning" nor measure . . . Its "logic" is the logic of deviation and transgression, it is rhetorical-strategic escalation or nothing at all'.[38] But if the Weinberger doctrine reduces to a piece of make-believe – a 'policy' that could never be implemented in any conceivable set of real-world circumstances – then the same must apply (so Derrida thinks) to those other, supposedly more 'rational' arguments put up by critics of the current US line. These critics complain that no *proofs* have yet been given – no convincing reasons, demonstrative arguments, or rational decision-procedures – that could possibly justify the preposterous notion of 'prevailing' in a limited nuclear exchange through application of the standard deterrence-theory. They assume that the principle of reason still holds, and that nuclear criticism – like everything else – must be subject to the same basic ground-rules of rational consistency, non-contradiction, predictive capability and so forth. On the contrary, says Derrida: 'there are no proofs in this area . . . There is only one proof, it is war, and moreover it proves nothing. The only thing the adversary discourse can oppose to the "Reagan" belief is another belief, its own hermeneutics and its own rhetoric'.[39] There is not much use in arguing fine points of strategy – and still less in criticizing the whole notion of 'deterrence' as a piece of sophistical doublethink – if the aporias of nuclear discourse are such as to reduce these issues to a bottom line of rhetorical undecidability. In fact it would appear from Derrida's remarks in this vein that the sole measure of 'competence' for nuclear criticism is the willingness to let speculation ride and abandon any thought of judging the issue in real-world consequentialist terms.

DECONSTRUCTION *VERSUS* POSTMODERNISM

But there is, as I have argued, another possible reading of the essay which maintains its link – however complex or qualified – with the values of Kantian enlightened critique. Derrida continues to raise the three central questions of Kant's philosophy (What can we know? What ought we to do? What can we reasonably hope for?), but does so from a standpoint of chastened historical and socio-political retrospect which no longer permits those questions to be answered with anything like Kant's measure of principled optimism.

Of course it may be argued that the bearing of these questions was always far from straightforward. Kant himself – in the three *Critiques* – went long and elaborate ways around in order to prevent any possible confusion between the realms of cognitive understanding and practical reason. He was also careful to distinguish between truth-claims entailing the existence of adequate (empirical or conceptual) grounds and those 'ideas of reason' which could never be confirmed or falsified by any such standard, since their ultimate appeal was to a *sensus communis*, a 'public sphere' of enlightened ethical and social values whose regulative force was in no way damaged by their failure so far to materialize in real-world terms.[40] For some recent commentators (Lyotard among them) this has opened the way to a postmodern reading of Kant that stresses the absolute heterogeneity – the lack of any common ground for judgment – between the various 'phrase-regimes', 'discourses' or 'language-games' involved.[41] From this point of view the greatest possible injustice is that which occurs when some particular phrase-regime oversteps the mark or threatens to annex neighbouring territory, as for instance when cognitive truth-claims (or judgments of truth and falsehood) lay claim to jurisdiction in the sphere of ethical or socio-political debate. The effect of this reading is thus to drive a wedge – a doctrine of downright incommensurability – between those various orders of knowledge and judgment whose relationship in Kant is indeed problematic (since subject to numerous boundary-disputes), but which Kant unlike Lyotard views as finally capable of reasoned adjudication. And a further consequence emerges clearly in Lyotard's treatment of the Kantian sublime – the limit-point of knowledge and representation – as a topos whose significance extends far beyond the realm of aesthetic judgment. The sublime, as theorized by Kant, sharpens our sense of the distance separating cognitive from ethical truth-claims, or sensuous intuitions that can be brought under adequate concepts (in the mode of theoretical understanding) from judgments belonging to the realm of 'suprasensible' ideas, values or principles.[42] Thus the sublime comes to figure, for Lyotard, as an index of the radical heterogeneity that inhabits our discourses of truth and value, or the kinds of injustice that inevitably result when one such 'phrase-regime' – most often the cognitive – seeks to monopolize the whole conversation.

On a superficial reading there is not much difference between Derrida's and Lyotard's approach to these issues. After all, they both set out to problematize the relation between those various faculties of knowledge and judgment that would claim – in more orthodox Kantian fashion – to provide *a priori* grounds for determining the powers and limits of cognitive enquiry, practical reason, aesthetic understanding and so forth. Moreover, they both pursue these questions to a point where language (or 'textuality') appears as something like an ultimate horizon, a field of contending regional truth-claims whose character is rhetorical through and through, and whose validity can never be more than a matter of suasive or performative force. Thus where Lyotard appeals to a broadly Wittgensteinian doctrine of 'language-games', 'phrase-regimes' etc, Derrida makes a similar point by questioning the categorical framework of Kantian philosophy, and showing how its arguments self-deconstruct, so to speak, through the play of a different ('supplementary' or 'parergonal') logic that cuts across the various terms and distinctions that Kant so strenuously seeks to hold in place.[43] This would certainly fit in with one possible reading of the 'nuclear criticism' essay, according to which that essay is an instance of the postmodern-textualist approach pushed to its giddy extreme, renouncing all hope that the issue might be treated in real-world or rationally accountable terms, and adopting (like Lyotard) an 'apocalyptic tone' – a rhetoric of the nuclear sublime – by way of reinforcing this desperate message.

But such a reading ignores both the structural logic of Derrida's argument and numerous passages (some of which I have cited above) where he expressly rejects any notion of abandoning the protocols, standards, or validity-conditions of reasoned philosophical debate. Thus if the 'logic' of deterrence turns out to be strictly nonsensical – a doctrine whose consequences cannot be thought through without running into all manner of absurd contradictions and non-sequiturs – then this argument *necessarily* assumes the existence of alternative, more rational grounds of judgment by which to demonstrate the point. And again: if nuclear war 'is for the time being a fable, that is, something one can only talk about', then one still has to acknowledge – as Derrida does – 'the massive "reality" of nuclear weaponry and of the terrible forces of destruction that are being stockpiled and capitalized everywhere, that are coming to constitute the very movement of capitalization'.[44] That he none the less chooses to place the word 'reality' in those queasy quotation-marks is a sign not so much of Derrida's retreating into a twilight realm of textualist solipsism as of his seeking to remind us to what extent the arms-race is a product of 'rhetorical-strategic escalation', of a discourse ('nukespeak') whose wildest fantasies might always give rise to some material shift in the perceived balance of power, some novel scenario which could have decisive – maybe catastrophic – real-world effects. It is in this sense precisely that 'the sophistication of the nuclear strategy can never do without a sophistry of belief and the simulation of a text'.[45] But to grasp Derrida's point is also to see that the 'aporias' of nuclear discourse are *not* just the symptoms of a generalized undecidability that affects all language and subverts any distinction between reason and rhetoric, truth and falsehood, real-world and imaginary threats, etc. On the contrary: they indicate the *specific* kinds of sophistry, the perversions of reason and the simulated pseudo-logic that prevail in a discourse so completely given over to the escalating rhetoric of nukespeak. In which case, despite appearances, it would be wrong to think of Derrida (in company with Lyotard) as rejecting the claims of critical reason, or – still worse – to lump him together with Baudrillard as just another purveyor of the current postmodern-textualist line.

3

HOW THE REAL WORLD BECAME A FABLE

FACT AND FICTION: TELLING THE DIFFERENCE

The Gulf War should have raised these issues with painful clarity for anyone concerned with the 'politics of theory' as a matter of more than specialized academic interest. For the idea has got around – among 'advanced' thinkers of various political persuasion – that realist epistemologies are a thing of the past; that truth-values in criticism have now been discredited (or shown up as just a figment of bourgeois ideology); that history and politics are textual (= fictive) phenomena on a par with poems, novels or whatever other 'kinds of writing' you care to name; and that henceforth the only 'discourse' that counts is one that cheerfully acknowledges all this, along with such presumed *faits accomplis* as the 'deconstruction' of the humanist subject as a locus of ethical choices, conflicts, and responsibilities. Mix in the notion – derived from a cursory reading of Hayden White and suchlike sceptical historiographers – that there is ultimately no difference between fictive and other (purportedly truth-telling) forms of narrative discourse, and it is not hard to see why Baudrillard's article on the Gulf War should have struck such a responsive chord.

What is so disturbing about all this is the conjunction of a vigorous expansionist mood among literary theorists – a desire to mount colonizing ventures into other disciplines like philosophy, law and history – with an attitude of wholesale scepticism as regards any notion that fictive or literary texts might themselves contain a measure of truth. As Tony Bennett remarks:

> if narratives are all that we can have and if all narratives are, in principle, of equal value – as it seems they must be if there is no touchstone of 'reality' to which they can be referred for the adjudication of their truth-claims – then rational debate would seem to be pointless.[1]

Not so long ago literary theorists – Marxists in particular – devoted great efforts of subtle (often wire-drawn) argument to the business of explaining the complex mediations between literature, ideology, and the order of real-world forces and relations of production.[2] Nowadays that project is mostly viewed by literary theorists with a kind of nostalgic fondness as the last vain attempt to salvage a version of the old 'enlightenment' meta-narrative, the idea of some ultimate 'truth at the end of enquiry' that would lay bare the various forms and mechanisms of ideological mystification.[3] The argument is not merely that literary critics, with their specialized techniques of close-reading, can offer a few lessons to historians, philosophers and others when it comes to examining the particular kinds of rhetorical or narrative structure that characterize these different forms of discourse. Rather, it is implied that the literary text – more specifically, the *postmodern* literary text – should serve as the paradigm instance of a language that disowns all truth-claims or realist illusions, and which thus points the way to an outlook in keeping with our current 'New Times' of pervasive hyperreality.

But this is to get things precisely upside-down, as happens so often in the more agitated regions of literary-critical debate. To begin with, it ignores the obvious point – self-evident from any but a thoroughgoing textualist perspective – that in reading works of fiction we always bring to bear a considerable range of real-world, factual, historical, 'commonsense' or extra-textual knowledge, the kind of information that is not to be had from the 'words on the page', but in the absence of which we could scarcely make a start in grasping what the work is all about. This knowledge extends from the basic regularities of human experience (cause-effect relations, ascriptions of agency, chronological sequence, spatio-temporal coordinates etc) to our presumed acquaintance with items of commonplace cultural knowledge and, beyond that, our capacity – if required – to figure out relevant background details on a straightforward inferential basis.[4] Thus it is simply not the case – as post-structuralists would argue – that critics fall into manifest naivety whenever they advance interpretive truth-claims beyond the scope of those signifying structures (or 'intertextual' codes and conventions) which define the limits of intelligibility for any given work. Such arguments will only look plausible if one adopts the thoroughly artificial standpoint of a reader whose competence extends to some brilliant feats of crypto-analytical decoding, but who lacks even the most elementary kinds of real-world cognitive grasp. Moreover, they take no account of recent developments in the theory of fiction which seek to explain the variety of ways in which truth-values (or elements of factual knowledge) enter into the reading of fictive texts. Among the most promising lines of approach is that which starts out from the notion of 'possible worlds', as debated by modal logicians and philosophers of language, and which examines the range of possible relations – or degrees of conceptual fit – between fictive and veridical modes of utterance.[5] This work demonstrates the extent to which any understanding of fiction depends upon our willingness to go 'beyond' the text, to engage in various – simple or complex – processes of inferential reasoning, and to eke out the paucity of given information by reference to our stock of real-world knowledge and beliefs. For otherwise we would be in no position to interpret even the most elementary forms of narrative discourse.

Among philosophers who have recently addressed this topic, Gregory Currie offers perhaps the strongest case for regarding fiction as essentially a hybrid genre, one that will always (by definition) contain at least *some* purely fictive assertions possessing no determinate truth-value, but whose character by no means excludes other statements with a genuine veridical import. Thus:

> If 'true fiction' sounds oxymoronic, it is because we haven't distinguished between truth *simpliciter* and reliable (i.e. counterfactually dependent) truth .... Homer turned out to be sufficiently reliable to lead Schliemann to the site of Troy. Most works of fiction are to some extent based on fact.... Walter Scott breaks off the narrative of *Guy Mannering* in order to tell us something about the condition of Scottish Gypsies, and it is pretty clear that what he says is asserted. A work of fiction is a patchwork of truth and falsity, reliability and unreliability, fiction-making and assertion.[6]

And this applies even to postmodernist works where the narrative may exploit all kinds of anti-illusionist or defamiliarizing techniques – often (as with writers like Borges, Calvino and Pynchon) to the point of radically disrupting our sense of a coherent fictional world – but where such techniques can only register by contrast with our normative habits of response. Making sense of these texts is therefore a matter of judging where the various anomalies, contradictions, incompatible viewpoints, chronological enormities, etc, cannot be reconciled with our knowledge of the way things stand in reality. So it is wrong to suppose that fiction involves a wholesale suspension of the truth-values that operate in other modes of discourse where truth is more directly or explicitly in question.

This is the point that Currie is making when he speaks of narrative reliability as a matter of 'counterfactual dependence', or how far the truth of some given utterance holds good across the various 'possible worlds' – each differing in respect of some more or less significant point of detail – to which that utterance might apply. 'We can sum all this up', he writes,

> by saying that the reports in a reliable newspaper *display counterfactual dependence on the facts*. What the paper says is true not only in the actual world but in other possible worlds too. Not, of course, true in every world, but true in those worlds which would make the following counter-factuals true: 1) If different events had occurred, the paper's report would have been correspondingly different; 2) Were those events, in correspondingly changed circumstances, to have occurred as they did, the paper would still have reported them.[7]

This is *not* to suggest – in postmodernist fashion – that newspaper reports, like fictional narratives, occupy a realm of unlimited 'counterfactual' possibility where nothing could finally decide the issue between truth and its various invented or imaginary analogues. On the contrary: fictional truth-values differ from the ordinary sort in so far as they involve reference to a world where *at least some* assertions will lack any kind of veridical force. They are, as Currie puts it, 'accidentally true' in the sense that 'the author's imaginative filling in of the plot does not depend on what actually happened', thus making it impossible to say in such cases (unlike the case of the newspaper report): 'if the events in which the historical characters were caught up had been different, the novelist's account would be correspondingly different'.[8]

It is here that fiction must be held distinct from those other kinds of discourse – historical, factual-documentary, etc – where assertions (if valid) are 'non-accidentally true', and are thus not subject to the novel-reader's willing suspension of disbelief. Even so, Currie argues, this difference applies only when considering this or that fictional world-view taken as a whole, that to say, as a sequence of true-seeming utterances *some* of which will always turn out to lack any genuine assertoric force. It doesn't exclude the possibility – indeed, the strong likelihood – that any such work will also contain a great number of assertions (or presuppositions) which do have determinate truth-values. Thus we are not reduced to positing a phantom realm of counterpart fictive entities ('Sherlock Holmes's London', 'Tolstoy's Napoleon', 'Balzac's Paris' and so forth) in order to preserve the ontological distinction between real-world and simulated orders of truth. Still less are we obliged – as Baudrillard would have it – to let go of such distinctions altogether and yield to the seductive 'hyperreality' of a postmodern world without cognitive or referential bearings. Quite simply, 'a work is fiction iff [i.e. if and only if] (a) it is the product of a fictive intent, and (b) if the work is true, then it is at most accidentally true'.[9] In which case there is no problem in conceiving of fiction as a mode of utterance that exhibits both feigned (make-believe) and veridical assertions, and whose proper understanding requires nothing more mysterious than an exercise of our normal, rational capacity for telling these functions apart.

Solomon, as we have seen, makes a similar point – albeit from a different philosophical perspective – when he argues for a form of 'potentialist realism', an approach to matters of historical fact that very largely depends on second-hand reports, archival sources, informed conjecture and so forth, but which none the less claims an access to truth through modes of probabilistic reasoning that best correspond to the real-world course of events. Thus he cites an apposite passage from *The Peloponnesian War* where Thucydides sets out to counter the objection that his history rests on dubious sources, and involves elements of *post hoc* speculative judgment that cannot be confirmed by any direct appeal to the facts of the case. 'With reference to the speeches in this history', he writes,

> some were delivered before the war began, others while it was going on, some I heard myself, others I got from various quarters. It was in all cases difficult to carry them word for word in one's memory, so my habit has been to make the speakers say what was in my opinion demanded of them by the various occasions, of course adhering as closely as possible to the general sense of what they really said.[10]

But this is no reason – Solomon argues – to treat *The Peloponnesian War* as an instance of the 'undecidability' that infects all forms of historical discourse, or the way that such narrative elements inevitably work to 'deconstruct' the difference between history and fiction. On the contrary: Thucydides knows very well that any *adequate* account of the war and its causes will at some point exceed the self-evident facts of the case, involving not only a reconstruction of probable interests and motives, but also an appeal to 'deep' explanations that cannot be simply read off from the record of events. Thus 'the real cause I consider to be the one that was formally kept out of sight. . . . The growth and power of Athens, and the alarm which this inspired in Lacedaemon, made war inevitable'.[11] Clearly such assertions go well beyond any manifest truth of the matter as determined by direct appeal to the documented facts. But this is not to say that we had therefore better view them as so many more-or-less plausible fictions, concerned not so much with relating what actually happened – in Ranke's famous phrase, *wie es eigentlich war* – as with fitting those 'facts' into a coherent story-line, a version of events whose characteristic features (plot, style, chronological sequence, authorial viewpoint, etc) embody a choice between the various 'master-tropes' of narrative discourse in general. Such arguments only hold good if there exists no alternative to the positivist notion of truth, that is to say, the strictly impossible idea of a direct equivalence – or one-to-one match – between historical facts and their corresponding structures of discursive representation. In Solomon's view this is just the kind of false dilemma that results when postmodern sceptics like Hayden White reject the naive realist position and embrace what amounts to a thoroughgoing version of the opposite (textualist) fallacy.

It is worth pursuing Solomon's arguments here since his choice of Thucydides as a test-case has an obvious relevance in terms of the Gulf War and its implications for critical theory. As we have seen, he proposes a form of 'potentialist realism' which takes account of the inherent probabilities attached to this or that sequence of actions, choices or events, and which thereby avoids the sceptical conclusion that historical narrative is a fictive construct, unrelated – so far as we can possibly know – to the real-world happenings it purports to describe. Such doctrines carry credence only if we accept the postmodern-textualist thesis according to which there is simply no appeal beyond the various structures of linguistic, rhetorical, or narrative representation. That is to say, they reject the very idea that historical explanations might be judged more or less truthful, convincing or adequate to the degree that they make good sense not only in story-telling (fictive) terms but in relation to our knowledge of the broader regularities that characterize human experience in general. It will then seem absurd – just a species of sceptical over-reaction – to dump all notions of historical truth for the sake of pursuing a textualist line that can scarcely explain how we manage to interpret postmodernist fictional texts, let alone those other forms of truth-seeking discourse that claim historical warrant. 'Let us hypothesize', Solomon writes,

> that the Peloponnesian referent refers to a dynamic synthesis of real, not subjective, historical actualities *and* potentialities. These do not absolutely determine our interpretations of the specific actualities that bear them, but they can help to guide them. They can, that is to say, help us both evaluate and hierarchize our possible interpretations. It will be asked: Why *should* we hierarchize our interpretational beliefs? Certainly there is no *scholarly* reason to do so. The scholar can certainly be content with a pluralistic analysis of the ways in which other scholars have sought to interpret the movement of history. But if the scholar wishes to move from the word to the world, from gnosis and analysis to praxis and decision, he or she will have to take some kind of stand, and to take that stand, he or she will require some ground to stand on. And as criticism begins to turn toward the nuclear referent, in particular, and the political referent, in general, it might well consider the potentialist 'ground' that is implicitly offered in Thucydides' own interpretation of the Peloponnesian referent. For in Thucydides' representation of the ways in which two rather uneasy allies finally fell out over ideological and geo-political differences, we may discern a not so very distant analogy to the super-power conflict of our own time, an analogy that is strengthened by the relative non-totality of both the nuclear and the Peloponnesian referents.[12]

In the same way – as I have argued – we are not without resources (historical, critical or ethical resources) when thinking about the Gulf War and the issues it raises for our knowledge of real-world events. We can still point out the various factual discrepancies, the distortions of truth and the massive *improbabilities* that have characterized much (but not all) of the media coverage devoted to events in the Gulf. And we can do this *despite and against* all the evidence that 'public opinion' – as sedulously monitored by the same media channels – came out decidedly in support of the war pretty much from beginning to end. Only on a thoroughgoing pragmatist view (i.e. that what is right or true is what's currently and contingently 'good in the way of belief') will this seem an adequate ground for accepting that the war was indeed, as its proponents would have it, a justified defence of 'democratic values' by the nations of the 'free-world' alliance.

It is not surprising that neo-pragmatist ideas have acquired such prominence in recent US philosophical and literary-critical debate. For they provide a useful means – along with opinion-poll sampling, mass-media manipulation and other such well-tried persuasive techniques – for marginalizing dissident views and ensuring that anyone opposed to the current consensus, no matter how articulate or well-informed, will be viewed as belonging to a fringe group whose arguments scarcely warrant serious attention. And it is no great distance from ideas like these – implicitly endorsed (sad to say) by a sizable number of 'advanced' critical theorists – to the populist talk of anti-war protestors as an 'unpatriotic' minority, failing to support 'our boys in the Gulf' and thus proving their utter lack of decent citizenly feeling. That this minority might nevertheless be right – right, that is to say, on factual, historical, and ethico-political grounds – was a notion unthinkable to most people at a time when so much effort had gone into swinging public opinion behind the war. And yet the fact remains: whenever the anti-war case was put by competent speakers in relatively open debate – and this was a relatively rare occurrence – then their arguments not only carried the day but reduced their pro-war opponents (government ministers, military historians, armchair strategists, 'experts' on Arab affairs, etc) to a state of silence or blustering outrage that signalled their lack of any genuine justifying grounds. Such encounters were, unsurprisingly, excluded from prime-time television coverage. And in the press there was an inverse correlation between the level of unqestioning support for this war and the level of informed or intelligent debate.[13] But the lack of space or air-time given to those opposing the war showed dramatically the way in which the values of 'free-world' liberal democracy – those values in whose name, after all, this war was being waged – can collapse when exposed to the coercive pressures of a wholesale ideological-conformist crusade.

The media coverage of the Gulf War is, however, no reason (I repeat) to go along with Baudrillard and take the view that 'truth' and 'reality' are nowadays *wholly indistinguishable* from the kinds of wholesale simulation – or the forms of institutionalized pseudo-debate – that exert such a hold upon the currency of thought and belief. For it is still possible to perceive the various blind-spots, gaps, contradictions, manifest non-sequiturs and downright lies that punctuate 'official' discourse, and which thus give a hold for constructing an alternative – more adequate and truthful – version of events. This applies just as much to those involved at the 'production' end – reporters, editors, programme producers, newspaper columnists, etc – as to those who 'consume' the resultant information and apply a greater or lesser degree of informed critical awareness. Of course the production people were subject to enormous pressures of censorship, whether in the form of explicit directives from government and military sources, or through the workings of a self-imposed professional code which told them (in effect) that their jobs were on the line if they put out news-reports or offered opinions at variance with the official account. Nevertheless there were occasions when (so to speak) the credibility-gap opened to such an extent that viewers could hardly fail to recognize the discrepancy between the authorized version – as given in the voice-over commentary, subject to military clearance – and what they were actually witnessing on screen.

Two examples stand out with particular vividness and will no doubt continue to provoke bitter controversy. One was the 'Allied' bombing of an air-raid shelter at Amiriyah that contained large numbers of civilian men, women and children, but which – according to US sources – was in fact an Iraqi operational command-centre, and thus a legitimate target. The television news reports (BBC and ITN, evening February 14 and thereafter) dutifully relayed the official explanation, along with the usual government talk of 'tragedy', 'collateral damage', 'unavoidable accidents of war', etc. But they also showed both the carnage inflicted (dead children, charred bodies, grieving relatives) *and* the evidence – presented noncommitally in the voice-over, but unmistakable to any alert viewer – that this bunker contained not the least sign of having served in a military, strategic or communications role. What thus came across was the *flat contradiction* between, on the one hand, the US and British propaganda version of events, and on the other the witness of visual images which succeeded at least for a while in challenging the official 'Allied' line. In this case the ground for alleging untruth was the perceived mismatch between those images and what was being said by way of justification or excuse by authorities with every motive for offering a false account. That is to say, their version lacked credibility even on a simple correspondence-theory of how assertions hook up with the domain of real-world, factual states of affairs. But in addition, the Americans then proceeded to claim (a) that their intelligence apparatus and surveillance systems were so advanced as to have given them proof positive that the Iraqis were employing the bunker for military purposes, and (b) that they had no knowledge of civilians using the shelter owing to some breakdown or localized fault in those same (supposedly infallible) systems. Here it is a coherence-theory that is needed – and no very subtle application of it – to see that one or the other claim is at very least open to doubt.[14]

The second incident that stretched credibility to something near breaking-point was the mass-bombardment of retreating Iraqi forces, carried out on the pretext of their still having their armour with them, despite their manifest incapacity to pose any further military threat. Here again, the visual evidence was so graphic (and appalling) that nobody – except those viewers completely hooked on the US propaganda line – could have doubted that this was a large-scale atrocity, and a war-crime on any reasonable definition of the term.[15] My point is that reporters and viewers alike were subject to a conflict of interpretations which involved on the one hand a rhetorical appeal to the 'realities' of war, the inevitability of 'collateral damage' and so forth, and on the other a knowledge – despite all these powerful suasive techniques – that such rhetoric was designed to conceal the truth of a needless and brutal attack against refugee forces. Now of course it might be argued (from a postmodern-pragmatist viewpoint) that what we have here is not so much an issue of 'truth' *versus* 'falsehood' but a pure and irreducible difference of opinion, a quarrel that cannot be resolved by appealing to the putative facts of the case, since those 'facts' exist only in the form of simulated media images, and are in any case subject to a wide variety of possible interpretations.

Lyotard would no doubt go further and insist that there is a manifest injustice – a domineering drive to monopolize the discourse of truth and right – in any thinking that presumes to adjudicate these differences, or to decide the issue between them on a basis of 'enlightened' critical judgment.[16] Michael Ignatieff adopted something very like Lyotard's position in a piece published in the *Observer* during the closing days of the Allied campaign. 'As the war ends', he wrote,

> everyone is exactly where they were when it started. The languages of moral concern hardly connect. Some people's radar of outrage is only picking up the criminal carnage on the Kuwait to Basra road [i.e., the saturation bombardment of retreating Iraqi troops]; others are only picking up the atrocities in Kuwait. . . . Those who supported sanctions can now point to the Iraqi dead and say: we told you so. Those who supported the war, as I have done, will reply: the cost would have been still higher had we delayed 18 months to wait for

sanctions to fail. Neither side has the slightest hope of convincing the other. To quote Edgar Morin in *Le Monde*: we are dealing here with an encounter between 'blind moralities', 'one-way indignations' and 'unilateral forms of pity'.[17]

This argument misses the point, however, since it ignores the special responsibility that we, as citizens of the 'Allied' countries, have with regard to the conduct of a war that was waged *in our name* by 'democratic' governments claiming a popular mandate for their actions. Of course Saddam's was a vicious and brutal regime which caused great suffering among his own people and the captive population of occupied Kuwait. But this does not mean that there is no room for argument on exactly those issues that Ignatieff thinks beyond hope of reasoned debate. These questions include the likely effectiveness of sanctions (had they been given time enough to work), the Allied strategy of air and missile attacks against centres of urban and civilian life, and the justice – or even the strategic value – of a war carried on with ferocious intensity well beyond the point of Iraqi military collapse. Moreover, such debates will *not* be just a matter of this or that preferred interpretation, but will involve the appeal to documented facts, the giving of good (adequately reasoned) arguments, and the willingness to weigh conflicting accounts from a standard of impartial truth-seeking enquiry.

These are issues that concern us in so far as they involve our assent to a certain understanding of the war, an understanding not only of its day-to-day conduct, tactical motives, propaganda claims and counter-claims etc, but also of the relevant background history, geo-political implications, and the long-term aims of the combatants. No doubt it is possible, as Ignatieff says, for thinking individuals to arrive at very different conclusions with regard to each of these questions; and also with regard to the overriding issue of whether or not the Gulf War was justified on moral and political grounds. But to suggest that these views are so completely at odds as to render meaningful argument impossible – since the parties would be talking at cross-purposes with no shared criteria or common grounds of debate – amounts to a vote of no confidence in the principles of reason, truth and justice.

This view also implies a version of the fact/value dichotomy that has plagued philosophy at least since Hume (or a certain misreading of Hume), and whose effects on recent critical theory have been nothing short of disastrous. For it is simply not the case – as Lyotard believes, and as Ignatieff likewise tends to suggest – that issues of fact have absolutely no bearing on issues of ethical judgment; or that (in the standard philosophical parlance) one cannot argue from an 'is' to an 'ought'. Hume's point, on the contrary, was that we *can and do* accomplish this feat very often as a matter of everyday, practical experience, i.e. whenever we base moral judgments on a knowledge of real-world antecedent facts or probable future consequences – although precisely how we do it *from a logical point of view* was a puzzle (as he thought) beyond hope of reasoned solution. Postmodernists like Lyotard standardly ignore the first point and seize on the second as justification for declaring the downright impossibility of moving across from the 'language-game' of cognitive judgment to the 'language-games' of ethics and politics. And this attitude finds voice in the opinion – endorsed by Ignatieff in his *Observer* piece – that differences of view on the rights or wrongs of the Gulf War cannot be a matter of argued debate about what *actually happened*.

Neopragmatism and the Rhetoric of Assent

Arguments such as those of Baudrillard or Lyotard would scarcely have achieved such prominence – or been taken seriously by so many commentators – had they not coincided with the widespread drift toward varieties of ultra-relativist thinking in matters of historical, political and ethical judgment. Postmodernism is merely the most extreme (or, as some would say, most consistent and consequent) version of this desire to have done with all truth-claims beyond what is presently and contingently 'good in the way of belief'. It goes along with the current neo-pragmatist line, as argued by thinkers like Rorty and Fish, that the only kind of truth that counts is the power to persuade members of one's own interest-group, 'interpretive community', or professional guild.[18]

In which case clearly the Gulf War issue must resolve into a matter of consensus opinion among those – chiefly the US and 'Allied' communities – whose understanding of events will dominate discussion and determine how the story gets told over the next few months, years or decades. It would then serve no purpose to resist or contest that account on factual, historical, political or ethical grounds, since such arguments could only prevail to the extent that there *already existed* a more or less receptive climate of opinion, a communal readiness to grant them a hearing and view them as somehow fitting in with a sense of what the war was really about. For if indeed it is the case – as these thinkers suppose – that all truth-claims eventually come down to a question of suasive appeal within this or that cultural context, then it follows that any appeal to 'the facts', to valid arguments, 'just war' principles and so forth could never do more than provide extra rhetorical or psychological back-up for beliefs that already commanded some measure of communal agreement. Thus rhetoric, in Fish's phrase, goes 'all the way down', and theory-talk is redundant – or self-deceiving – except in so far as it consents to occupy this drastically diminished role.

The first generation of American pragmatists – James, Dewey and Peirce – would scarcely have acknowledged any kinship with the doctrine now offered in their name. Rorty himself finds problems with Peirce on account of the latter's unfortunate desire to hang on to some ultimate, regulative notion of 'truth at the end of enquiry'.[19] Dewey – undoubtedly the hero of Rorty's narrative – was none the less a stickler for factual truth when he chaired the unofficial US tribunal investigating the trumped-up charges of espionage laid against Trotsky during his period of exile by Stalin's secret police.[20] And William James provides perhaps the most significant contrast in his staunch opposition to US involvement in another 'war of liberation', the Philippines campaign of 1910–11 which can now be seen as setting the pattern for numerous subsequent military adventures dressed up in a rhetoric of high moral purpose.[21] In short, there is a world of difference – in philosophical and ethico-political terms – between the stance adopted by those early proponents of the pragmatist outlook and the current (postmodern) use of their ideas as a knock-down argument against all forms of dissident or critical-interventionist thought. And this difference has a lot to do with the turn – clearly evident in Rorty and Fish – toward post-structuralist ideas of language, discourse or representation that deny any access to reality and truth except by way of signifying systems which would render such access strictly impossible. If one accepts all this, then of course the way is open for neo-pragmatists to draw the familiar conclusion: that truth is *always and only* what counts as such within a given 'interpretive community' (Fish) or at a given stage in the ongoing cultural 'conversation of mankind' (Rorty). And it will then appear flatly impossible that any counter-argument on factual, historical, or ethically principled grounds could ever carry weight or even make sense to members of the relevant community.

It seems to me that literary theory has a lot to answer for when it comes to assessing the extent and the damaging influence of these modish ultra-relativist ideas. What has occurred across a range of disciplines – and often in the most 'advanced' sectors of speculative thought – is a full-scale reversal of the commonsense view that holds language to be normally and properly accountable to standards of truth-telling probity, and which regards fiction – or the various forms of non-truth-conditional utterance – as construable only in terms of its relation (albeit a complex and hybrid relation) to those same normative standards. Tony Bennett again provides a useful gloss on the effects of such thinking when carried over into subject-areas (especially historiography) that have registered the impact of post-structuralist ideas. 'Given the difficulties associated with literary conceptions of literature', he writes,

> little is to be gained from granting these an extended sphere of operation such that all documents fall within their compass. Textualizing the past in such a way that it can be rendered permanently undecidable serves little purpose. Keeping the past open in the cause of keeping present possibilities open and fluid serves every politics in principle but none in practice. For the latter requires, however provisionally, that the past be fixed, that what can be said of it – what can surface there and be 'in the truth' – be subject to definite limitations, substantive and procedural, if those truths, and the contest over them, are to count for much. This is not a matter of closing down the past but simply of recognising that its openness cannot be infinite if the truths produced there are to prove actionable.[22]

In other words, there is a path that leads directly from the textualist (or neo-pragmatist) suspension of determinate historical truth-claims to the attitude of supine moral and political acquiescence that equates truth with some existing state of received consensus belief. For on this view there could be no warrant – no intelligible reason or justification – for any argument that went clean against the prevailing socio-cultural drift, or that challenged the consensus from a standpoint outside its agreed-upon values and assumptions. In which case opponents of the Gulf War would be caught in one or other of the two rhetorical predicaments which – according to Rorty and Fish – offer the only possible alternatives for anyone who sets out to argue a case. In so far as their objections made enough sense to persuade some (more or less sizable) proportion of the relevant 'interpretive community', they would already be arguing from a position of relative strength, 'preaching to the converted', so to speak, or at any rate falling in with certain predisposed habits of belief. So any principles, grounds or factual arguments adduced in support of their claim would amount to nothing more than a morale-boosting gesture – a source of added rhetorical appeal – for themselves and their like-minded audience. On the other hand, if their arguments *didn't* possess some measure of foregone suasive appeal, then it would be no use claiming factual or principled warrant for a position which simply lacked credibility according to the current consensus view. In either case – so the neo-pragmatists urge – it is persuasive force (or the rhetoric of assent) that finally decides such issues.

An event like the Gulf War throws these questions into sharp relief by stressing the sheer distance that exists between consensus-belief (as represented by the opinion-polls, newspaper coverage and mass-media feedback mechanisms) and those issues of real-world truth and falsehood that provide the only basis for reasoned opposition on the part of conscientious objectors. That so many thinkers are currently concerned to collapse or 'deconstruct' such distinctions is a standing indictment of much that now passes for 'advanced' theoretical wisdom. Where these arguments fail most conspicuously is in backing the idea that truth is nothing more than a figment of the social imaginary, a name that gets attached to whatever sorts of truth-claim happen to prevail from time to time within one's own 'interpretive community'. Nothing succeeds like success, so these doctrines hold, and 'success' can be measured only by the degree to which one's beliefs fit in with the consensual status quo. Thus for Rorty it is a matter of sustaining the 'conversation' on terms laid down by membership of a community whose geo-political parameters are those of 'North Atlantic Postmodern Bourgeois Liberal Democracy'.[23] Such is the last, best hope for intellectuals like himself – who after all are well placed to enjoy the benefits on offer, and who can have no sensible reason for wanting to disrupt the conversation on behalf of other, less privileged mortals. That those others might feel themselves excluded – if not forcibly dragooned or bombed into compliance – in the name of a New World Order conceived on the US model is, of course, a possibility that Rorty can scarcely entertain, concerned as he to relegate such conflicts to the margins of civilized debate. And for Fish likewise it is strictly inconceivable that anyone, bar a few self-deluded radical theorists, should think to stand outside the existing 'interpretive community' and criticize its values and beliefs from a viewpoint at odds with the current consensus wisdom.

In short, what these thinkers are proposing is just another version of the 'end-of-ideology' thesis, devised in the late 1950s by Daniel Bell and other apologists for the previous (Cold War) phase of US expansionist policy, and now revived by think-tank intellectuals with different geo-political ends in view, but working to much the same political agenda.[24] All the more convenient that, just at this moment, the high ground of cultural debate should be captured by a group of theorists (or anti-theorists) who proclaim the obsolescence of enlightened critique, the ubiquity of consensus values, and the advantages to be had by going along with this emergent sense of a New World Order equated – so it happens – with the interests and priorities of current US strategic policy.[25] From this point of view, opposition to the Gulf War could only be seen as a tedious irrelevance, an appeal to that old (late-1960s) ethos of counter-hegemonic protest and dissent which in the end produced nothing more than a kind of short-lived collective neurosis. Whence the much publicized mood of 'post-Vietnam' euphoria, the notion – put about by George Bush and his publicity machine – that Allied victory in the Gulf War had somehow laid the Vietnam trauma to rest and enabled Americans to feel once again that sense of well-being or manifest destiny which had suffered only a momentary setback, a 'crisis' brought about by whinging left-liberals who greatly exaggerated the extent of US 'defeat' in that earlier war of liberation. In short, history could now be re-written in keeping with a new-found spirit of upbeat expansionist vigour. All of which might seem to bear out the Fish-Rorty line of argument, i.e. the relativity of truth-values and the idea that our representations of the past are the upshot of present-day consensus beliefs or notions of how history ought to shape up according to the current self-image of the age.

Such doctrines involve a peculiarly vicious version of the so-called 'hermeneutic circle', the notion that we are always, inescapably confined to the order of taken-for-granted values (or the structures of tacit pre-understanding) that determine what shall count as a viable argument at any given time.[26] So if the 'cultural conversation' has entered a phase where topics like 'victory in the Gulf War' and 'kicking the Vietnam trauma' tend to dominate discussion, then there is no point trying to resist such talk by appealing to historical realities or pointing out the various well-practised propaganda techniques by which the mass-media have managed to create this mood of euphoric abandon. Any counter-arguments will only take effect once the mood has already passed, by which time talk of 'facts' and 'principles' will again be beside the point, since the majority of people (or a large enough number) will by then have been persuaded to accept the justice of the anti-war case without need for further demonstration. And if this happened somewhat belatedly in the case of Vietnam – too late for public opinion to prevent many acts that were subsequently viewed as atrocities or war-crimes – then this merely goes to show that high-toned principled arguments count for nothing against the weight of received consensus-values. Moreover, the fact that opinion is shifting yet again – back toward a mood of 'post-Vietnam' triumphalism – is still further evidence, if any were needed, that the rhetoric of assent goes all the way down, and that truth is indeed purely and simply a matter of what is 'good in the way of belief'.

There are few things more depressing on the current intellectual scene than this collapse of moral and political nerve brought about – or at any rate deeply influenced – by various forms of postmodern-pragmatist thought. For the result of such ideas is firstly to undermine any sense of the *epistemological* distinction between truth and falsehood, and secondly to place *ethical* issues beyond reach of argued, responsible debate by making them contingent upon this or that state of consensus opinion, no matter how ill-informed or subject to the pressures of distorted mass-media coverage. Of course it may be said that the relation between knowing and willing (or, in Kantian terms, cognitive understanding and 'practical reason') has long been a vexed topic, not least within that discourse of enlightenment thought which postmodernists like Lyotard interrogate in order to bring out its concealed value-agenda, along with its attendant blind-spots and aporias. But what emerges at the end of this revisionist line is an outlook of deep-laid scepticism with regard not only to the truth-telling claims of Enlightenment *Ideologiekritik* but also to the ethical values bound up with those claims, i.e. the principle – central to Kantian philosophy – that it is our duty as responsible citizens to *think for ourselves* on matters of significant moral and political choice, and to base such commitments on the *best available knowledge* of their real-world conditions and consequences.[27] Thus, however complex their relations in Kant, understanding and practical reason cannot be separated, at least not to the point of viewing them (like Lyotard) as belonging to entirely 'heterogeneous' language-games beyond all hope of eventual arbitration on jointly epistemic, historical and ethico-political grounds. The trouble with so much current theorizing, whether in the postmodernist, post-structuralist or neo-pragmatist vein, is that it reduces all these orders of truth-claim to a mere play of competing 'discourses' devoid of any warrant beyond what is supplied by the current conversational rules of the game. In so doing it effectively revokes the idea (the outmoded 'enlightenment' belief) that there exists a significant margin of choice on issues of ethical conscience, and furthermore, that our judgments of right and wrong need not – and should not – be simply a matter of consensus-values, but should involve the critical scrutiny of conflicting arguments and the effort to adjudicate between them on a basis of good-faith, rational debate.

Of course such talk will sound hopelessly old-fashioned after (e.g.) Foucault's demolition of the Kantian subject, his claim that it was really just a figment of language, a transient 'fold' in the order of discourse or representation, a curious 'transcendental-empirical doublet' which has now disappeared from view with the advent of a different (post-humanist or genealogical) paradigm. But there is no good reason to regard this argument as anything more than a piece of fashionable late-1960s rhetoric, trading on a mixture of Nietzschean and Heideggerian irrationalism, together with the vaunted linguistic (or post-structuralist) 'turn' across various disciplines of thought. That it has continued to exert such widespread appeal – to the point of becoming a veritable *doxa* among thinkers like Lyotard and Baudrillard – is just another sign of the lamentably fashion-prone character of present-day 'critical theory'.

4

FROM THE SUBLIME TO THE ABSURD (LYOTARD)

OF LIES AND LANGUAGE-GAMES

Of course I am not claiming that the 'truth' of the Gulf War is a matter of plain, self-evident fact, or that simply by assembling the relevant details – the casualty figures, the extent of ecological damage, the diplomatic record, the history of previous US and British involvements in the region, etc – one could overcome Hume's famous dilemma and move straight on from an 'is' to an 'ought'. That is to say, there will continue to be deep disagreements both as regards the facts of the case and the justice (or the moral defensibility) of the 'Allied' war campaign.[1] Moreover, these differences are unlikely to be settled as the propaganda smokescreen gradually clears and the historians, investigative journalists and others begin to provide a more adequate account of the war and events leading up to it. Undoubtedly there will still be those who maintain that the action was justified on several counts, among them the manifest evil and brutality of Saddam's regime, the atrocities inflicted on Kuwait and its citizens during the period of Iraqi occupation, the threat of further acts of aggression against Saudi Arabia and other Gulf states, the prospect of continuing instability in the region, and so forth. Clearly it would be wrong for the anti-war party to discount these arguments *tout court* as so many items of US propaganda served up to justify its own pursuit of economic self-interest, control over the oil supplies, and long-term hegemonic influence. But the fact that such events are always subject to differing interpretations is no reason to regard them as simply beyond reach of constructive, truth-seeking argument, or – in Lyotard's terms – as belonging to heterogeneous language-games where any attempt to convince the other party, on factual or ethico-political grounds, would amount to a form of speech-act coercion, an injustice or infraction of the conversational ground-rules. For if this were the case then there could be no prospect of advancing discussion beyond the mere exchange of personal opinion or idiosyncratic belief. Any claim to do more – to offer good reasons or grounds for distinguishing valid from invalid arguments – would at best be a useless endeavour, and at worst a totalitarian gesture that aimed to silence competing voices.

Such thinking has nothing to commend it beyond the vague appeal to a liberal-pluralist ethos that rules out the more blatant forms of authoritarian thought-control. Even here it runs into obvious problems as soon as one asks what exceptions might exist – what permissible forms of reasoned counter-argument or objection on conscientious grounds – in the case of beliefs (like right-wing revisionist 'readings' of the Holocaust) that flouted every standard of historical truth or ethical accountability.

To be fair, Lyotard confronts this issue at its most sensitive point, namely in connection with Faurisson's outrageous thesis that we cannot know for sure that the gas-chambers existed, since there survived no witnesses to corroborate the fact as a matter of first-hand experiential proof.[2] But his position makes it difficult for Lyotard to denounce this imposture as a downright lie, a massive falsification of the truth whose political motives are evident enough, and which could only win credence by playing upon the ignorance, stupidity or malice of a like-minded readership. Thus, according to Lyotard, Faurisson's argument constitutes an 'injustice' chiefly in discursive or speech-act terms, that is to say, as an affront to the victims that results from illicitly applying the criteria of one language-game (i.e. the factual-documentary) to another kind of discourse where the truth-claims in question are of a wholly incommensurable order. As Lyotard puts it: 'if the demand to have to establish the reality of the referent of a sentence is extended to any sentence . . . then that demand is totalitarian in its principle'.[3] And in Geoffrey Bennington's words, summarizing Lyotard:

> positivist historians are at the mercy of a Faurisson if they imagine that justice consists solely in the application of cognitive rules in such cases. If history were merely a question of such rules, it is hard to know how Faurisson could be accused of injustice.[4]

This is all very well in so far as it makes the point – as against sophists and hard-line ideologues like Faurisson – that historical truth rarely (if ever) comes packaged in bite-sized chunks of information that can then be checked against the evidence in a straightforward empirical way. It is precisely this simplified, positivist notion of truth whose unworkability has lately given rise to the various forms of modish ultra-relativist doctrine. But Lyotard promptly confuses the issue by arguing that the only way out of this false dichotomy is the road that leads on to postmodernist talk of 'language-games', 'phrase-regimes', 'discursive differentials' and so forth, thus falling back into the relativist trap of making truth-claims solely and exclusively a product of socio-linguistic convention.

As a result, Lyotard can envisage no way of debating such issues with justice except through the adoption of a pluralist outlook wherein each litigant respects the other's difference of viewpoint, even to the extent of suspending his or her own truth-claims for the sake of maintaining this liberal *modus vivendi*. Any attempt to do otherwise – to suggest that some arguments are just flat wrong on factual or ethical grounds – must be seen as an unwarranted discursive move designed to monopolize debate and silence one's opponent. In so doing, it not only tends to perpetuate the cycle of repression and victimization – even if aimed toward establishing the truth of such claims, as in the case of the death-camps – but puts one in a disadvantaged position *vis-à-vis* the antagonist (e.g. Faurisson) who can likewise decline to play by the rules. Thus, according to Lyotard:

> the historian need not strive to convince Faurisson if Faurisson is "playing" another genre of discourse, one in which conviction, or, the obtainment of a consensus over a defined reality, is not at stake. Should the historian persist along this path, he will end up in the position of victim.[5]

But this conclusion only follows if we accept Lyotard's major premise, namely that the various speech-act 'genres' (cognitive, ethico-political etc) are so radically heterogeneous that their truth-claims exist in a state of perpetual conflict, or (at best) in a stand-off achieved by acknowledging their strictly incommensurable character. What he thus fails to recognize – for reasons bound up with his doctrinaire postmodernist stance – is the fact that in the great majority of cases there is no such conflict between truth-telling motives (or cognitive interests) on the one hand, and issues of ethical accountability on the other. Getting things right – or as right as one can get them by the best methods of empirical, historical or factual-documentary research – may itself be a prime responsibility in matters of ethico-political judgment. And never more so, *pace* Lyotard, than in cases where the victims are subject to a campaign of disinformation – or a conspiracy of silence – which compounds the original injustice by denying (like Faurisson) that their wrong can be a matter of proven, indubitable knowledge. For on Lyotard's reckoning the only way to counter such flagrant abuses of the truth is to shift into a different register, a 'phrase-regime' where issues of factual record or empirical warrant give way before the claims of an ethical tribunal under whose jurisdiction those criteria simply don't apply. But this offers little more than a strategy of evasion, a recourse to the kind of last-ditch relativist position that effectively lets the whole argument go by default.

LYOTARD ON KANT

One measure of Lyotard's extreme anti-cognitivist stance is the prominence he gives to the Kantian sublime as a category of ethical and socio-political thought. For Kant, the sublime is that which exceeds all our powers of determinate representation, an experience for which we can find no adequate sensuous or conceptual mode of apprehension, and which differs from the beautiful in so far as it affords no sense of harmonious balance or agreement between those faculties.[6] And yet there is something in us, a responsive capacity, that gives the word 'sublime' its meaning (however indeterminate), and whose nature Kant associates with the realm of 'suprasensible' (i.e. inward or non-phenomenal) ideas and judgments. Thus it is precisely at the point where understanding comes up against the limits of its power to comprehend experience – to 'bring intuitions under concepts', in Kant's phrase – that we achieve an insight into that which lies beyond the domain of phenomenal cognition, namely our existence as autonomous, free-willing agents who are *not* entirely subject to those laws or necessities that operate in the other (causal-determinist) realm. In short, the sublime figures for Kant as a means of expressing – albeit by analogy – what would otherwise be strictly inexpressible, since it is in the very nature of ethical judgment (or practical reason) that its dictates issue from a realm beyond the grasp of determinate concepts or phenomenal cognition. Hence also its importance for Lyotard, offering as it does an index of the radically disjunct or heterogeneous character of the various phrase-regimes and language-games whose differences must always be borne in mind when seeking to render justice to the rival litigants in any given case. Above all, it signifies the wrong that may always be inflicted on one of those parties when the other appeals to cognitive (factual or evidential) criteria which cannot be satisfied – as with Faurisson's thesis on the death-camps – or which allow the opponent no effective right of reply on his or her own behalf.

The Kantian sublime thus serves as a reminder of the gulf that opens up – the 'differend', as Lyotard terms it – between truth-claims lacking any common measure of justice by which to resolve their dispute. In such cases, Lyotard writes,

> one side's legitimacy does not imply the other's lack of legitimacy. However, applying a single rule of judgment to both in order to settle their differend . . . would wrong (at least) one of them (and both of them if neither side admits this rule). . . . A wrong results from the fact that the rules of the genre of discourse by which one judges are not those of the judged genre or genres of discourse.[7]

But it is clear that the sublime – on Lyotard's reading – has a tendency to weigh such disputes in favour of the non-cognitivist phrase-regime, or the party whose claims rest not so much on an appeal to the facts of the case as on the basis of a purely ethical injunction divorced from issues of veridical warrant. And indeed it could hardly be otherwise, given his stress on that aspect of Kant's thinking that equates the autonomy of practical reason with its belonging to a phrase-regime maximally distant from the claims of empirical cognition on the one hand and conceptual understanding on the other. What justice requires in such matters of non-self-evident truth is that one should always be willing to judge 'without criteria', or to keep an open mind with regard to the various protocols, stakes or decision-procedures that mark out the 'differend' – the conflict of interests – in any given case. Above all, it should prevent us from seeking to impose some single, uniform criterion (e.g. that of empirical truth or cognitive accountability) where the issue involves a quite different order of ethical or socio-political judgment. And it is here – according to Lyotard – that the Kantian sublime takes on its most significant role, not only in relation to matters of aesthetic taste but also as concerns the powers and limits of practical reason. For it is the mark of the sublime that it 'has no concept for which to present its sensible or imaginative intuition'; that it 'cannot determine a realm, but only a field'; and that the field in question 'is only determined to a second degree, reflectively, so to speak: not by the commensurability between a presentation and a concept, but by the indeterminate commensurability between the capacity for presenting and the capacity for conceptualizing.'[8]

In other words – and here Lyotard follows Kant very closely – the sublime brings us up against that limit-point of thought where judgment has to recognize its own lack of resources (or the absence of agreed-upon criteria) for dealing with cases that exceed all the bounds of rule-governed, 'rational' adjudication. With his treatment of the sublime 'Kant advances far into heterogeneity', that is to say, into regions where the conflict of truth-claims cannot be resolved – as happens with the beautiful – by appealing to ideas of an ultimate reconciliation, a *sensus communis* where the faculties achieve a kind of working accord between their various interests. Such ideas can have no place in our experience of the sublime since here it is a question of feelings (obscure intimations) that so far overwhelm our capacity to discover any adequate sensuous or cognitive analogue that the mind registers an initial sense of utter failure or abjection, followed – as Kant describes it – by a wakening knowledge of the inward ('suprasensible') powers which occasioned that response in the first place. Thus, if 'the solution to the aesthetic antinomy appears much more difficult in the case of the sublime than it does in the case of the beautiful', then this is good reason for regarding the sublime as a salutary check upon our habits of premature judgment, especially our tendency to bring all cases under one particular phrase-regime – e.g. the cognitive – whose application outside its proper domain would represent an injustice, an ethical affront to those with different interests at stake.

What is required of us, therefore, in such situations is that we should 'venture forth by lending [our] ear to what is not presentable under the rules of knowledge. Every reality entails this exigency in so far as it entails possible unknown meanings. Auschwitz is the most real of realities in this respect'.[9] That is, we must answer the ethical challenge posed by a 'revisionist' ideologue like Faurisson by rejecting not only his sophistical 'proofs' but also, along with them, the very idea that questions of this order could properly be treated in terms of empirical or factual-documentary truth. For with the advent of the death-camps, Lyotard argues,

> something new has happened in history (which can only be a sign and not a fact) which is that the facts, the testimonies, which bore the traces of *heres* and *nows*, the documents which indicated the meaning or meanings of the facts, and the names, finally the possibility of diverse kinds of phrases whose conjunction makes reality, all this has been destroyed as much as possible.[10]

In which case the sublime would offer the most fitting analogy for an event which defies all forms of adequate representation, which reason (especially Enlightenment reason in its critical-speculative mode) is totally unable to assimilate, and which therefore demands that we respond to its summons without falling back on established criteria or protocols of validating judgment. Henceforth – after Auschwitz – we are indeed 'without resources' in the sense that such a name utterly repudiates all our preconceived notions of reason, humanity, truth and historical progress. It is no longer possible to think (like Hegel, or like Kant in his more sanguine moments) that history might be viewed as unfolding under the sign of a rational 'meta-narrative' whose various episodes – events like the French Revolution – were so many tokens of future promise, signposts on the road to perpetual peace and truth at the end of enquiry. All that is left to us now is the melancholy knowledge that this promise has failed to materialize, that history has turned against any form of affirmative dialectic, and that the names which are those of 'our' history ('Berlin 1953, Budapest 1956, Czechoslovakia 1968, Poland 1980' etc) are such as to destroy any lingering faith in that old Enlightenment project.[11]

The only possible response, as Lyotard sees it, is to maximize the range of first-order 'natural' language-games or narrative discourses, each of them judged according to its own criteria so that none can ever claim to dominate the others from a standpoint of ultimate, self-assured truth. This would provide at least the minimal condition for a just settlement of disputes, i.e. that all parties should receive an equal hearing and not find their arguments summarily dismissed through the appeal to some ground-rule or adjudicative precept that rejects their case out of hand. And for Lyotard it is the phrase-regime of cognitive judgments – the recourse to notions of empirical self-evidence, historical proof, first-hand documentary witness and so forth – that most often exerts this distorting pressure on the conduct of civilized debate. Of course he is not denying that such judgments are *sometimes* legitimate, that they possess (so to speak) a regional validity or appropriate sphere of jurisdiction, specifically in those cases where issues of factual truth and falsehood are a) by common assent the chief topic of dispute, and b) resolvable without having recourse to criteria that override the interests of one or another contending party. They can thus be applied without prejudice to instances of straightforward cognitive self-evidence, cases in which – as Lyotard puts it – 'the phrase of cognition requires the presentation of a corresponding intuition: the concept is then determined by means of the presentation that suits it, namely the schema'.[12] But clearly a problem arises when it comes to questions of a factual-documentary or historical nature, questions (that is to say) where there is no possibility of 'bringing intuitions under concepts', since the evidence exists only in the form of statements, texts, archival sources, scholarly reconstructions etc, all of which are open to dispute on the part of rival litigants or seekers-after-truth. At this point, Lyotard argues, we are confronted with issues that cannot be resolved within the 'phrase-regime' of cognitive judgment, and whose character is much better grasped by analogy with the Kantian discourse on aesthetics, especially where that discourse invokes the sublime as a figure for modes of experience or feeling that exceed all the powers of sensuous (phenomenal) cognition on the one hand, and conceptual understanding on the other. This is where the sublime differs from the beautiful: in the fact that it entails 'not only a disinterested pleasure and a universal without a concept', but also 'a finality of antifinality and a pleasure of pain, as opposed to the feeling of the beautiful whose finality is merely without an end and whose pleasure is due to the free agreement of the faculties with each other'.[13]

It is worth attending closely to Lyotard's argument at this point since it claims Kantian warrant for what can only be seen as a thoroughly un-Kantian (or anti-Enlightenment) approach to questions in the ethical and political domain. More specifically, it reflects the widespread tendency – among postmodernists and some deconstructors – to exploit Kant's notion of the sublime (or the analogous relation between aesthetics and ethics) to a point far beyond anything licensed by the relevant passages in the third *Critique*.[14] The effect of such readings is to render the commentators blind to those other, equally important passages where Kant warns against the confusions created by forgetting that these are analogies only – heuristic strategies or figures of thought – and are not to be taken as in any way conflating the two distinct realms of practical reason and aesthetic judgment. To be sure, they play an essential role in the overall argumentative structure of the three *Critiques*, providing Kant with an indirect (figurative) means of expression for that which inherently lies beyond reach of clear-cut explanatory treatment. Thus, in Lyotard's words,

> the *sensus communis* is, in aesthetics, what the whole of practical, reasonable beings is in ethics. It is an appeal to community carried out *a priori* and judged without a rule of direct presentation. However, in

the case of moral obligation [i.e., as figured in the sublime], the community is required by the mediation of a concept of reason, the Idea of freedom, while in the phrase of the beautiful, the community of addressors and addressees is called forth immediately, without the mediation of any concept, by feeling alone, inasmuch as this feeling can be shared *a priori*. The community is already there as taste, but it is not there yet as rational consensus.[15]

One could raise no serious objection to this as a straightforward paraphrase of Kant's thinking on the matter of ethical judgment as conceived *by analogy* with issues in the aesthetic domain. But where Lyotard decidedly parts company with Kant is in promoting the sublime – the aesthetic sublime – to a position of such transcendent authority that it becomes, in effect, the *sine qua non* of judgment in its ethico-political aspect. For with the sublime, we recall, 'Kant advances far into heterogeneity', that is to say, into regions where no single language-game (least of all that of cognitive judgment) is able to give the rule, and where thinking must own itself 'without resources' as regards the criteria – the operative standards – that should properly apply from one case to the next.

One can see why postmodernism attaches such significance to the Kantian sublime since it figures – for Lyotard and others – at that limit-point of language and representation where thought comes up against insoluble antinomies, and is thus forced to recognize the lack of common measure – or the radical heterogeneity – that inhabits both its own and other discourses. 'To give the differend its due', Lyotard writes, 'is to institute new addressees, new significations, and new referents in order for the wrong to find an expression and for the plaintiff to cease being a victim.'[16] Such an ethics should in principle be open to the widest possible variety of language-games, truth-claims, phrase-regimes etc, including – presumably – those that involved some appeal to the known or discoverable facts of the case. But in practice – as we have seen with Lyotard's comments on the Faurisson affair – it is this kind of truth-claim that he regularly views as striving to monopolize the whole conversation, and hence as an obstacle to the interests of justice.

Where Lyotard goes wrong in his reading of Kant is also – more importantly – where postmodernism errs in its broad diagnosis of the ills that have afflicted 'Enlightenment' thinking during the past two centuries and more. There are several sources of confusion here, each of them tending to reinforce the others through a process of circular confirmation that admits of no possible counter-argument. Thus: 1) It is assumed (mistakenly) that values like truth, reason and critique are on the side of a repressive 'monological' discourse that entertains no question as to its own grounding rationale; 2) This supposition gives rise to the further – equally erroneous – idea that any truth-claim resting on an argued appeal to the facts of the case is likely to involve some injustice with regard to other possible ways of viewing the matter, modes of understanding that show more respect for the ethics of open dialogical exchange; 3) Such injustices most often come about through an illicit extension of the cognitive phrase-regime into realms where different criteria apply, and where cognitive judgments should properly be ruled out of court; 4) There is no principle of justice more important than the maintenance of a pluralist ('language-games') approach that acknowledges the range of incommensurable values, beliefs or criteria, and which thus makes a virtue of abstaining from judgments of determinate truth and falsehood; 5) Any passage from facts to values – from an 'is' to an 'ought' – must be seen (after Hume and Kant, among others) not only as a logical impossibility but also as a species of ethical injustice, an infringement of the incommensurability rule; 6) The sublime thus moves to stage-centre as the name for whatever exceeds all those forms of conceptual knowledge, phenomenal intuition, self-evident truth etc. which normally govern our idea of what counts as a valid contribution to debate. And finally (7), as a consequence of all the foregoing: 'the sense pertinent for the criterion of justice and the sense pertinent for the criterion of truth are heterogeneous'.[17]

In other words there is simply no bridging the gulf between these different orders of discourse. Thus:

> phrases under the cognitive regimen, which undergo the sifting by truth-conditions, do not have a monopoly on sense. They are 'well formed'. But poorly formed senses are not absurd. . . . A phrase which attaches a life-ideal to a man's name and which turns that name into a *watchword* is . . . an ideal of practical or political reason in Kant's sense. The phrase presents what ought to be done, and simultaneously it presents the addressee who ought to do it. It does not arise from the true/false criterion because it is prescriptive. . . . In the case of the young Bonapartist, the stakes placed in *Bonaparte* are aesthetic, ethical, and political, not cognitive.[18]

In which case we should err in supposing, for example, that zealous adherents to the Reagan-Bush line on America's 'manifest destiny' as defender of free-world, democratic values could be argued out of their naive belief by an opponent who adduced – among other things – the record of US strategic interventions in Korea, Vietnam, Grenada, Panama, the Gulf and elsewhere; the massive casualties inflicted during the Gulf War on civilian populations despite all the talk of 'precision bombing', 'minimal collateral damage' etc; the evidence of large-scale diplomatic pressure brought to bear on other governments in order to achieve an appearance of 'Allied' resolve; and the fact (albeit a different order of truth-claim) that American war-aims not only exceeded but blatantly contravened the provisions of the relevant UN edicts, constantly invoked – though rarely spelled out – by way of moral justification. Such arguments would be simply beside the point, presuming as they do that matters of fact (or judgments in the cognitive/truth-telling mode) have a direct bearing on issues in the realm of ethics, politics, and historical understanding. For Lyotard, these issues can only be approached through a different ('incommensurable') language-game, one that discovers its closest analogy in the aesthetic – more specifically, the Kantian sublime – as a figure that exceeds all mere determinations of factual-documentary truth.

Thus 'historical cognition itself arouses a throng of senses (hypotheses, interpretations) in order to sift them out through the sieve that is the adducing of the proof'.[19] This is indeed 'what is called historical criticism'. But any 'proofs' in this area will be wholly ineffective as against the far stronger ethical claims of that 'throng of senses' that attach to certain sublime 'watchwords', and which thus stand beyond any possible reduction to the phrase-regime of cognitive judgment. For it is the mark of the differend, in Lyotard's words, that it inhabits 'the unstable state and instant of language wherein something that must be able to be put into phrases cannot yet be'. And again:

> The referent of a proper name, *Bonaparte, Auschwitz*, is both strongly determined in terms of its location among the network of names (worlds) and feebly determined in terms of its sense by dint of the large number and of the heterogeneity of phrase universes in which it can take place as an instance.[20]

In short, we fail to respect the diversity of language-games if we take just one (e.g. the cognitive, referential or factual-documentary) and treat it as enjoying a privileged status *vis-à-vis* questions of historical truth and ethical accountability. For history is always a 'sublime' referent in the sense that it calls forth differing responses which cannot be resolved *either* by appealing to 'the facts' (since those facts are inescapably a product of narrative interpretation), *or* by invoking established concepts of truth, justice or ethical principle (since those concepts are precisely what is at issue between the contending parties in any given case). From which it follows, according to Lyotard, that 'reality does not result from an experience', but has more to do with 'speculative logic' and with the kind of 'novelistic poetics (observing certain rules that determine narrative person and mode)' provided by literary theorists like Gérard Genette or textualist historiographers like Hayden White.[21] Thus the turn toward the sublime as an analogue for history, politics and ethical judgment goes along with a turn toward literary (textual) models by way of bringing home the relativity of 'truth' and the lack of any adequate criterial basis for deciding between rival language-games or narratives.

NARRATIVE AND HISTORICAL KNOWLEDGE

The trouble with all this is not only that it gets Kant wrong – a matter, one might think, of fairly specialized concern – but that it opens the way to some dangerous forms of moral and political obfuscation. Among them is the idea (pushed to the limit in Baudrillard's Gulf War article) that reality is indeed nothing more than the play of fictive strategies, war-game scenarios, media simulations etc, all of them inhabiting a space of sublime ('hyperreal') pseudo-referents where issues of truth and falsehood are neither here nor there. Thus, the misreading of Kant takes on a wider relevance, as part of this postmodernist drive to deconstruct – for which read 'demolish' or 'obliterate' – the legacy of Enlightenment thought. For in Kant there is no question of aestheticizing ethics and politics in the way that Lyotard wants, and that other thinkers – Walter Benjamin and Paul de Man among them – have pointed to as a major source of right-wing political mystification.[22] Nor does Kant ever go as far as Lyotard in divorcing ethical judgment (or practical reason) from the interests of truth-seeking enquiry, the need – that is to say – that moral agents should base their choices and decisions on the *best possible knowledge* of the real-world circumstances, antecedent conditions and likely future consequences that alone give their actions a claim to genuine ethical significance.

Of course Kant lays great stress on the distinction between issues in the realm of epistemology (where the validating rule is that intuitions should be 'brought under' adequate concepts), and questions that cannot be addressed in these terms since they belong to the order of 'suprasensible' ideas, having to do with thinking (*Denken*) in its ethical or speculative aspect, and not with knowing (*Erkennen*) as a matter of phenomenal-conceptual grasp. His grounds for so doing are evident enough: that the autonomy of practical reason would otherwise be compromised – even destroyed – in so far as it turned out to be dependent upon, or analogous to, that realm of determinate truth-claims where necessity is the absolute rule.[23] Hence the notoriously abstract character of Kant's 'categorical imperative', its failure – as many critics have noted – to provide a sufficiently 'thick' description of real-life ethical predicaments, or to take account of the manifold complexities, doubts and ambivalent motives that often crowd in upon the process of ethical reflection.[24] But readers of Kant will surely be aware that this isn't the whole story, and that he often fills out the picture with examples, instances and illustrative cases that go at least some way toward rebutting that charge. As Habermas puts it:

> neither Kantian ethics nor discourse ethics lays itself open to the charge that since it defines the moral principle in formal or procedural terms, it can only make tautological statements about morality. . . . The issue is whether we can *all* will that a contested norm gain binding force under given conditions. The content that is tested by a moral principle is generated not by the philosopher but by real life. The conflicts of action that come to be morally judged and consensually resolved grow out of everyday life. Reason as a tester of maxims (Kant) or actors as participants in argumentation (discourse ethics) *find* these conflicts. They do not create them.[25]

What is remarkable about Lyotard's reading, on the other hand, is that it thoroughly obscures this situational or worldly aspect of Kantian ethics by exploiting the sublime as a kind of blocking agent, a wedge that is driven between the two realms (i.e. those of knowledge and suprasensible ideas) to the point where their interests diverge absolutely, so that ethical injunctions are conceived as issuing from a voice of conscience utterly indifferent to real-world practical concerns. In short, he makes Kant sound more like the Kierkegaard of *Fear and Trembling* than a proponent of enlightened autonomy in matters of ethical, political and religious conscience.

This is all the more surprising given Lyotard's stress on 'narrative pragmatics' as a means of understanding how communities arrive at a sense of their own cultural identity and negotiate the various legitimation-crises thrown up by conflicting value-systems.[26] For on this account it would seem that ethical issues could only be treated in 'thick' contextualist terms, i.e. from a viewpoint that took full cognizance of the social situation, historical background, motivating interests, modalities of judgment etc, which helped to make sense of some given utterance at a given point in cultural space and time. There are two kinds of narrative strategy, according to Lyotard. The first kind is repressive and monological, aimed toward an ultimate, self-authorized knowledge and tending to reinforce existing structures of privilege and power, while the other resists such forms of preemptive closure and affords opportunities for multiplying language-games beyond the control of any single master-discourse or privileged voice of reason and truth.

This second sort of narrative pragmatics may be seen as analogous to the sublime, or 'what Kant calls an Idea of the imagination (intuitions without a concept)', and hence also bears a striking resemblance to what 'today . . . are called scenarios or simulations'. In this context, according to Lyotard, 'a multiplicity of possible, probable, and improbable stories are told heedless of their verisimilitude, in anticipation of what could be the case'.[27] Such would be the status of those 'first-order natural narratives' that circulate in an open economy of discourse subject to none of the validity-conditions, the coercive checks and restraints brought to bear from a higher ('meta-narrative') level of self-authorized meaning and truth. Thus

> there is a privileging of narrative in the assemblage of the diverse. It is a genre that seems able to admit all others. . . . There is an affinity between narrative and the people. Language's popular mode of being is the deritualized short story. Short because it is faithful to phrase regimes and to differends. . . . The wisdom of nations is not only their scepticism, but also the 'free life' of phrases and genres. That is what the (clerical, political, military, economic, or informational) oppressor comes up against in the long run. Prose is the people of anecdotes.[28]

In other words, the great virtue of these narrative language-games is that they show – like the sublime – just how many possibilities are closed off when one resorts to some single, privileged phrase-regime (e.g. the cognitive) and allows it to dictate what shall henceforth count as a valid (or 'well-formed') mode of utterance. Hence what I take to be Lyotard's postmodernist rewriting of Kant's categorical imperative: 'always maximize the range of alternative narratives on offer', or 'act always in accordance with the maxim that no single narrative will have the last word'.

But again one has to ask what defence such arguments can muster against a strong revisionist (or downright perverter of historical truth) like Faurisson, that is to say, an 'historian' who wilfully flouts all the protocols of reason, factual warrant and ethical accountability in order to promote a racist and right-wing ideological agenda. On Lyotard's account the only line of response is to acknowledge that Faurisson is simply not playing by the same rules, and that no amount of reasoned argument – or documentary proof – could ever bring him round to accepting the historical reality of the death-camps. Thus

> it remains that, if Faurisson is 'in bad faith', Vidal-Naquet [one of his opponents in this controversy] cannot convince him that the phrase *There were gas-chambers* is true. The historian bitterly notes that, in analogous fashion, 'there are still anti-Dreyfusards'. Consensus may be missing even in such a case, such as that of the falsehoods fabricated by Colonel Henry, whose reality has been established as much as the procedures for establishing reality will permit. Thus bad will, or bad faith, or a blind belief (the ideology of the League for the French Fatherland) can prevent truth from manifesting itself and justice from being done. – No. What you are calling bad will, etc, is the name that you give to the fact that the opponent does not have a stake in establishing reality, that he does not accept the rules for forming and validating cognitives, that his goal is not to convince.[29]

In which case one will not only fail to convince Faurisson but will also be at risk of *doing him an injustice* – ignoring his 'differend' with the interests and values of enlightened, truth-seeking discourse – if one judges the issue from a standpoint that requires him to play by the accepted (cognitive or ethical) rules of the game. For at this point the tables between victim and oppressor are very easily turned, and Faurisson can always turn them yet again to present himself in the role of persecuted advocate for a suppressed minority opinion. Moreover, his enlightened opponent will then be cast as a persecuting figure backed up by all the sanctions of a right-thinking liberal consensus. 'Should the historian persist along this path, he will end up in the position of victim.'[30] Much better abandon this hopeless endeavour and acknowledge that the differences go so far down that no amount of reasoned argument will ever serve to settle the dispute.

If Lyotard is right in all this then it amounts to a terminal collapse not only of the so-called (and much-maligned) Enlightenment 'meta-narrative', but also of every last standard or criterion of truth, reason, and ethical accountability. Thinking is indeed 'without resources' if it is unable to refute an ideologue like Faurisson by appealing to the manifest facts of the case and the massive wrongdoing involved in all attempts to argue those facts away, or to treat them as so many products of interpretation, neither more nor less biassed than the Faurisson view.

Lyotard gets into this unfortunate position for a number of reasons, all of them connected with what I have here described as the wider postmodern-neopragmatist drift. Firstly, there is the tendency to reduce all truth-claims to the level of so many rhetorics, narrative strategies or Foucauldian 'discourses', conceived as existing solely by virtue of the differences or rivalries between them, so that no single claimant can assert itself at the expense of any other. In effect, this amounts to a curious grafting of the Hobbesian *bellum omnium contra omnes* onto a model of linguistic structure and system originally derived from Saussure, but now developed into a wholesale postmodern *ideology* of language, thought, and representation. A second feature of this trend is the appeal – most prominent in Lyotard – to the Wittgensteinian notion of 'language-games' and cultural 'forms of life', pushed to the point where every such discourse disposes of its own *sui generis* criteria, so that litigants (like Faurisson) who flout all the rules of cognitive, historical or moral accountability must simply be seen as playing a different game. Finally, there is the turn toward the Kantian sublime – or a certain angled misreading of Kant's reflections on that topic – as a means of devaluing cognitive truth-claims and elevating the notion of the *unrepresentable* (i.e. intuitions or Ideas of Reason that cannot be 'brought under' adequate concepts) to absolute pride of place in the ethical realm. Taken together, these factors help to account for the prevailing anti-realist strain that has characterized recent speculative work in literary theory and the human sciences at large.

5

ALTERNATIVE RESOURCES: AGAINST POSTMODERNISM

TEXTS AND PRETEXTS

It seems to me that a challenge to this orthodoxy is long overdue, and that an event like the Gulf War can sharpen the issues by showing what follows when scepticism is pushed to the point where it becomes just a pretext for strategies of moral and political evasion. These strategies range all the way from Baudrillard's caricature postmodernist stance to the Fish-Rorty line of passive acquiescence in whatever currently and contingently passes as 'good in the way of belief'. In Lyotard's case, the war would figure as a referent for many 'heterogeneous' language-games, each involving a different set of cognitive, historical, or ethico-political criteria, thus demanding that we treat it with a due respect for those strictly 'incommensurable' truth-claims, and not apply standards belonging to some other self-appointed critical tribunal.

In this sense the war would be a 'sublime' referent, one that challenged our principles of justice in so far as it involved the suspension of determinate judgments (truth and falsehood, right and wrong) in the interests of allowing all parties a fair and equal access to the dialogue of contending viewpoints. Hence the value that Lyotard attaches to his notion of '*dis*sensus' – the maximization of differends – as opposed to the kind of consensus-thinking espoused by the current neo-pragmatists. To cultivate dissent as a principle of radical heterogeneity is to ensure the greatest possible freedom for litigants to state their case (so to speak) in open court, and not become the victims of a judicial (or prejudicial) frame-up designed to swing the verdict against them from the start. The first rule here would be to discount any kind of presumptive 'evidence' that staked its claim on a cognitive appeal to the manifest facts of the case, and which sought to pass straight from that particular 'phrase-regime' to pronouncements of an ethical, socio-political, or kindred evaluative order. For this move would clearly constitute a massive infringement of the ground-rules established for fair and open debate, i.e. that each litigant should tell his or her own story without the intrusion of some 'higher' (meta-narrative) voice of authority and truth that treated them as mere unreliable narrators subject to correction from outside and above.

Apply this to the Gulf War and the message is plain enough: that we should take all the various language-games on board – from Bush's moral-crusading rhetoric to the UN resolutions, military briefings, Pentagon scenarios, media campaigns, anti-war protests, investigative news-reports, historical and political analyses etc – and treat them as *in principle* belonging to different (heterogeneous) genres of discourse, to judge any one of which according to the operative standards, values or truth-conditions of another would constitute a violent suppression of the differend and hence an unjust proceeding. For all its appearance of fine even-handedness this doctrine amounts to nothing more than a posture of moral and political indifference, a refusal to weigh the rights and wrongs of the case by attempting to separate truth from falsehood, or the pseudo-truths of consensus belief from the factual details that can yet be established through a critical sifting of the available (albeit partial and fragmentary) evidence. Talk of the 'sublime' is no help here, any more than it helps when Derrida (and others) invoke a vague notion of the 'nuclear sublime' as that which exceeds all the powers and capacities of representational thought, since it belongs to a realm of as-yet unexampled – and strictly inconceivable – future catastrophe which would totally obliterate all our means of recording, describing or comprehending such an event. Of course this argument has a certain predictive or probabilistic force, given the fact that nuclear war could yet break out and (according to the worst-case scenario) destroy every vestige of civilization, right down to the last human witness and the archives of cultural memory to date. But this is not to say – as Derrida does, on occasion, tend to suggest – that we are *now already* placed in this terminal predicament, confronted with a 'sublime' nuclear referent that somehow baffles, suspends or incapacitates our powers of rational judgment. Still less is it to go along with the strain of apocalyptic endgame thinking that has characterized much discussion of the nuclear issue in postmodernist and deconstructive circles.[1] For the fact is simply that an all-out nuclear exchange *hasn't yet occurred*, and the chances of preventing it depend very largely on the prospect that some sizable number of people will manage to think their way through and beyond the aporias of Nukespeak, the perversions of reason which have led to the nonsensical doctrine of deterrence and what Derrida terms its pseudo-logic of 'rhetorico-strategic escalation'.

The sublime may perhaps be an apt enough analogy in the speculative or future-hypothetical mode, a figure for that which indeed (by definition) cannot be known or represented since a) we have no experience of it, and b) there would be nobody around to represent it should the unthinkable actually occur. But it is wrong to extend this analogy to our current predicament, suggesting that we *already inhabit* such a realm of 'sublime' hyperreality, and that henceforth we can be in no position to reason, criticize, or debate nuclear issues in 'realistic' terms. And it is a short step from here to Baudrillard's absurd 'theses' on the Gulf War, as well as to Lyotard's kindred (if philosophically more articulate) ideas about the sublime as a limit-point of knowledge and representation, a name for that which suspends all judgments of determinate truth and falsehood and which thus gives voice to an ethical demand unaccountable to any but its own self-authorizing criteria. For there would then be no arguing *on reasoned or principled grounds* against anyone who held a false, irrational or morally offensive belief, provided only that they managed to maintain it with sufficient conviction and rhetorical-persuasive force.

This principle would apply to Faurisson's denial that the death-camps actually existed; to the apostles of nuclear-strategic doublethink with their various simulated doomsday scenarios; and to champions of 'freedom' and 'democracy' like President Bush whose rhetoric conceals the less palatable truth of US interventionist designs. It is one thing to argue that the 'facts' in such cases are always to some extent open to dispute, and even more so the judgments of right and wrong which usually rest their claims on an appeal to those same contested facts. But it is quite another thing to find a whole school of thought – including some of the most 'advanced' speculative theorists of our day – committed to the viewpoint that there is *just no deciding* between rival interpretations of an event like the Gulf War, since 'facts' and 'values' are likewise subject to a generalized relativity-principle which means that different parties will always be judging in light of radically different criteria, and will hence have no common ground of dispute.

Alternative resources are not hard to find if one looks outside the narrow domain of post-structuralist thinking about language, discourse and representation. The trouble with post-structuralism – as

I suggested briefly above – is that it takes up a series of working hypotheses first developed by Saussure in the specialized context of structural linguistics, and erects them into a wholesale methodology for the human sciences with marked metaphysical (anti-realist) overtones. For Saussure, that is to say, it is a technical requirement, a condition of possibility for constituting the field of synchronic language study, that the linguist should attend to the twofold order of structural articulation obtaining at the levels of the signifier and the signified, and should therefore exclude – or provisionally suspend – any dealing with language in its referential aspect.[2] For his followers, conversely, this doctrine becomes a high point of principle, the basis for a full-scale theoretical assault on reference, truth and that mythical bogey, the 'classic realist text'. The first major phase of this colonizing drive was to show – in the manner of Barthes's *S/Z* – that textuality indeed went 'all the way down', that texts could be shown to unmask or deconstruct their own bourgeois-realist pretensions, and moreover, that this applied not only to *avant-garde* writings like *Finnegans Wake* but also to novels (e.g. those of Balzac or George Eliot) that seemed to belong squarely within the great realist tradition.[3] And from here it was just a short step to the argument – zealously promoted by Barthes, Hayden White and others – that historical discourses are similarly dependent on a range of highly varied rhetorical and narrative structures, and must therefore be seen as strictly undecidable as regards their factual-documentary or truth-telling warrant.[4] Postmodernists like Baudrillard merely push this doctrine to its 'logical' (but none the less absurd) endpoint by systematically inverting the received order of priority between truth and falsehood, knowledge and belief, fact and fiction, reality and its 'hyperreal' counterparts.

The alternative resources I mentioned above would include not only a good deal of work in the analytical philosophy of language – work that provides a much stronger grasp of the relation between sense, reference and truth – but also various (Marxist and other) contributions to the better understanding of history as a mode of discourse with its own, highly specific standards of truth-telling accountability.[5] Tony Bennett, for example, puts up a robust defence against cognitive scepticism. His target is the kind of all-purpose narrative theory which ends by effectively sinking the difference between historical and literary (fictive) modes of representation. Thus, as Bennett points out, if there is no touchstone of 'reality' to which to refer the adjudication of competing truth claims then rational debate would seem wholly pointless.

If the non-accessibility of a referent means that the theorist is drawn into labyrinths of textual 'undecidability' where any kind of systematic truth-claim could only tell the tale of its own undoing – then why bother? The political consequence of such a relativism . . . can only be quietism.[6]

Such arguments derive their suasive appeal only from a false, all-or-nothing view of the contested relation between historical truth and its forms of discursive or narrative transmission. On this account, 'truth claims must be able, under some specifiable set of conditions, to be established absolutely, or they cannot be established at all; or, if there is no way of escaping the constraints of narrative and language, then all narrative and linguistic orderings of reality must be regarded as equally valid'.[7] In which case, given the extent of informed disagreement on matters of historical truth, one would have little choice but to go along with the sceptical-relativist line and acknowledge that history is indeed just the product of various competing narrative views, with nothing to adjudicate between them except the appeal to this or that interpretive (i.e. ideological) persuasion. For the alternative – positivist – conception of truth is one that the sceptics can safely regard as no longer possessing any claim to credibility among historians, critical theorists, or even philosophers of science.

But as Bennett rightly says, there is no good reason to accept this sharply polarized view of the issue regarding historical truth-claims. What such arguments fail to recognize is the extent to which various discourses of knowledge evolve their own procedures, validity-conditions, standards of documentary proof and so forth by which to adjudicate the issue in any given case. I can't improve on Bennett's formulation of this point, so will quote the relevant passage at length. 'It is these truths', he writes,

> truths comprising 'the historical past', which serve as a check, and as the only possible check, on the forms in which earlier epochs are represented. Of course, it is not an absolute check. Nor could it be to the degree that the historical past is constituted, and necessarily so, by areas of marked uncertainty and instability in consequence of the historiographical disputes concerning the forms of evidence pertinent to particular enquiries and the rules of reasoning to be applied to them. The effect of such disputes – and it is such disputes which *constitute* the discipline rather than being its accidental by-products – is to introduce

a degree of indeterminacy into the 'historical past'. But only a degree, for this indeterminacy is located against a bedrock of what are taken to be determinate historical truths. This bedrock may be shifted in the sense that some truths may be added to it while others are subtracted as specific historiographical disputes are worked out. Yet such disputes never throw the totality of the historical past into question. Indeed, it is a condition of its intelligibility that historical debate should take place within a horizon of both determinacy and indeterminacy: it requires both – the former to supply conditions of resolution, the latter to be purposive.[8]

Despite the rather queasy scare-quotes surrounding its appeals to the 'historical past', this passage takes a firm and principled stand against any notion that history can be reduced to just a play of 'discourses', 'language-games', narrative representations or whatever. And it does so in full cognizance of the fact that historical truth-claims may always be contested, since the kinds of dispute that take place in this area – as in the other (natural and human) sciences – are precisely what constitute history as a discipline of thought. But this is not to say, like Lyotard, that such disputes must at some point involve a differend – an irreducible conflict of interests – that cannot (or should not) be settled by reference to established criteria of proof, valid argument, or adequate documentary grounds. For there would then be no escaping the relativist conclusion, the idea that history is *wholly and exclusively* a product of the various hermeneutic paradigms – the sense-making strategies or narrative schemas – that happen to prevail within some given 'interpretive community'. And this relativist doctrine itself fails to make sense, as Bennett shrewdly remarks, since it takes no account of the enabling assumptions – the 'conditions of intelligibility' – which operate in all historical discourse and which provide the only grounds for meaningful argument on this or that specific point of dispute.

One could put the case from a slightly different angle by returning to Solomon's discussion of the nuclear issue and his defence of a 'potentialist' (or revised Aristotelian) theory of truth and reference that avoids the worst excesses of present-day cognitive scepticism.[9] In particular, Solomon brings out what is wrong with post-structuralist talk of the 'nuclear referent' as an instance of the quasi-Kantian sublime, a topos that so far exceeds our powers of deliberative thought and judgment that it can only be figured by recourse to a rhetoric of crisis, communicative breakdown or terminal catastrophe, a language (that is to say) beyond all forms of adequate representation or conceptual grasp. Such talk understandably possesses great appeal for literary theorists keen to establish their credentials in a field – that of 'nuclear criticism' – where they might not appear very expert or competent, at least according to current ideas of the professional-academic division of labour. But such strategic interventions are hardly to be welcomed if they produce nothing more than a novel species of nuclear-rhetorical sophistry, a mystification of the 'nuclear referent' which asks us to view it (like the Kantian sublime) as belonging to a 'fabulous' or 'fictive' realm where hypperreality is the postmodern name of the game, and where rational judgments are henceforth played off the field. On the contrary, says Solomon: here more than anywhere we need to summon the most adequate resources of critical-realist thought in order to resist the endgame scenarios, the simulated strategies, the pseudo-logic of 'deterrence', and all the other forms of irrationalist rhetoric that have so far managed to capture the high ground of nuclear-strategic debate.

Solomon applies this notion of 'potentialist' realism to a range of specific historical issues, in particular the problem of assessing historical truth-claims (for instance, those put forward by Thucydides in *The Peloponnesian War*) which to some extent rely on hearsay, second-hand sources, probabilistic reasoning, or techniques of imaginative reconstruction. 'To what does the Pelopponesian referent refer?', Solomon asks, given that our knowledge of the war derives largely (though of course not exclusively) from Thucydides' text, and moreover, that his text makes a point of acknowledging its own frequent use of indirect or conjectural 'evidence'.

> Certainly not to any monadic identity, not to any full historical presence, not to the simple totality of the Peloponnesian War, because the text in which the referent appears not only is incomplete but also was written, at least in part, as the war itself was being fought. The Peloponnesian referent, we might say instead, refers not to a completed totality but to a dynamically unfolding situation, a situation, what is more, with certain calculable propensities that Thucydides apprehended in his interpretation of the causes of the conflict. . . . [Thus] may we not discern, within the actual empirical circumstances of the rivalry between Athens and Lacedaemon, a certain factor that would 'weight', so to speak, Thucydides' interpretation more heavily than another and render it more probable? In other words, do not such political circumstances as those that led to

the outbreak of the Peloponnesian War bear a certain empirical potentiality, a certain propensity for conflict, that we can take into account as we seek to interpret the course of similar events?[10]

And of course there is a sense – an everyday, familiar, practical sense – in which we know all this perfectly well without benefit of having read Thucydides, Aristotle, Hegel, Marx, Frege, Russell, Kripke, or any of the other historians and philosophers whom Solomon calls to witness. That is to say, we possess a fair working grasp of the criteria for distinguishing historical from fictive (imaginary) forms of discourse, for assessing historical truth-claims where these are subject to dispute, and for weighing the balance of real-world probabilities in cases where the issue cannot be resolved by appealing to any kind of first-hand, factual, or documentary evidence. We make such judgments all the time, at whatever tacit or preconscious level, not only when reading narrative works that occupy various positions on the scale between history and fiction, but also when attempting to sift out the elements of truth and falsehood in the media coverage of events like the Gulf War. To come up with an account of just how we perform this complex (though by no means impossible) task is a challenge to philosophers, historiographers, discourse-analysts and others. But to treat it as a wholly superannuated issue amounts to nothing more than a species of irrationalist mystery-mongering.

THE CULT OF THE SUBLIME

I have argued that the kinds of speculative thinking most in vogue among present-day cultural theorists are such as to leave them little room for genuine, effective engagement with matters of real-world ethical and political concern. More specifically: the turn toward post-structuralist, postmodernist and neo-pragmatist doctrines of discourse and representation is one that can only lend support to prevailing (consensus) notions of reality and truth by making it strictly *unthinkable* that anyone could offer good arguments – or factual counter-evidence – against the elective self-images of the age, or ideas of what is (currently and contingently) 'good in the way of belief'. Join this to the fashion for postmodernist misreadings of Kant that treat the sublime as an ultimately privileged category, a figure for whatever exceeds the powers of adequate representation or conceptual grasp, and one arrives at a form of extreme anti-realist thinking that would render criticism totally powerless to challenge the dominant mass-media treatment of a 'simulated' event like the Gulf War. Moreover, this version of the Kantian sublime is one that thoroughly mystifies issues of social and ethico-political judgment by treating them, in effect, as modalities of *aesthetic* understanding, questions that cannot be settled – or intelligibly raised – except by suspending all reference to matters of empirical truth and falsehood. In Kant this is offered as an *analogy* – nothing more – between on the one hand the sublime as a limit-point, a check to our powers of adequate phenomenal cognition and conceptual understanding, and on the other hand practical reason (or ethical judgment) as that which belongs to the domain of 'suprasensible' ideas, and which therefore cannot be brought under any such rule. But postmodernists like Lyotard disregard Kant's warnings against literalizing these various analogical hints, and thus come to treat the sublime as pretty much *coextensive or synonymous* with the realm of practical reason. In so doing, they empty ethical judgment of any reference to real-world (social and political) states of affairs, and end up – as in J. Hillis Miller's recent book *The Ethics of Reading* – at a point where issues of right and wrong can be reduced to so many textual aporias, instances of 'sublime' unrepresentability, or products of what Miller (following de Man) calls the 'structural interference' between various, incompatible linguistic codes.[11]

Three things follow from this inflated treatment of the Kantian sublime that pushes it so far beyond the limits assigned in Kant's elaborate 'architectonic' of the faculties. One is the tendency – visible in Lyotard and even more marked in Hillis Miller – to dissociate questions of ethical judgment from issues of factual-historical understanding, especially where these latter involve some appeal to cognitive criteria of truth and falsehood. The second has to do with the status of the subject, that is to say, the locus of those choices, ethical principles, and commitments that for Kant mark out the 'suprasensible' domain of practical reason, conceived as distinct from – but not in downright opposition to – the realm of phenomenal experience and conceptual understanding. For post-structuralists and those of a kindred persuasion – notably Foucault – this 'subject' is nothing more than a momentary 'fold' in the order of discourse and representation, an imaginary figure whose advent can be dated historically (with the rise of the so-called 'human sciences'), and whose demise is close at hand with the dawning awareness that *all* our most basic or 'self-evident' categories (truth, knowledge, reality, selfhood) are really just fictive, transient constructions out of this or that currently prevailing discourse. And this applies above all to the Kantian subject, that curious 'empirical-transcendental doublet' (as Foucault memorably puts it in *The Order of Things*) whose sovereign prerogatives were once taken to include both the attainment of a truthful knowledge of the world through the accurate matching-up of concepts with phenomenal intuitions, and a knowledge of its own 'suprasensible' nature as vouchsafed in the mode of practical reason.[12] But, according to Foucault, these ideas only made sense in the context of a period-specific 'discourse' (roughly speaking, that of 18th and 19th century liberal humanism) whose eclipse has been brought about by the contemporary passage to a post-Enlightenment, post-humanist, non-subject-centred epoch of knowledge. Quite simply, it is no longer possible to place any credence in those old concepts and categories.

Hence the third main aspect of this turn toward the sublime as a model or analogue for the movement 'beyond' truth, knowledge, representation, and ethical judgment in its enlightened (Kantian) mode. This is the 'textualist' argument endorsed most vigorously by Miller in *The Ethics of Reading*, and pursued to a point where Derrida's much-quoted and widely misconstrued slogan ('there is nothing outside the text') seems to be taken pretty much at face value, as a statement of downright principled indifference to matters of worldly or socio-political concern.[13] Thus when Miller reads Kant – or certain problematical passages in Kant – what emerges is a generalized undecidability: between fact and fiction; between constative and performative modes of discourse; or between the moral law as a matter of absolute, categorical duty and ethics as a realm of purely *contingent* choices and events that can only be figured by way of narrative ('literary') instances and parables. In short, 'it is never possible to be sure that duty is not a fiction in the bad sense of an ungrounded act of self-sustaining language, that is, precisely a vain delusion and chimerical concept, a kind of ghost generated by a sad linguistic necessity'.[14] For Miller, it is the very act of *reading* – of textual exegesis in this rigorous, un-self-deceiving, deconstructive mode – that properly merits the name of 'ethical' criticism, as opposed to those other approaches (New Historicist, Marxist, feminist etc) which blithely pass over such problems in pursuit of their own preconceived ideological agenda. Where these latter modes of reading are always to some extent 'vague and speculative' – appealing as they do to a context of real-world interests and priorities beyond what is manifestly there in the text – deconstruction has the signal virtue, as Miller sees it, of engaging directly with 'the real situation of a man or woman reading a book, teaching a class, writing a critical essay'.[15]

Not that he wishes to exclude all reference to extra-textual realities, to those pressures of circumstance, historical context, gender-role assumptions, etc, which do undeniably bear upon the act of reading and thus lay claim to the theorist's attention with varying degrees of urgency. 'No doubt', Miller concedes, 'that "situation" spreads out to involve institutional, historical, economic, or political "contexts", but it begins with and returns to the man or woman face-to-face with the words on the page.'[16] And to this extent the deconstructive 'ethics of reading' should apply not only in the case of literary (poetic or fictional) texts, but also to those other kinds of writing – historical, political, sociological etc – which will likewise be found to place obstacles in the way of a naive referentialist account. Clearly Miller is here staking a claim for the priority of deconstruction over those rival schools of thought (especially New Historicism) that have lately threatened to usurp its place as the most advanced and prestigious form of textual-interpretive practice. But there is more at issue in these arcane disputes than a contest for power and influence among the high priests of US academic fashion. For the result of this widespread textualist turn – closely allied (as we have seen) to post-structuralist assaults on the notion of the subject, and to the cult of the sublime as a limit-point of knowledge and representation – is to encourage a retreat from any theory capable of mustering resistance to received ideologies and forms of manufactured consensus-belief.

VERSIONS OF CATASTROPHE: KAL 007

One striking example of this textualist cult is an essay by Richard Klein and William B. Warner which appeared in *Diacritics* in 1986 shortly after the Soviets shot down a Korean civilian airliner that had 'wandered off course' (as US sources maintained) and infringed Soviet airspace around sensitive military installations and radar-tracking systems.[17] According to another version of events, the aircraft had in fact been directed onto this alternative flight-path – one that involved a wide detour and considerable risk to its passengers – in order to trigger the Soviet alarms, to bring the new radar network into action, and hence provide US intelligence agencies with a great deal of valuable strategic information. Among the arguments adduced in support of this 'reading' were 1) the well-documented evidence that civilian flights had previously been used for similar intelligence-gathering purposes, 2) the otherwise unaccountable fact that the aircraft had taken on a large quantity of extra fuel for that part of its journey, 3) the odd 'coincidence' by which it happened that a US spy satellite was passing over the area in question at just that moment, and 4) the sheer unlikelihood that the plane's navigational equipment – along with its duplicate back-up systems – should have suffered such a massive and unprecedented failure as to send the aircraft some hundreds of miles off course in a region known to be bristling with top-secret Soviet military bases. To begin with, therefore, the event produced two conflicting narrative explanations, each with its own preferred candidate for the villain's role (Soviet paranoia or US conspiracy) and its supporting cast of more-or-less innocent injured parties. As further details emerged through the usual combination of rumour, investigative journalism, and unattributed Pentagon leaks, so the ground of debate started to shift, from a straightforward (US *versus* Soviet) contest of views to a discussion of various less dramatic alternatives, including – as so often – the cock-up theory which stopped somewhat short of detecting a full-scale, deliberate US conspiracy, and which blamed both sides for their disastrous failure to predict, interpret and manage the course of events. In short, we are here confronted – so the *Diacritics* essay argues – with a set of utterly heterogeneous narratives, each of which can lay some claim to consistency on its own (intradiegetic) terms, but none of which can possibly establish its *truth* as a matter of real-world, historical or factual warrant.

It seems to me that Klein and Warner have argued themselves into this position simply through their habit of unquestioning adherence to the current postmodern-textualist doxa. All the familiar signs are there, among them the presumption that facts become fictions (or wholly 'undecidable') as soon as they are cast in narrative form; that the referent – in this case the destruction of the aircraft and events leading up to it – must therefore elude the best efforts of truth-seeking enquiry; that this gives such events a 'fabulous' or 'sublime' aspect in so far as they stand beyond reach of determinate representation; and (most absurdly) that certain effects of language, albeit purely random or gratuitous effects – like the flight designation 'KAL 007' – may be as significant as anything else in predisposing us to read the evidence according to this or that narrative schema.

When things have got as loony as all that, as William Empson once remarked, it is time to enounce a few simple truths that literary theorists seem bent upon forgetting. One is the fact that textuality *doesn't* go 'all the way down', at least in the simplified (sub-Derridean) sense of that slogan embraced by postmodernists, neo-pragmatists and some decon-structors. On the contrary: when reading we bring all kinds of extra-textual knowledge to bear, some of it (of course) derived from our reading of other texts, but a sizable proportion having to do with our grasp of real-world events, probabilities, or factual states of affairs. And this applies not only in the case of those discourses that standardly claim veridical warrant (e.g. works of history, investigative journalism, documentary analysis etc) but also in the reading of fictional texts where our responses are always – *pace* Miller – reliant on sources of knowledge and information beyond what is given by the 'words on the page'. For otherwise we should find ourselves over and again in the predicament of Quine's 'radical translator', confronted with a text (or a cultural sign-system) whose meanings, truth-claims or ontological commitments were totally opaque from our own point of view, and which therefore required that we start out afresh each time through some extraordinary effort of crypto-analytical skill.[18] No doubt there are some works of postmodern fiction – experimental, *avant-garde* or self-deconstructing narratives – that strive to place the reader in exactly this predicament through their various anti-realist or defamiliarizing techniques. But it is a singular perversity – albeit widespread among present-day critics and theorists – that raises this doctrine into a high point of principle and then applies it to *every* sort of text, realist novels and historical narratives included.

Gregory Currie makes the point as follows in a passage from his book *The Nature of Fiction* that cuts a swathe through much of the fashionable nonsense currently talked on this topic.

> Philosophers and critics have sometimes argued that fictional works do not possess semantic features, that they are neither true nor false, and make no reference to anything outside the text. These claims are sometimes the product of a general scepticism about semantics according to which no text ever succeeds in making extralinguistic reference. This strikes me as one of the great absurdities of the contemporary cultural scene.... After all, even if the theory were correct, it would leave us where we began: without a means of distinguishing between fiction and non-fiction.[19]

Currie's point is that we *can and do* make such distinctions with a fair degree of assurance, not only between works belonging to different (veri'ical and fictive) orders of discourse, but also at what might be called the 'micro-textual' level, i.e. from one passage or sentence to the next in works – especially realist novels – that partake of both orders in varying proportion. What his argument brings out is the sheer *impossibility* of doing what the postmodern-textualists would have us do, that is to say, reading always on the fixed principle that language is a self-enclosed system of signs without referents or truth-values, that texts possess meaning solely by virtue of their immanent signifying structures, and – following from this – that there is *simply no difference* between factual and fictive (imaginary) narrative modes. And this helps us to see more precisely what is wrong with the textualist approach when extended to matters of a real-world, historical, or factual-documentary import. For such matters – like the Gulf War or the Korean airliner incident – can then just as well be treated as rhetorical constructs, episodes that we learn about only through various (incompatible) narrative accounts, and whose referential status is thereby rendered strictly undecidable, along with the truth-value of any proposition regarding the putative facts of the case, or any argument that claims to falsify some other version of events. On this account there is simply no appealing to evidence of an 'extra-textual' nature, even when that evidence – as in the case of KA 007 – piles up to a point where the balance of probability swings strongly in favour of one interpretation. Much better suspend judgment, so these theorists advise, and disregard all truth-claims save those arrived at through a sedulous attention to the 'words on the page'. In which event truth becomes entirely a product of *post hoc* rhetorical or narrative reconstruction.

Here of course we are back on Lyotard's favourite terrain, faced with a variety of rival ('incommensurable') language-games, and forbidden to treat any one of them as possessing superior – cognitive or veridical – warrant for fear of committing an injustice against all the others. But the argument collapses into manifest nonsense as soon as one asks what could possibly *justify* this refusal to credit any evidence, truth-claims, or validating grounds beyond the strict protocols of textual close-reading devised in the first place by literary theorists as an advertisement for their own special skills. For it is simply not the case – whatever these adepts might say – that our knowledge of such matters comes solely from the scanning of texts or narrative representations that constitute the limits of intelligibility for this or that sequence of historical events. Any reader who brings some degree of critical intelligence to bear on the various accounts of the Korean airliner incident will find him- or herself compelled to draw certain obvious conclusions, among them the fact that the official (US) version of events was a fabricated story shot through with contradictions, non-sequiturs, evasions, or downright lies. To call them 'aporias' – in the deconstructive parlance – is already to risk falling in with the idea that such anomalous details are only to be expected, given the complexity of the issues involved and the fact that all truth-claims, on whatever side, are caught up in a contest of rhetorical and narrative strategies where no single viewpoint either can or should prevail. In this case the only justified response would be an open verdict, a willingness to treat the incident as belonging to that realm of 'sublime' pseudo-referents where fact and fiction are inextricably mixed, where judgments of determinate truth and falsehood have no application, and where textuality is the bottom line of appeal. For such is the end-point of deconstruction when it becomes (as in Miller) just a geared-up version of the 'old' New Critical techniques of rhetorical exegesis, and where it gets out of touch with those countervailing standards of truth, argumentative rigour, and ethical accountability that Derrida for his part has always striven to maintain.

CHOMSKY VERSUS FOUCAULT

One thing that emerged with painful clarity during the months of the Gulf War was the failure of many intellectuals to adopt anything like a principled stand against the atrocities inflicted on the Iraqi population by a US-led 'free-world' coalition whose pursuit of strategic advantage in the area involved a massive falsification of the historical, political, and moral issues. This is one index of the complicitous relation that exists between 'theory' in its currently most prestigious (post-structuralist, postmodernist, or neo-pragmatist) forms and the interests of a hegemonic drive to repress or to marginalize dissident opinion in the name of a popular 'consensus' achieved through the usual techniques of media control, 'public opinion' management and government and military propaganda.

The most striking counter-example to all this is of course Noam Chomsky, the eminent linguist-philosopher and implacable opponent of US foreign policy in its various global adventures over the past three decades and more.[20] What sets him decidedly apart from the avatars of post-structuralism, postmodernism and the rest is Chomsky's defence of a rationalist philosophy of mind and language that derives from the Kantian Enlightenment tradition, or the heritage that he sees as beginning further back with Descartes and the Port-Royal grammarians.[21] More specifically, Chomsky equates the interests of a genuine participant democracy – one in which citizens would enjoy the greatest measure of intellectual freedom, moral autonomy, and political choice – with the exercise of those same capacities of human intelligence that are elsewhere manifest in the process of language-acquisition and in our everyday 'competence' as language-using creatures.[22] His rationalism therefore has a twofold (theoretical-descriptive and ethico-evaluative) aspect, on the one hand involving work on those 'deep' transformational structures of thought and language that can best explain how we *do* in fact achieve such remarkable (though commonplace) levels of communicative grasp, while on the other appealing to a set of social and political values, an enlightened 'public sphere' – in Habermas's phrase – where these capacities would attain their fullest scope of collective realisation. As against the post-structuralists (Foucault in particular) Chomsky maintains the continuing relevance of a critical-rationalist outlook that rejects the *tout court* equation of reason and truth with current consensus-beliefs. In linguistic terms, this leads him to criticize both behaviourists like Skinner and structuralists like Bloomfield and Saussure, since on their understanding language reduces either to a product of stimulus-response psychology or to a pre-given system of signifying structures and relationships which functions according to its own immanent laws. In both cases the theory excludes any reference to the subject (speaker or interpreter) in whom these capacities are creatively realised to a point far beyond the explanatory powers of any such reductive account.

Thus for Chomsky there is a link between 'technical' issues in the realm of linguistic theory and larger questions of ethical and socio-political responsibility. For if language-users can be shown to possess a 'competence' – a power of rational-interpretive grasp – that cannot be adequately explained in behaviourist (or structuralist) terms, then this finding clearly has crucial implications for anyone who seeks to vindicate the truth-claims of Enlightenment critique against the argument of those, Foucault among them, who would regard such claims as just a reflex product of pre-given cultural beliefs, or as resulting from ideological values acquired (along with language) through exposure to the dominant conventions of this or that social order. It is in this way that Chomsky's work has extended beyond the relatively specialized sphere of transformational-generative grammar to issues in epistemology, cognitive psychology, and the philosophy of mind. And it can also be seen to have a direct bearing on his dissident stance with regard to the US foreign policy record, especially in cases – like the various strategic-interventionist wars from Vietnam to Nicaragua, El Salvador, Grenada, Panama and the Gulf – where economic interests or motives of regional dominance have sheltered behind a high-sounding rhetoric of freedom, democracy or self-determination, and where 'public opinion' has been mobilized, as usual, through a large-scale campaign of disinformation or straightforward lying propaganda.

No one has done more than Chomsky to expose these forms of state-sponsored hypocrisy and to set the record straight in face of massive opposition from the censors, watchdogs, and well-placed arbiters of what properly counts as 'open discussion' in a self-styled liberal democracy. One need only consult the items collected in a volume like *Language and Politics* (1988) to appreciate the extraordinary range and depth of Chomsky's political engagement, his persistence in hunting out the relevant facts behind the smokescreen of Pentagon briefings and compliant mass-media coverage, and – not least – his sheer moral courage in maintaining this stance despite the campaign of slander and abuse launched against him by those same agencies, along with their supporting interest-groups in the national press, the universities, and other such 'representative' public institutions.[23] Of course there have been other left-liberal dissident thinkers in recent times – Bertrand Russell among them – who have sought to achieve some degree of correspondence between their philosophic principles and their socio-political beliefs. But Chomsky is unique in both the strength of his convictions and the extent to which they do manifestly link up with his other, more specialized areas of concern. One would need to go back to a figure like Voltaire if one wanted to find a comparable case of the voice of intellectual conscience raised against all the pressures of conformist self-interest and cynical acquiescence that operate to stifle any form of principled or reasoned dissent.

Needless to say, such arguments would carry little clout with the arbiters of current postmodern-neopragmatist debate. From their point of view, Chomsky would figure as a relic of the old

Enlightenment tradition, a thinker still hooked on grandiose 'meta-narrative' ideas of reason, critique, and truth at the end of enquiry. As it happens there is a little-known dialogue between Chomsky and Foucault, originally broadcast as part of a Dutch television series in the early 1970s, which raises these issues with particular clarity and force.[24] According to Foucault, it is the merest of illusions – just a self-promoting ruse on the part of ideologues like Chomsky – when individuals who have worked in some particular field of research (e.g. linguistics or cognitive psychology) then exploit their position in order to pose as the intellectual 'conscience' of their age, as if it somehow followed that knowing a lot about this or that specialized topic was sufficient guarantee that they could speak with authority on issues of a wider socio-political import. Such had been the case with those charismatic figures – 'universal intellectuals' in the line running from Voltaire, through Kant and Hegel to a latter-day guru like Sartre – who could still count on the respect accorded to this myth of the philosopher or the grand theorist, the subject 'presumed to know' about questions that transcended all the narrow, workaday limits of acquired professional expertise. Moreover, it traded on the Enlightenment idea of truth as a moral imperative, a matter of criticizing false ('ideological') habits of thought, and thus arriving at a knowledge that would not be just a matter of what is (locally and contingently) 'good in the way of belief'. But this myth had now collapsed, along with the role of self-conceived 'universal intellectuals' like Chomsky, those who set up to criticize the dominant self-images of the age – or the various forms of untruth, state-sponsored falsehood, ideological misrecognition and so forth – from a standpoint of supposedly superior truth-telling warrant.

For it was no longer possible – so Foucault opined – to believe in the various articles of faith that had once propped up this delusive Enlightenment creed. One was the notion of 'the state' as an agency of centralized repressive surveillance and control, an agency whose powers were exerted *over and against* those individual subjects whose interests, freedoms and citizenly rights were in constant danger of infringement, and had thus to be defended by – who else? – the upholders of enlightenment and truth. On the contrary, Foucault argues: power is not a matter of sovereign imposition by governments, bureaucracies, or (in Althusser's slightly less naive formulation) 'ideological state apparatuses'. Rather, it consists in the 'micro-politics' of localized struggles and specific power-relations, at a level where subjects are themselves the meeting-point of numerous competing 'discourses', and where resistance may on occasion come about *not* through the effort of 'enlightened' intellectuals to explain what is wrong with the system, but simply through the various conflicts engendered by the plural, decentered, non-self-identical character of the 'subject-positions' (or discursive strategies) available at any given time. In which case it is futile for old-fashioned 'radical' intellectuals like Chomsky to set up as purveyors of a privileged, truth-speaking discourse, one that would somehow redeem or revive that superannuated figment of Kantian-Enlightenment discourse, the autonomous knowing and willing subject, thus providing a bedrock of cognitive and ethical truth-claims as against this present (postmodern) dispersal of power, resistance, and subject-positions. Nowadays there is only a role for what Foucault calls 'specific intellectuals', those who have given up such overweening claims and reconciled themselves to the prospect of working in particular, well-defined areas of local expertise.[25]

On the one hand this is taken to indicate – again *contra* Chomsky – the dangers of extrapolating from one, highly specialized branch of academic-professional research to a wholesale politics of knowledge and truth appealing to the old universalist paradigm. On the other, it means that intellectuals should indeed become actively involved with pressure-groups, resistance movements, anti-war lobbies, campaigns for legal reform etc, but only as participants with certain specific kinds of knowledge and advice to offer, and not as experts whose intellectual standing provides them with automatic leadership credentials. Thus Foucault wrote books about the history of penal institutions, about clinical practices, the treatment of the 'insane', the discourse of psychiatric medicine, about sexual politics, the policing of gender-role relations, the social construction of 'deviant' or 'pathological' cases, and so forth. And he was also very active in various pressure-groups that enabled him to pursue this work at the level of specific local interventions, e.g. by campaigning for legal reforms, for improved prison conditions, for changes in the practice of clinical psychiatry, and for the liberalization of attitudes (legal, medical and popular) toward sexual minorities. To this extent – simply as a matter of consistency – the intellectual was justified in carrying his or her specialized interests across into forms of active involvement and resistance that could best make use of their acquired expertise, their strategically deployable 'discourses' of power/knowledge. But there was no role left for 'universal intellectuals' of the type that Sartre had once represented for a whole self-deluding generation of French seekers-after-truth, and which Foucault found oddly and pathetically revived in Chomsky's high-toned rationalist approach to questions of language, philosophy and politics.

Such notions had suffered a fourfold blow to their once near-hegemonic prestige among the custodians of enlightened critical discourse. Firstly, intellectuals now had to acknowledge that the 'Enlightenment' was indeed just that, one particular, historically dated and culture-specific discourse – or ensemble of discursive relations – whose truth-claims and values amounted to no more than a transient episode in the modern history of ideas. Secondly, the demise of the 'transcendental subject' – the knowing, willing, judging subject of Kantian epistemic and ethical discourse – removed the very ground of truth-telling moral authority that intellectuals like Chomsky still claimed to occupy. And thirdly, this meant that any effective 'politics of truth' must henceforth adopt a Nietzschean or genealogical perspective, one that renounced any idea of truth as something that could actually be *known or attained* by subjects dedicated to that purpose, and which treated all truth-claims as products of the ubiquitous will-to-power within language, discourse or representation. From all of which it followed – fourthly – that 'specific intellectuals' in Foucault's sense of that term were the only ones willing to accept this sharply deflated self-image, to give up universalist aspirations of whatsoever kind, and to regard themselves *not* as autonomous subjects in the Kantian-Enlightenment mode, but as strategists engaged in producing various sorts of discourse, from various (often contradictory) subject-positions, without any claim to ultimate authority or truth. That is to say, they could live with the manifest breakdown of those old 'meta-narrative' paradigms, and moreover turn it to advantage by adopting a rhetoric of multiple, 'decentred' discourses that effectively took this predicament on board as a matter of principled choice.

So one can see why the Chomsky-Foucault debate figured as the high-point of that Dutch TV series. For it raised all the issues that were just then emerging in the quarrel between defenders of a broadly 'Enlightenment' tradition – Habermas preeminent among them – and apostles of a new (postmodernist) outlook which rejected that tradition root and branch, along with the idea that intellectuals like Chomsky could ever be entitled to enunciate truths at odds with the currency of popular belief. In the dialogue, Chomsky comes out – true to form – with a sturdy defence of those principles and values that Foucault regards as having long outlived their erstwhile progressive or emancipatory role. Intellectuals have a duty to question the prevailing ideologies or beliefs that make up the 'political economy of truth' in a social order increasingly subject to the pressures of censorship, mass-media control, manufactured consent and other such forms of direct or indirect state intervention. They are (or they should be) well equipped for this task on account of their access to the documentary sources, their relative freedom of thought and speech as compared with workers in other, more vulnerable areas, and – above all – their presumed capacity for critically sifting the available evidence and arriving at a reasoned, impartial assessment of the rival truth-claims in any given case.

This is not to say that Chomsky obligingly assumes the role of an old-style 'universal' intellectual as envisaged by Foucault for his own (mainly polemical) purposes. He is *not* claiming to speak from a position of superior moral and political wisdom on behalf of all those other, less fortunate individuals who lack the ability to think for themselves and who therefore need instructing in the virtues of truth, enlightenment and citizenly duty. There may be some justice to Foucault's claim when applied to intellectuals in the grand continental line of descent, from Hegel to Sartre and the *Nouveaux Philosophes*. But it amounts to nothing more than an absurd caricature of Chomsky's position, or indeed of those other Enlightenment figures – from Kant to Habermas – whose arguments evince not only a respect for the capacities of human reason, but a principled commitment to asserting and defending those capacities against the various forms of stupefying influence exerted by the agencies of censorship, thought control, or mass-induced consensus belief. This position bears absolutely no resemblance to the stance of condescending, self-authorizing arrogance portrayed by Foucault in his composite image of the 'universal intellectual'. In so far as Chomsky appeals to standards of truth, reason and enlightened understanding, he does so in the name of those common human interests that are actively suppressed – or marginalized to the point of near-invisibility – by the numerous mechanisms of covert propaganda and state-sponsored media disinformation.

Of course there are points on which Foucault and Chomsky can make common cause despite their far-reaching disagreements. Thus they both see the role of the critical intellectual as that of resisting, contesting or challenging the forms of taken-for-granted belief that masquerade as authoritative truth. Moreover, they are agreed in locating the source of such resistance in the sphere of those various oppositional or counter-hegemonic discourses that can work to destabilize the dominant relations of instituted power-knowledge. But they differ most profoundly over the question of whether truth-claims can still have any role to play beyond the point where – in Foucault's Nietzschean genealogical account – there emerges a plurality of rival, incommensurable 'discourses', all of which embody some particular nexus of power-seeking motives or knowledge-constitutive interests, and none of which possesses any truth-telling warrant beyond its own realm of performative efficacy. To Chomsky's way of thinking, conversely, the fact that truth is so often a contested or conflictual domain is no good reason to embrace the kind of all-out sceptical or relativist outlook that provides a handy refuge, not only for postmodern sophisticates like Foucault and Baudrillard but also for the various ideologues, media pundits, sources 'close to the White House', compliant academic 'experts', and other such willing purveyors of official disinformation. 'Perhaps this is an obvious point', he writes,

> but the democratic postulate is that the media are independent and committed to reporting and discovering the truth, and that they do not merely reflect the world as powerful groups wish it to be perceived. Leaders of the media claim that their news choices rest on unbiased professional and objective criteria, and they have support for this contention in the intellectual community. If, however, the powerful are able to fix the premises of discourse, to decide what the general populace is allowed to see, hear, and think about, and to 'manage' public opinion by regular propaganda campaigns, the standard view of how the system works is at serious odds with reality.[26]

One can easily imagine what a well-versed Foucauldian would make of this passage, appealing as it does to a range of those typecast 'Enlightenment' criteria – truth, responsibility, ethical choice, honest reporting, democratic values, intellectual integrity, freedom of information etc – which we are now asked to view as just one 'discourse' among others, and a discourse (moreover) that has lost all claim to persuasive credibility or force.

A Foucauldian counter-argument would fasten on three main aspects of Chomsky's critical-realist position. One is the supposedly naive or old-fashioned idea that truth and falsehood can indeed be distinguished, no matter how difficult the task, and that critical intellectuals (or investigative journalists) have a special responsibility in such matters. The second, following directly from this, is Chomsky's belief that individual subjects have a genuine margin of ethico-political choice, that they can (on the one hand) lend themselves *knowingly and willingly* to the purposes of public-opinion management, or (on the other) decide to resist those suasive pressures and establish the facts in any given case to the best of their knowledge, professional skills, or available information-sources. And the third major premise of Chomsky's argument – again placing him completely at odds with Foucault – is the idea that self-styled 'liberal democracies' can be judged according to the measure in which they live up to this professed ideal, or (conversely) by the fact that, as Chomsky puts it, 'the standard view of how the system works is at serious odds with reality'. For such judgments will evidently lack all force if one assumes, like Foucault, that 'reality' is a product of the current institutional-discursive *status quo*, that there is simply no truth behind ideological appearances, and that every socio-political order – from the Gulag to the various (however partial or compromised) forms of liberal democracy – displays the same workings of a ubiquitous 'power/knowledge' that effectively levels the difference between them. On all three counts it would appear that Chomsky is still in the grip of an outmoded quasi-universalist 'discourse', a meta-narrative view of history and social institutions whose progressive or emancipatory character no longer commands any credence.

Let us take these arguments one by one as they relate to Chomsky's recent writings on the 'political economy' of truth. Now of course there is a sense – and Chomsky concedes as much – in which dissident truth-claims are always *to some extent* bound up with existing forms of power/knowledge, or necessarily reliant on sources of information which circulate (in however marginal or clandestine a form) among other documents in the public domain, and which therefore should be subject to the same degree of scepticism that applies, for example, in the case of Pentagon briefings or government pronouncements. But this is not to say – as Foucault would have it – that there is no judging between these various 'discourses' in point of credibility or factual truth since they all give voice to some particular set of self-interested, power-seeking, knowledge-constitutive values and beliefs. Chomsky addresses the point as follows in a passage that makes short work of such sophistical arguments.

> In criticizing media priorities and biases we often draw on the media themselves for at least some of the facts. This affords the opportunity for a classic *non-sequitur*, in which the citation of facts from the mainstream press is offered as a triumphant 'proof' that the criticism is self-refuting, and that media coverage of disputed issues is indeed adequate. That the media provide some facts about an issue, however, proves absolutely nothing about the adequacy or accuracy of that coverage. . . . More important in this context is the question of the attention given to a fact – its placement, tone and repetitions, the framework of analysis within which it is presented, and the related facts that accompany it and give it meaning (or preclude understanding). That a careful reader looking for a fact can sometimes find it with diligence and a sceptical eye tells us nothing about whether that fact received the attention and context it deserved, whether it was intelligible to the reader or effectively distorted or repressed. What level of attention it deserves may be open to debate, but there is no merit in the pretence that because certain facts may be found in the media by a diligent and sceptical researcher, the absence of radical bias and de facto suppression is thereby demonstrated.[27]

In other words, the attempted *non-sequitur* strategy comes back like a boomerang, proving not so much that dissidents like Chomsky are unknowingly trapped in a version of the hermeneutic circle, but rather that arguments against the possibility of adopting a dissident stance – arguments such as those very knowingly adopted by critics like Rorty and Fish – are themselves based on a simplified idea of what counts as truthful utterance in any given context of debate. And the same applies to Foucault's sceptical genealogy of power/knowledge, his contention that all truth-claims come down to a level of conflicting discourses or representations where nothing – or nothing aside from strategic self-interest – could possibly count as a valid reason for regarding some statements as truthful (since adequately borne out by the evidence), and others are lacking such warrant on account of their partial, distorted, or politically-motivated character. For if this were the case then clearly Chomsky would have wasted his time in compiling such a mass of detailed case-histories documenting the various media-propagated falsehoods, cover-up campaigns, conspiracies of silence, abuses of trust, techniques of public-opinion management and so forth that his writings have persistently sought to expose. From Foucault's point of view this labour would amount to nothing more than a multiplication of discourses, an addition to the range currently on offer which might have the useful strategic effect of generating local points of resistance, but which couldn't be regarded as in any way bringing us closer to the truth on any given issue.

THE POLITICAL ECONOMY OF TRUTH

It seems to me that the superior cogency of Chomsky's arguments should be obvious to any reader whose mind remains open to persuasion on rational grounds. There are factual truths (and counter-factual falsehoods) which *don't* come down to a mere disagreement between rival viewpoints, language-games or discourses, but which involve determinate standards of veridical warrant and accountability. For example, popular support for the Gulf War was secured through a large-scale campaign of media disinformation that suppressed many truths – historical, geo-political, and factual-documentary – and which traded on widespread ignorance of what was *actually occurring* from day to day, in the bombing of civilian populations, the extent of so-called 'collateral damage', and the pursuit of war-aims that greatly exceeded the official UN provisions with regard to the Iraqi occupation of Kuwait.

Thus for instance it is a claim borne out by knowledge of the relevant background history that the 'Allied' campaign was fought with the object of securing Western hegemony in the region through the survival of a client regime (Kuwait) which could then be relied upon to keep the oil-supplies flowing and to exert a 'stabilizing' influence on adjacent territories. It is also a matter of documentary record 1) that Saddam Hussein was brought to power and maintained over a long period by US intelligence and 'long-arm' strategic agencies; 2) that his regime was backed up *until the very last moment* by constant supplies of weapons and resources (not to mention diplomatic support) provided by the US and other Western powers; 3) that this invasion of Kuwait was prompted – or at least given what appeared to be the green light – by indications that the US would not intervene since it also wished to push up the oil-prices by exerting pressure on Kuwait; 4) that the Gulf War was fought *first and foremost* as a war of retribution against an erstwhile ally who had proved too difficult to handle; 5) that its conduct involved not only enormous military and civilian casualties but also – contrary to professed 'Allied' war-aims – a full-scale campaign of aerial bombardment launched against electricity generating stations, water-supply systems, sewage disposal plants, and other components of the urban infrastructure whose collapse could be predicted to cause yet further death and suffering through the breakdown of emergency services and the spread of infectious diseases; 6) that the attacks on retreating Iraqi forces (along with civilian hangers-on and hostages) continued to the point where any justifying talk became merely a cover for mechanized mass-murder; and 7) – still within the realm of documentary evidence – that the war might well have been averted had the 'Allies' held out against US pressure and listened to those well-informed sources who argued that sanctions were already (in early January) taking their toll of Iraqi war-fighting capabilities. Of course all these claims are properly subject to reasoned argument and counter-argument, some of them (like items 3, 4 and 7) involving a considerable measure of interpretive hindsight. But to treat such disputes – in the Foucault-Lyotard manner – as so many rival, incommensurable 'discourses' beyond any hope of just and truthful arbitration is to adopt the kind of doctrinaire relativist outlook that leaves no room for genuine debate.

This leads on to the second point at issue between Foucault and Chomsky, namely the question whether anything survives of that subject-centred epistemological and ethical 'discourse' whose epoch coincided (according to Foucault) with the rise of the modern human sciences, and whose imminent demise is now widely heralded by the followers of postmodern fashion. For it is among the most basic suppositions in Kant and for thinkers (like Habermas) still committed to the 'unfinished project of modernity' that there exists a close relation between truth-telling interests – including the claims of enlightened *Ideologiekritik* – and those ethical values that likewise depend upon a free and open access to the 'public sphere' of rational, informed discussion. There are two requirements here, the first having to do with the conditions of possibility for such debate within a given set of institutional, cultural and socio-political structures, and the second relating to the duty that devolves upon responsible individuals – especially politicians, journalists, academics, 'expert' commentators and others with opinion-shaping influence – to establish the facts to the best of their ability and then *tell the truth* concerning those facts despite any countervailing pressures of censorship, political interference, professional self-interest or whatever. For, as Chomsky remarks, most biased choices in the media arise from the preselection of right-thinking people, internalized preconceptions, and the adaptation of personnel to the constraints of ownership, organization, market, and political power. Censorship is largely self-censorship, by reporters and commentators who adjust to the realities of source and media organizational requirements, and by people at higher levels who are chosen to implement, and have usually internalized, the constraints imposed by proprietary and other market and governmental centers of power.[28]

Now of course this passage could be read as supporting one of Foucault's major theses: that power no longer operates (if ever it did) through a straightforward 'top-down' mechanism where those in authority – 'the state' or its high-level executives – exert various forms of coercive restraint upon the mass of more or less compliant subjects. Rather it is a question, according to Foucault, of complex differential power-relationships that extend to every aspect of our social, cultural and political lives, involving all manner of (often contradictory) 'subject-positions', and securing our assent not so much by the threat of punitive (legal or other) sanctions, but by persuading us to internalize the norms and values that prevail within this or that social order. In which case it is pointless, according to Foucault, to invoke the old theories – Marxist 'meta-narratives' among them – that envisage power-relations on a two-term model (oppressor and oppressed) where the terms are strictly non-reversible, and where any resistance can only take rise from the overthrow of existing social structures by an oppressed working class that has at last, with the help of enlightened intellectuals, come to recognize the conditions of its own servitude. To Foucault, such ideas are wholly misguided, resting as they do on a false (outmoded) notion of the critical 'vanguard' thinker as a source of truths inaccessible to other, less privileged or knowing individuals.

This error is compounded by a constant appeal to what Foucault calls the 'repressive hypothesis', that is to say, the naive conception of power/knowledge that identifies power with the various agencies of state-sponsored ideological command, and knowledge with the liberating will-to-truth – the progressive or emancipatory impulse – that enables us to break with existing forms of authority, surveillance, and control.[29] On the contrary, Foucault argues: knowledge is itself just an epiphenomenon of that ubiquitous Nietzschean will-to-power whose genealogy encompasses all the truth-claims of 'enlightened' reason, and whose workings cannot be grasped – much less resisted – by appealing to those old (Kantian or Marxist) notions of knowledge and truth. Still less can one continue to invoke the subject – the knowing, willing, autonomous, self-critical or 'transcendental' subject of Kantian discourse – as if that figment of humanist ideology had somehow survived the epochal shift to a different order of discursive relations, an order where (in Foucault's celebrated phrase) 'man' is already facing extinction, his self-image remaining like a figure drawn in sand at the ocean's edge, about to be erased by the incoming tide.[30] Thus we cannot any longer think of 'truth' in its various Kantian aspects or modalities, i.e. as a matter of adequate cognitive (epistemological) warrant, of ethical good faith, or of *Ideologiekritik* as a process of reflective, self-disciplined enquiry that enables us to see *through and beyond* the structures of ideological misrecognition. Rather, we should now view the subject as a locus of multiple, dispersed or decentered discourses, all of which involve power-seeking interests, but some of which may generate localized effects of resistance by virtue of their incompatability one with another. 'No power without resistance, no resistance without power' is the basic (and strikingly Hobbesian) message of Foucault's work in the areas of penal history, medical practice, psychiatric treatment, and sexual politics. Moreover, it is a lesson that he sees as inescapable for anyone who surveys the dubious record – the high hopes contrasted with the bleak realities – of 'enlightenment' reason over the past two centuries of failed emancipatory promise. Confronted with this melancholy spectacle, so Foucault believes, we have no option but to relegate the subject (the Kantian 'transcendental-empirical doublet') to the history of outworn ideas, and adopt a different rhetoric of 'subject-positions', 'enunciative modalities', 'signifying practices' and so forth by which to register the chronic obsolesence of all such delusive truth-telling claims.

As I remarked above, there is a measure of agreement between Foucault's and Chomsky's positions on this issue. Thus Chomsky goes some way toward conceding the point that our ideas of truth are very largely the product of 'internalized preconceptions'; that subjects may indeed be conditioned to accept certain facts as 'self-evident' merely by virtue of their fitting in with some established, consensual, or professionalized code of belief; that censorship often operates not so much 'from above' as through forms of self-imposed discipline and restraint that don't involve the exercise of overt, coercive powers; that there may be 'honest', 'right-thinking' individuals (as Chomsky is willing to describe them) who are none the less involved in propagating falsehoods that service the 'political economy of truth'; and moreover, that resistance to those falsehoods or abuses of power must always be *to some extent* reliant on the 'discourses' – the available sources of information – that circulate at any given time. But he differs very sharply with Foucault when it comes to the latter's ultra-relativist (Nietzschean) argument that 'truth' is *nothing but* a reflex product of these power/knowledge differentials, and that the 'subject' – the subject-presumed-to-know – is likewise *nothing more* than a point of intersection between those multiple, transient and shifting orders of discourse that admit of no appeal to truth-telling standards beyond what is currently 'good in the way of belief'. For Chomsky, there is still the possibility of judging that some individuals in positions of authority, influence or power hold out against the pressures of conformist ideology and attempt to tell the truth to the best of their knowledge, while others lend themselves – whether knowingly or not – to the purposes of media disinformation, state propaganda, or public-opinion management. To deny these distinctions, as Foucault does with his resolutely post-ethical talk of 'subject-positions', 'discourses', 'power/knowledge' etc, is to go all the way with Nietzsche's amoralist pronouncement that truth is nothing more than a particular kind of lie (or variety of self-promoting fiction) which happens to suit prevailing conventions or forms of consensus-belief.

Chomsky's objections to this cynical doctrine are not just a matter of high-toned abstract principle, but are everywhere manifest in his large body of work on US foreign policy, on the abuses of state, corporate and media influence, and on what might be called – without benefit of Foucault – the politics of power/knowledge as applied to issues of media representation. The following passage gives a fair indication of the distance that separates Chomsky's critique from the currency of postmodern-pragmatist thinking, a fashion that derives in large part from Foucault's sceptical 'genealogies' of truth, knowledge, and ethical value-systems. I must quote at some length since the argument is crucial to all the main issues that are raised by the Foucault/Chomsky debate.

> In the media, as in other major institutions, those who do not display the requisite values and perspectives will be regarded as 'irresponsible', 'ideological', or otherwise aberrant, and will tend to fall by the

wayside. While there may be a few exceptions, the pattern is pervasive, and expected. Those who adapt, perhaps quite honestly, will then be free to express themselves with little managerial control, and they will be able to assert, accurately, that they perceive no pressures to conform. The media are indeed 'free' – for those who adopt the principles required for their 'societal purpose'. There may be some who are simply corrupt, and who serve as 'errand boys' for state and other authority, but this is not the norm. We know from personal experience that many journalists are quite aware of the way the system operates, and utilize the occasional openings it affords to provide information and analysis that departs in some measure from the elite consensus, carefully shaping it so as to accommodate to required norms in a general way. But this degree of insight is surely not common. Rather, the norm is a belief that freedom prevails, which is true for those who have internalized the required values and perspectives.[31]

What is important here – and throughout Chomsky's work – is that the argument finds room for differences (even shades and nuances) of ethico-political judgment that would scarcely register on Foucault's scale, since for him there is no question of truth-claims that possess a factual warrant quite apart from this or that given nexus of motivating 'power/knowledge' interests. And on his account likewise there is no conceiving of *individually responsible* agents – politicians, intellectuals, journalists, editors, think-tank consultants or whatever – whose varying degrees of complicity or resistance should be seen (in most cases) as matters of moral conscience, and not just as signs of their having been recruited by one or another 'discourse' among the range currently on offer. For Chomsky, the whole purpose of a dissident or counter-hegemonic critique of state and media interests is first to establish the truth of such matters as far as it can possibly be known, and second to expose the lies, hypocrisies and techniques of mass-disinformation that have so far prevented citizens from attaining an adequate (factual and moral) perspective. And this applies above all to those persons whose privileged status – whose political authority, opinion-shaping power, intellectual prestige, or relative freedom of access to the relevant documentary sources – renders them morally accountable to a higher degree than others with no such advantages.

Chomsky makes this point most tellingly when he acknowledges the limits of his 'propaganda model' (a model that comes, on the face of it, fairly close to Foucault's way of thinking) if set against the actual diversity of viewpoints that characterize media debate on matters of so-called 'national interest'. In such cases, he writes,

> the humanity and professional integrity of journalists often leads them in directions that are unacceptable in the ideological institutions, and one should not underestimate the psychological burden of suppressing obvious truths and maintaining the required doctrines of benevolence (possibly gone awry), inexplicable error, good intentions, injured innocence, and so on, in the face of overwhelming evidence incompatible with these patriotic premises. The resulting tensions sometimes find limited expression, but more often they are suppressed either consciously or unconsciously, with the help of belief systems that permit the pursuit of narrow interest, whatever the facts.[32]

Here again, Chomsky is able to invoke standards of good faith, integrity and truth-telling warrant which don't come down – as they do for Foucault – to a mere illusion of ethical choice on the part of subjects whose range of possible 'positions' is always (so to speak) staked out in advance by the discourses that happen to circulate at any given time. Not that Chomsky for a moment underrates the pressures of institutionalized 'power/knowledge', or the extent to which 'right-thinking' individuals can avoid becoming aware of their own complicity in campaigns of media disinformation by having thoroughly internalized the various belief-systems, societal norms, interests of state, forms of 'voluntary' self-censorship and so forth which make up the moral or professional code of their particular interest-group. Indeed, the above passages – along with many others – bear ample witness to Chomsky's understanding that journalistic bad faith can take numerous forms, from the 'errand-boy' attitude of cynical acquiescence or knowing and willing mendacity, to the wholly unconscious adoption of an outlook in line with prevailing consensus-beliefs. But these are extreme cases, he argues, and shouldn't distract us from the more representative middle-ground, the area where genuine conflicts or 'tensions' arise, and where people typically find themselves faced with an issue of conscience that involves either telling the truth as best they can or falling in with some standard, acceptable line that requires them to suppress certain relevant facts. It is here that Chomsky locates the 'psychological burden', the strain to which certain individuals are subject – at whatever 'conscious' or 'unconscious' level – when required to choose between the rival claims of 'humanity and professional integrity' on the one hand, and careerist self-interest on the other.

Foucault quite simply has no vocabulary – no descriptive resources of an ethical, psychological or socio-political kind – with which to account for such varieties of good and bad faith. This follows from his all-purpose, levelling rhetoric of 'power/knowledge', a rhetoric that reduces issues of conscience to a play-off between various (morally indifferent) discourses, and which relegates the subject – the locus of ethical conflict and choice – to the status of a mere 'transcendental' illusion, a mirage of bourgeois-humanist ideology. To Chomsky's way of thinking, conversely, such arguments amount to a wholesale *trahison des clercs*, a convenient refuge for jaded intellectuals who have not only renounced all claims to distinguish between truth and falsehood, right and wrong, but raised that failure to a high point of principle, a doctrine that falls in with the worst (i.e. the most knowing and cynical) varieties of journalistic bad faith. For on this account – to adopt a more homely idiom – the buck wouldn't stop anywhere, but would circulate endlessly in a system where nobody had reason, authority, or conscientious grounds for contradicting this or that accredited item of state-sponsored media untruth.

Most crucially, Chomsky rejects the Foucauldian premise that power/knowledge operates *always* by inserting the subject into discourses – or pre-given 'subject positions' – that involve no significant margin of choice on his or her part, and which therefore offer no hold for judgments of ethical, social or political accountability. On the one hand there are those – some few intellectuals, some very few journalists – whose principles conflict outright with the dictates of professional or media complicity, and who therefore (like Chomsky) find themselves excluded from the mainstream of socio-political debate, obliged to publish and lecture where they can, mostly in specialized or minority contexts. At the opposite extreme are those other, ideally compliant types who are willing to toe the official line and whose consciences offer no resistance, either through their having 'internalized' the standard requirements or – more often – out of a straightforward concern for their livelihoods, prospects of promotion or whatever. Then again, there are journalists of a principled but canny disposition, individuals who know (as Chomsky puts it) 'how the system operates', and who can thus 'utilize occasional openings' in order to 'provide information and analysis that departs in some measure from the elite consensus'. But in each of these cases (*contra* Foucault) there is a question of more or less conscious *agency*, of subjects whose relation to the dominant 'discourse' – whether of complicity or resistance – involves some measure of humanly-accountable motive, interest, or intent.

Thus, as Chomsky writes,

> there are important actors who do take positive initiatives to define and shape the news and to keep the media in line. It is a 'guided market system' that we describe here, with the guidance provided by the government, the leaders of the corporate community, the top media owners and executives, and the assorted individuals and groups who are assigned or allowed to take constructive initiatives. These initiators are sufficiently small in number to be able to act jointly on occasion, as do sellers in markets with few rivals. In most cases, however, media leaders do similar things because they see the world through the same lenses, are subject to similar constraints and incentives, and thus feature stories or maintain silence together in tacit collective action and leader-follower behavior.[33]

From a Foucauldian standpoint this could only appear as yet another instance of Chomsky's regressive (liberal-humanist) habits of thought. But Chomsky would just as surely respond by pointing to the *consequences* of Foucault's doctrine if it were taken on board – 'internalized' as a working system of belief – by those various individuals (journalists, academics, media analysts etc) who in practice exert a good deal of influence on the currency of social and political debate. For as Foucault sees it these subjects would be indulging in a species of illusory wish-fulfilment – a fantasy projection of their own will-to-power – if they thought themselves capable of uttering truths at odds with the prevailing consensus-view, or of taking a principled, conscientious stand against falsehoods put about through the standard channels of media disinformation. At best, such figures would occupy a place somewhere toward the 'radical' end on a scale of pre-given subject-positions where the various roles were scripted in advance, and where any effective resistance came about through conflicts of interest – or power/knowledge differentials – that operated wholly beyond the grasp of the knowing, willing subject.

In which case the 'critical' intellectual would have no option but to take up the middle-ground (tactical-opportunist) stance among the range that Chomsky describes, and rest content with exploiting those occasional 'openings' – blind-spots or chinks in the official discourse – that turned up once in a while. And even so he or she would be deceived if they construed such resistance as resulting from an act of principled *choice*, a decision on their own part – having weighed the evidence – not to let the standard version of events go entirely unchallenged. For whatever its undoubted appeal on a sheerly pragmatic or psychological level – as a motivating impulse among investigative journalists, political dissidents, conscientious intellectuals etc – this belief is just another item of outworn 'Enlightenment' baggage, and one (moreover) that we can easily dump once equipped with Foucault's alternative project of discursive-strategic intervention.

REVERSING THE DRIFT: REALITY REGAINED

What would be the upshot of Foucault's arguments if applied to the Gulf War, its media representation, and the responses to it displayed by various (approving or dissenting) commentators? To be sure, the press and television coverage offered ample evidence tending to support Foucault's major premise, namely that there soon emerged a dominant 'discourse' whose values, beliefs and normative assumptions were not so much imposed 'from above' by some clumsy mechanism of overt censorship, but were readily internalized by the great majority of journalists, editors and on-hand purveyors of 'expert' opinion. This is not to say that the consensus was by any means monolithic, or that one couldn't – by reading the 'quality' papers or watching late-night TV discussion programmes – find at least a few people ready to challenge the official line and give reasons (historical, factual-documentary, and ethico-political reasons) for rejecting the justificatory arguments put forward by the US and its client 'Allied' powers. But these debates hardly encroached onto prime-time coverage or into the pages of the mass-circulation tabloids where (as always) the 'public opinion' monitors chose to focus their attention.

Nor is this in any way surprising since, as Chomsky remarks, there are numerous factors that cooperate to swing the balance in favour of the official (state-sponsored) view. One of these is 'elemental patriotism', the 'overwhelming wish to think well of ourselves, our institutions, and our leaders'. As a result of this desire

> we see ourselves as basically good and decent in personal life, so it must be that our institutions function in accordance with the same benevolent intent, an argument that is often persuasive even though it is a transparent *non-sequitur*. The patriotic premise is reinforced by the

119

belief that 'we the people' rule, a central principle of the system of indoctrination from early childhood, but also one with little merit, as an analysis of the social and political system will quickly reveal. There are also real advantages in conformity beyond the rewards and privileges that it yields. If one chooses to denounce Qaddafi, or the Sandanistas, or the PLO, or the Soviet Union, no credible evidence is required. The same is true if one repeats conventional doctrines about our own society.... But a critical analysis ... must meet far higher standards; in fact, standards are often imposed that can barely be met in the natural sciences. One has to work hard, to produce evidence that is credible, to construct serious arguments, to present extensive documentation – all tasks that are superfluous so long as one remains within the presuppositional framework of the doctrinal consensus.[34]

In short, it is only to be expected that most commentators (especially those in the popular or prime-time media) will tend to endorse the government line, or at any rate restrict their criticism to matters of tactics, short-term regional aims etc, rather than offering the kind of in-depth factual and socio-political analysis that would challenge the entire currency of orthodox belief. And, as Chomsky notes, their motives in this may range all the way from cynical self-interest, through various shades of (conscious or unconscious) complicity, to the 'benevolent' – if culpably naive – idea that liberal democracy, US-style, should be taken pretty much at its own valuation as the best guarantee of freedom and truth.

Again, one could argue that this leaves Chomsky in a position of broad agreement with Foucault, at least as regards the ubiquitous character of power/knowledge, the insertion of subjects into 'discourses' that set the agenda for relevant debate, and the sheer *impossibility* of adopting a standpoint – a principled, truth-telling standpoint – that would claim to expose (and thereby discredit) the working of those same mechanisms. But it should be apparent from the above passage that Chomsky both rejects the logic of this argument and offers an alternative 'propaganda model' which avoids such ultimately cynical, reductive or nihilist conclusions by affirming the role of human agency and choice in issues of ethical and political conscience. Unlike Foucault, he attaches real significance to the values, principles and elective self-image by which most citizens in a liberal democracy prefer to think themselves (and their governments) guided. That is to say, he rejects the Foucauldian option of viewing them as so many ruses or alibis in the service of an omnipresent will-to-power, one that operates indifferently across all social orders or 'political economies of truth', and which scarcely leaves room for any meaningful distinction between democratic systems – however badly compromised in practice – and other (e.g. totalitarian) regimes. For Chomsky, such differences not only exist but require just the kind of critical vigilance that prevents power-interests from advancing their hegemony to the point where a sceptic like Foucault might be justified in professing his Hobbesian theses.

Thus it is not – or not only – with ironical intent that Chomsky cites the verdict of a US judge in the *Pentagon Papers* case, ruling that publication was indeed in the national interest, that it threatened no breach of state 'security', and moreover that 'a cantankerous press, an obstinate press, a ubiquitous press must be suffered by those in authority in order to preserve the even greater values of freedom of expression and the right of the people to know'.[35] Certainly the citation is double-edged to the extent that its claims show up in an ironic light when set against the evidence of media unfreedom, complicity, self-interest, systematic bias etc which Chomsky provides in such abundant detail. But the irony doesn't, in Fish-Rorty parlance, go all the way down to the point where any notion of journalistic truth or honesty would appear just a species of naive illusion carried over from the Enlightenment *ancien regime*. For as Chomsky reads them, 'these ringing declarations express valid aspirations, and beyond that, they surely express the self-image of the American media'.[36] It is the distance between image and reality that needs to be exposed, and not – as would appear on Foucault's account, and from the viewpoint of postmodernists like Baudrillard – the absence of any such notional 'reality' against which to measure the image.

That this distance can become momentarily visible even under conditions of near-blanket censorship is one hopeful message that emerges from the otherwise bleak panorama of the Gulf War and its media representation. I have already drawn attention to several such instances, among them the moments of perceived disparity between, on the one hand, official talk about 'precision bombing', 'pinpoint accuracy', 'minimal collateral damage' etc, and on the other the documentary TV evidence of urban destruction and large-scale civilian casualties. Ocular proof or first-hand witness is of course the most powerful dispellant of propaganda falsehood, even if the evidence comes – as in this case – through media channels where the saturation coverage creates a high level of sensory and cognitive overload, tending to blur our sense of the critical image/reality distinction. That is to say, there is a sense in which commentators like Baudrillard were justified in claiming that this was a different kind of war, one that involved such a massive concentration of media resources (along with – and allied to – the weapons technology) that it took on a 'hyperreal' aspect unprecedented in the history of modern warfare. But it is quite another thing to push this argument all the way to Baudrillard's desperate conclusion, i.e. that issues of truth and falsehood were therefore wholly irrelevant, since all those concerned – whether TV viewers, journalists, war-cabinet members, military strategists, front-line combatants, or whoever – were likewise dependent on a communications network that dictated their perception of events at every stage, and which thus blocked any possible access to 'the facts' as apart from their various modes of electronic or media simulation. For this is to confuse an ontological question (what happened?) with an epistemological issue (what difficulties do we face in getting to know what happened?). Such confusions are rife among those, like Baudrillard, who would seize every pretext for proclaiming an end to the 'epoch' of enlightened truth-seeking discourse.

Perhaps there was nothing here to match the experience of soldiers in the First World War, witnessing the horrors and catastrophic setbacks as a matter of brute, self-evident fact, and then reading reports in the British press – geared entirely to the propaganda effort – which falsified the casualty figures, treated the conflict as a tolerably civilized affair, and echoed the standard morale-boosting line that victory was just around the corner. Indeed, what comes across most strikingly in many 'first-hand' (journalistic or combatant) recollections of the Gulf War is the curious sense of not really having *experienced* these events at all, but having witnessed them only at a distant remove where 'reality' could scarcely get into conflict with the steady stream of images, war-game scenarios, media liaison exercises and so forth. Then there is the fact – less often mentioned – that Iraqi losses, military and civilian, may never be known with any degree of accuracy, given the sheer destructive power of the weaponry involved and its capacity to well-nigh obliterate the evidence. In light of all this it would be idle to pretend that the Gulf War didn't pose special problems for anyone seeking to report truthfully on events, or to analyse the media coverage in respect of its factual honesty, its access to the best, most reliable sources of information, or its critical attitude when dealing with suspect (government or military) sources. But there is still a great difference between conceding that truth in such matters is peculiarly hard to come by, and recommending – as Baudrillard does – that we give up the attempt forthwith since war has now entered a realm of postmodern 'hyperreality' where those standards no longer apply.

These issues were confronted most explicitly in an article by Dick Hebdige, written during the early phase of the Gulf War and published shortly afterwards in *Marxism Today*. It is a significant piece for two main reasons, firstly as the statement of a left intellectual known for his 'postmodern' sympathies, and secondly as having appeared in a journal whose aim has been to update Marxist thinking in response to precisely such challenges. It is also – I would argue – exemplary of the problems that arise for any good-faith commentator broadly sympathetic to postmodernist ideas, but confronted with a series of events which effectively shake that facile creed and demand something more in the way of intellectual and moral integrity. Hebdige starts out with the following reflections, appearing to situate his essay very much in the Baudrillard camp. 'We are involved', he writes,

> in the most thoroughly mediated war in history but now more than ever vicarious contact with the front line via blanket news coverage fails to guarantee comprehensibility, still less access to the truth. The battlefield today is electronic. Wars are waged, as ever, over real territories and real spheres of influence. But conflicts between 'major players' are now also conducted in a 'virtual space' where rival hypothetical scenarios, 'realised' as computer simulations, fight it out over the data supplied by satellites. Meanwhile, hygienically edited highlights of the action get replayed nightly on the news through ghostly green videos shot through the night-sight viewfinders of airborne artillery. In this screened space anything can happen but little can be verified.[37]

One can scarcely deny the truth of all this as a piece of diagnostic commentary, that is, in so far as it accurately describes the experience of many viewers faced with a barrage of media (dis)information and hard-put to separate the elements of fact from the mass of simulated pseudo-truths or downright propaganda footage. But as Hebdige himself points out, 'the mere accumulation of data doesn't confer an automatic advantage unless it is accompanied by quality analysis and contextual detail'. Of course it may be said that 'quality' and 'context' are discourse-specific values, defined only through their playing a part in this or that mode of media presentation. But Hebdige's next sentence makes it clear that he is appealing to certain argumentative criteria – standards of consistency, non-contradiction, or adequate evidential grounds – that cannot be so easily dismissed by recourse to the glib postmodernist line. Thus: 'witness, for example, the wildly discrepant assessments of the effectiveness of allied air-raids in the first days of the war, or the "classification error" which led to the deaths of hundreds of civilians in Baghdad'. There is no question here of simply levelling the difference between events-as-they-occurred and events as represented in the 'virtual space' of media hyperreality.

My point is not at all to score points off Hebdige for his endorsement of the Baudrillard position but – quite the contrary – to show that he abandons that position as soon as he reflects on a real-world issue that exposes such sophistries for what they are. In fact there are numerous details of his argument that go clean against the postmodernist drift of that opening paragraph. For Hebdige knows as well as anyone that reality continues to exert a claim on our attempts to make sense of the world; that it is still possible to verify certain factual propositions (and to falsify others) through investigative journalism, documentary research, or the critical sifting of evidence; and that where such evidence is hard to come by – or subject to effects of mass-media simulation – we can none the less apply alternative (probabilistic) standards of truth and falsehood. Thus his article goes on to criticize the war and the manner of its press and television coverage in terms that involve a continued appeal to standards (critical and ethico-political values) that could find no place in Baudrillard's universe of free-floating hyperreality. As Hebdige puts it:

> the role of information in an internationally mediated environment has sinister implications when combined with the new high-tech modes of warfare currently being tested in the Gulf. As TV onlookers we are placed at the centre of events no human being could ever witness, by close-ups of a bomb's-eye view of the interior of a ventilator shaft right up to the moment of impact. But the larger picture is systematically distorted by the military and political calculations concerning the strategic uses of information and disinformation. Whole chunks of 'enemy territory' are 'disappeared' by means of censorship, radar and the wholesale destruction of Iraqi communications facilities. . . . With the BBC 'illustrating' the cluster bombing of Iraqi airfields with an arms manufacturer's demonstration video, TV's claim to 'show it like

it is' in 1991 appears as obscene as it did in the Falklands. . . . For the
world's first totally screened war has placed a mirror at our disposal. In
it we can see reflected the ecological, psychological, spiritual damage
and the massive human waste of this war.

It hardly needs saying that these judgments would lack all force if we
had really moved on – as Baudrillard contends – into an epoch of
terminal indifference with regard to truth-claims or the values of
enlightened critical debate. What emerges most forcefully in the above
passage is Hebdige's conviction first that the Gulf War was unjustified
on moral, social or political grounds, and second that the mainstream
press and television coverage was in large part responsible for
suppressing information – or producing a distorted perception of
events – in line with 'Allied' propaganda interests. The vocabulary of
moral outrage ('sinister', 'obscene', 'spiritual damage and massive
human waste') goes along with his clear understanding that this was a
war whose conduct involved not only 'systematic distortion' of a
wholly unprecedented kind but also a degree of hyperreality brought
about by the illusion of 'total screening' and the consequent lack of
that critical distance required for an adequate comprehension of
events.

To this extent (i.e. at the diagnostic level) Hebdige concurs pretty
much with Baudrillard in analyzing the sources of confusion and
treating them as symptomatic of a wider postmodern predicament. But
he differs on one crucial point: his insistence that these are *pathological*
symptoms, resulting from a definite malaise in the body politic, and
not just the signs – as Baudrillard would have it – of a generalized drift
toward forms of cognitive and ethico-political scepticism whose
advent leaves us utterly devoid of alternative critical resources. If this
'totally screened war' has indeed placed a 'mirror at our disposal' it is
not the same mirror that Baudrillard holds up in order to convince us
that everything is illusion, that criticism is henceforth a pointless
activity, and that nothing now counts as valid argument except those
various rhetorics, discourses or elective self-images that happen to be
currently 'good in the way of belief'. On the contrary, Hebdige writes:
'the challenge – more urgent now than it was even in the cold war – is
to think differently and to act otherwise'.

6

THE 'END OF IDEOLOGY'
REVISITED

NEOPRAGMATISM AND THE 'NEW WORLD ORDER'

It is a sad reflection on the currency of 'advanced' intellectual debate in the human sciences that so much of what passes for radical theory is in fact quite incapable of mustering resistance to a downright conformist or consensus-based account of knowledge, truth and reality. For some – Rorty and Fish among them – this appears a consummation devoutly to be wished, a sensible acknowledgment of the plain fact that we just can't get outside the values, conventions or habits of belief that make up our particular 'interpretive community', and would therefore do better to take them on board and cease the vain quest for argumentative grounds that might somehow escape this predicament.[1] In the end such thinking leads to a point where minority or dissident views can be accounted for only by treating them as localized options within this or that marginal community, language-games whose 'truth' is entirely a matter of suasive or rhetorical appeal, and which don't so much win converts by arguing a case as preach to the converted – however few in number – by playing on their preexistent habits of belief. From this point of view ('North Atlantic postmodern bourgeois-liberal neopragmatist', in Rorty's capacious definition) it is simply unthinkable that anyone could come up with *reasons* – factual, historical, ethical, political or otherwise principled reasons – for rejecting the dominant consensus belief as regards, for example, the extent of Iraqi civilian casualties in the Gulf War, the motives for US involvement in the region, or the interests at stake in that 'New World Order' envisaged by Bush and his supporters in the Allied camp. Any putative resistance would amount to nothing more than a predisposed choice among the various language-games currently on offer, a position arrived at not through the exercise of reasoned critical thought but through mere force of habitual adherence to one or another rhetorical strategy.

It is not hard to see how this line of neo-pragmatist talk comes down to a species of thinly-disguised apologetics for the current socio-political status quo. Applied to the Gulf War, it would yield the following arguments: 1) that opposition was largely unavailing, given the existence of a majority pro-war consensus and the effectiveness of Allied propaganda techniques; 2) that any dissident views could only gain a hearing in so far as they appealed to some in-place 'community' of beliefs, values and ideological assumptions that went against the dominant consensual grain; 3) that to this extent objectors were relying on their own kind of rhetoric, albeit one whose suasive force was confined to a much more restricted community, but still involving the same basic mechanisms of predisposed habitual assent; and 4) that one should therefore regard their claims as pretty much on a level with all the other 'discourses' or strategies of argument produced by the various contending parties.

What completely drops out of this ultra-relativist picture is any notion that there might be grounds for deciding between good and bad arguments, truths and untruths, reasons for adopting some particular position as opposed to the varieties of suasive rhetoric adopted in the effort to justify this war in accordance with official (state-sponsored) forms of media disinformation. In short, neo-pragmatism – or the version of it espoused by adepts like Fish and Rorty – amounts to nothing less than an all-purpose pretext for rubbishing the claims of oppositional thought, of intellectual conscience, political dissent, or any such naive ('Enlightenment') belief in the continued relevance of *Ideologiekritik* as a means of challenging false consensus beliefs. Whatever their particular views about the Gulf War – and neither, to my knowledge, has so far ventured an opinion – their theoretical (or anti-theoretical) arguments are such as to cast opponents in the role of *either* an ineffectual fringe movement *or* a relatively vocal minority whose views might just prevail through some future shift in the currency of 'informed' public debate. Even so, such a change would come about for purely contingent (indeed quite inscrutable) reasons having to do with the drift of consensus values, the periodic revisions of historical perspective, or the simple need – as Rorty puts it – that we invent new 'vocabularies' from time to time in order to relieve the monotony and keep up the ongoing 'cultural conversation of mankind'. To imagine that truth might at length win out through a detailed, critical, investigative treatment of the relevant source-materials is merely to demonstrate one's lingering attachment to that old Enlightenment paradigm.

Of course there is a sense in which the Gulf War and the discourse surrounding it exemplify exactly the point that Fish and Rorty are making. That is to say, it has already – as of June 1991 – become a source of new-found rhetorical and narrative strategies for those proponents of the US 'New World Order' who see it as a heaven-sent opportunity to re-write history, to advertise the virtues of a strong military-interventionist stance, and thus – in Bush's memorable words – 'kick the Vietnam syndrome' once and for all. Nothing could better illustrate Rorty's idea that reality and truth are just what we make of them according to the narratives, the preferential idioms or 'final vocabularies' that set the agenda of public debate from one period to the next. What this argument amounts to is a seemingly benign (liberal-pluralist) version of Orwell's grim prognosis in *1984*: that history can always be revised in accordance with the interests, priorities or modes of selective hindsight that inevitably change with the passage of time and the pressure of contemporary social needs. But it fails to take account of the manifest fact – brought home with such brutal directness by Bush's phrase – that those needs are most often a matter of cynical *Realpolitik*, imposed from above by government agencies, think-tanks, military information-sources, press and TV control mechanisms etc, and scarcely answering to what Rorty regards as the open dialogical exchange of beliefs in a 'postmodern bourgeois liberal pragmatist' culture. That history is always written from the standpoint of the victors is the kind of truism that can cut both ways, on the one hand challenging alternative histories that seek to do justice to forgotten causes and victims, while on the other bringing welcome news to those – like US foreign policy hawks – who can fully exploit the opportunities it offers for the knowing manipulation of consensus belief. Neither possibility seems ever to have struck Rorty, wedded as he is to a notion of liberal democracy which requires nothing more than that the 'cultural conversation' should be kept going, that truth-claims (or criticism of false claims to truth) shouldn't be allowed to disrupt it, and that nobody should henceforth spoil the party by raising awkward questions, for instance as to whether this self-image corresponds to the real-world character of US domestic and foreign policy conduct. Such questions are politely but firmly ruled out of order, not least because they offer a sizable challenge to any argument premised on the non-availability of justifying grounds or reasons.

In Rorty's view, any claim to take a stand – as Chomsky does – on ethical, political or truth-telling grounds is both misguided and pointless: misguided in so far as it fails to acknowledge the consensual character of *all* our beliefs, minority or dissident beliefs included, and pointless in so far as it fails to appreciate the virtues of a liberal-pluralist culture where everyone is entitled to have their say and nobody is any longer hooked on those old, conversation-stopping notions of truth, critique, intellectual responsibility and so forth. That the consensus might be swung – or the dialogue distorted by manipulative pressures of various kinds – is a notion that can scarcely be allowed to obtrude upon this placid postmodernist variant of the late-50s 'end-of-ideology' thesis. Still less can Rorty entertain the idea that certain ways of re-writing history – like Bush's strong revisionist line on Vietnam – might actually go so far as to create a massively falsified consensus, one that offered a pretext for powerful interest-groups to push for the resumption of an aggressive stance in promoting US commercial, military and hegemonic interests. For if history is conceived in postmodernist fashion as a field of constantly shifting rhetorical strategies – or as a product of the various narrative paradigms that predominate from time to time – then we might as well accept that historical 'truth' is the prerogative of those (government agencies, PR experts, Pentagon spokesmen, think-tank pundits and the like) who are best placed to exert their influence on the currency of popular belief.

Rorty is understandably keen to avoid any such desperate conclusion. But it is hard to envisage an escape-route from this relativist impasse if rhetoric is indeed the last court of appeal, if truth-claims are nothing more than a species of suasive utterance, and if questions of factual or argumentative validity can only be settled on the terms laid down by some existing communal discourse. For one major lesson of the Gulf War and its aftermath is that the mere existence of media debate – of 'conversation' pushed to unprecedented levels of intensity and saturation coverage – is no guarantee against the distorting mechanisms of censorship, state intervention, and vested military-industrial interests. In the end, there seems little reason to share Rorty's faith that democratic values will surely prevail if only we can keep the dialogue going and prevent all those earnest seekers-after-truth from attempting to have the last word. What this argument ignores is the simple point: that *getting things right* as regards the historical record is the only adequate means of counteracting the various myths, pseudo-histories, propaganda ploys or strong revisionist narratives that can otherwise be invented pretty much to order by those with the power to intervene in the production of socially-acceptable truth. That such techniques can be used to very practical effect in the management of public opinion through the mass media, current affairs 'debate', school curriculum guidance and other forms of subtle (or not-so-subtle) interventionist strategy is a lesson one might expect critical theorists to have learned during the past decade of concerted right-wing ideological offensives.

Of course it may be argued that the most effective line of response is one that plays by the same rules, that accepts the postmodern-neopragmatist challenge, and that sets out to offer a range of attractive counter-narratives (left-liberal, Marxist, feminist, post-colonial or whatever) by way of recapturing the cultural high ground and steering the conversation onto a more congenial course. But again, this fails to reckon with the forces ranged against any version of events – any story-telling mode or conversational gambit – that goes clean against the officially sponsored view. It is clearly not enough for opponents of Bush's strong-revisionist line on the Gulf War ('kicking the Vietnam syndrome') to come up with an alternative account that lays no claim to historical truth but contents itself with giving the story a different narrative twist, one more suited to their own rhetorical or ideological purposes. For this move lays them open to the obvious objection that theirs is just another self-interested viewpoint, a 'discourse' or 'language-game' (in Lyotard's parlance) which operates according to certain *sui generis* criteria, and which cannot – or should not – seek to give the rule in areas where different (incommensurable) truth-claims are in play.

Thus, the Fish-Rorty line of set-piece neopragmatist argument is politically and culturally worlds apart from the stance of active, critical-interventionist concern espoused by thinkers like James and Dewey.[2] In part it is a matter of willing adjustment to the mood of unresisting acquiescence – more charitably, the 'new realism' – which has won so many converts over the past few decades, from the 'end of ideology' ideologues to the apostles of so-called 'New Times' and their flirtation with postmodern, post-Marxist, end-of-history rhetoric. But it also has to do with the linguistic (more precisely, the textualist) turn across various disciplines, the idea – common to Rorty, Fish, Foucault, Lyotard, Baudrillard and others – that there is simply no appeal beyond the structures of representation, the discourses, language-games, rhetorics or 'final vocabularies' that determine what shall count as knowledge or truth within a given interpretive context.

Take this as self-evident – ignoring the numerous objections that arise from other (non-post-structuralist) philosophical quarters – and it will then follow surely enough that opponents of the Gulf War were wasting their time if they thought to find reasons or justifying grounds in the record of US conduct in this and other military adventures. That is to say, their arguments would only carry weight if the current of opinion (or some sizable part of it) was already running their way, so that any opposition on factual-documentary or principled grounds would at once be rendered *de facto* convincing and perfectly beside the point. And if they were *really* striving against the whole drift of currently acceptable consensus belief then of course – *vide* Rorty and Fish – they wouldn't get a hearing in the first place.

If this were the case then the following passage (by the editorial collective of *Socialist Review*) would count as just one more story-telling line, a line whose appeal depends entirely on whether or not one happens to go along with its particular (anti-war) narrative bias. Of course I am not arguing that this is by any means an objective or unbiased source. But it does serve to show how evaluative (ethico-political) judgments can follow directly from the application of historical and factual-documentary criteria. Again I need to quote the passage at length since it raises some crucial issues in a specific and highly relevant context of debate.

> This war is also importantly a battle over history: over the meanings and lessons of the past, and particularly of the 1960s. Even before the fighting began in the Persian Gulf, comparisons and analogies between this conflict and the Vietnam War proliferated, and conflicting interpretations of the significance of that war have shaped much of the discussion about the war with Iraq.
>
> What were – and are – the 'lessons' of Vietnam? Many . . . drew the conclusion that the US should avoid direct military involvement in regional conflicts in the third world. This widely held view lay behind the uncharacteristic lack of US involvement in the 1975 Angolan civil war or the 1979 Sandanista revolution in Nicaragua; as late as the 1980s, the slogan 'no more Vietnams' was used with considerable success to mobilize opposition to US involvement in Central America.
>
> The first set of responses to the 'Vietnam syndrome' was war by proxy or surrogate: US arms, funds and advisers were sent overtly or covertly to 'friendly governments' fighting insurgencies or to guerrilla armies fighting leftist regimes. . . . The second approach – now bearing

fruit with the war against Iraq – has been a concerted effort to attack the syndrome head-on by means of an ideological campaign to recast the meaning of the Vietnam war, coupled with a gradually escalating pattern – from Grenada to Panama to Iraq – of direct use of the military as a tool of US foreign policy.

According to the revisionist school of thought, Vietnam teaches us not to avoid direct military conflict, but that limited war is dangerous. Vietnam was not, as many liberals pictured it, a 'quagmire' that we wrongly walked into; it was, in Ronald Reagan's words, 'a war our government wouldn't let us win'. Never mind that there were half a million US soldiers in Vietnam and horrendous casualties on all sides; never mind that the US dropped more bombs there than the Allies did during all of World War II (a record quickly eclipsed by Desert Storm) or that the United States secretly and illegally invaded and bombed neighboring neutral countries for years. . . . The revisionist 'lesson' of Vietnam proved to be one of the most successful and clever ideological myths of Reaganism, effectively reversing 'no more Vietnams' from an antimilitaristic slogan to a rallying cry for rearmament, more weapons systems, and new strategies for fighting regional wars.[3]

My point is that this passage *doesn't* just present a kind of plausible counter-narrative designed to challenge the 'official' (state-sponsored) account by adopting alternative rhetorical strategies more attuned to the currency of left-liberal opinion. On the contrary: it offers a series of determinate truth-claims whose validity can always be checked out against the best available sources of factual-documentary information, and whose bearings in the sphere of ethical choice and political commitment are a matter of reasoned critical debate among those willing to question the received consensus view. Of course there is a sense in which the issue comes down to rival narrative paradigms, or to a conflict of interpretations where the outcome depends on which particular story-line one happens to prefer. But this is not to say that the preference can only be based on foregone beliefs or consensus ideas as to just what counts as a satisfying mode of narrative reconstruction. What makes all the difference between *this* version of events and the Reagan-Bush revisionist scenario is the fact that the latter can only gain credence through a falsification of the documentary record and a manipulative handling of the sources on offer. Such an argument would cut no ice with Rorty and Fish, convinced as they are that 'truth' in these matters is purely and simply a product of consensus belief. But their position can best be understood diagnostically as itself just a sign of the times, a reflex symptom of that widespread drift toward a rhetoric of assent – or an attitude of willing acquiescence in the taken-for-granted values and beliefs of 'postmodern bourgeois liberal' culture – which these thinkers adopt as a matter of course.

Terry Eagleton pinpoints the blind-spot in their argument when he remarks that neopragmatists like Rorty and Fish show a deep reluctance to address the topic of ideology, or to consider what might be the motivating interests bound up with their desire to have done with such old-hat Enlightenment or Marxist notions.[4] Of course these thinkers are much too canny to be caught out by any direct application of the standard *tu quoque* rejoinder, that is to say, the objection – deployed against relativists down through the history of Western philosophical debate – that their scepticism applies to every kind of truth-claim *except* the claim that 'all truths are relative' or that rhetoric, as a matter of demonstrable fact, goes 'all the way down'. Thus Rorty and Fish are quite willing to concede that in their own case also there can be no appeal beyond the question of what is currently 'good in the way of belief', or the extent to which their arguments fit in with existing modes of consensus thought. But they typically fight shy of asking the further, more awkward question as to just what political interests are served by this espousal of an 'end-of-ideology' thesis on the part of thinkers with considerable influence on the conduct of debate in the present-day human sciences. Thus, in Eagleton's words,

> those who today press the sophistical case that all language is rhetorical . . . are quite ready to acknowledge that the discourse in which they frame this case is nothing but a case of special pleading too; but if Fish is genially prepared to admit that his own theorizing is a bit of rhetoric, he is notably more reluctant to concede that it is a bit of *ideology*. For to do this would involve reflecting on the political ends which such an argument serves in the context of Western capitalist society; and Fish is not prepared to widen his theoretical focus to encompass such embarrassing questions. Indeed his response would no doubt have to be that he is himself so thoroughly a product of that society – which is undoubtedly true – that he is quite unable to reflect on his own social determinants – which is undoubtedly false.[5]

The same applies to Baudrillard with his placid postmodernist assumption that truth and critique are hopelessly outmoded concepts, notions scarcely to be thought of in a world given over to the infinitized play of simulacra. Here again, the one question that Baudrillard never asks is a question concerning the social determinants – the specific modes of knowledge-constitutive (or knowledge-denying) interest – that have worked to engender this outlook of terminal cognitive and ethico-political abandon. And so it becomes possible, as Eagleton writes, 'in a cynical "left" wisdom, to celebrate this catatonic state as some cunning last-ditch resistance to ideological meaning – to revel in the very spiritual blankness of the late bourgeois order as a welcome relief from the boring old human nostalgia for truth, value and reality'.[6]

There could be few more striking demonstrations of Eagleton's point than the ease with which media coverage of the Gulf War managed to create not only a majority consensus in support of US aims, but a climate of opinion clearly receptive to the rhetoric of Bush's 'New World Order' and its concomitant – though somewhat less high-toned – agenda of 'kicking the Vietnam syndrome'. That such strategies were highly effective as a matter of suasive or rhetorical technique can hardly be doubted by anyone who registered the absence of informed critical debate, at least in those quarters (prime-time TV and the mass-circulation tabloid papers) where 'public opinion' was subject, as usual, to a process of specular self-confirmation designed to elicit, to monitor and thus to reinforce the predominance of acceptable (i.e. pro-war) attitudes.[7] But these signs of the times can still be read as *pathological* symptoms, indicative not so much – as Baudrillard would have it – of a wholesale irreversible shift in our modes of knowledge and perception, but resulting from specific abuses of state interventionist power and pressures brought to bear upon the various channels of (supposedly) open, democratic debate.

Here of course I am invoking Jürgen Habermas's postulate of an 'ideal speech-situation', a regulative idea (in the Kantian sense) which manifestly cannot be realised under present conditions, but which holds out the prospect of a *genuine* dialogue – an uncoerced exchange of differing arguments and viewpoints – from which truth might yet emerge at the end of enquiry.[8] It is against this standard, Habermas contends, that we can best gauge the extent of those distortions, vested interests, manipulative pressures, mechanisms of censorship, inequalities of access to the relevant information sources and so forth that constitute the difference – the critical difference – between liberal democracy as a public sphere of enlightened communal exchange and 'liberal democracy' as a slogan in the service of this or that ideological interest-group. For otherwise (as he argues) there can be no appeal to criteria of truth or argumentative validity outside the terms currently provided by some given – no matter how false or distorted – system of consensus values and beliefs.

In his recent work Habermas adopts what might appear a position much akin to Rorty, Fish and other exponents of the so-called 'linguistic turn'. That is to say, he registers the impact of recent anti-foundationalist arguments, even to the point of describing his project as a form of 'transcendental pragmatics', one that keeps faith with the Kantian tradition of *Ideologiekritik*, but which does so in the knowledge that truth-claims must be grounded in a theory of speech-acts or communicative reason, and not through the epistemological appeal to *a priori* standards of cognitive accountability. But he also insists – as against Rorty, Fish and the purveyors of postmodern-pragmatist fashion – that those claims cannot be levelled down to a question of what is currently 'good in the way of belief', but must always be subject to a critical appraisal of the various distortions, communicative blind-spots, or pressures of manipulative thought-control that conspire to prevent such dialogue from occurring under present socio-political conditions.

This is what Habermas means by the apparently oxymoronic phrase 'transcendental pragmatics': a philosophy of knowledge and human interests that on the one hand concedes the linguistically or discursively mediated character of all such debate, while on the other holding open the further possibility of criticising consensus-values from a standpoint of enlightened communicative grasp. This is not to deny that Habermas has travelled some considerable distance from the position adopted in his early works, where the approach is more decidedly Kantian in matters of epistemological and ethico-political critique, and where issues of language or speech-act implicature as yet have no explicit role to play.[9] No doubt this shift came about in large part through his persuasion that thinkers like Rorty were right *up to a point*, and that the effort to redeem what he (Habermas) calls 'the unfinished project of modernity' would have go by way of a detailed engagement with the various schools of discourse-analysis and post-Wittgensteinian linguistic philosophy. But it is just as important – in fact rather more so when confronted with the excesses of current postmodernist thought – to understand why Habermas continues to reject any version of the 'linguistic turn' that excludes all truth-claims save those endorsed by some existing interpretive community or set of consensus beliefs. He does so for two main reasons: first, because it offers no means of distinguishing between false (systematically distorted) and genuine, enlightened or rational forms of consensus thinking, and second because it takes no account of the interests – the critical or emancipatory interests – bound up with maintaining a 'public sphere' of informed dialogical exchange. For otherwise clearly we shall have to go along with that line of least resistance (the Fish-Rorty line) which amounts to a standing justification for whatever seems 'good in the way of belief' to those with a stake in deciding such matters.

Eagleton puts the case more concisely than one finds it expounded anywhere in Habermas, so I shall quote him (again) at sufficient length to bring out the main points at issue. The 'ideal speech-situation', he writes,

> would be one entirely free of domination, in which all participants would have symmetrically equal chances to select and deploy speech acts. Persuasion would depend on the force of the better argument alone, not on rhetoric, authority, coercive sanctions and so on. This model is no more than a heuristic device or necessary fiction, but it is in some sense implicit even so in our ordinary, unregenerate language dealings. . . . Our most despotic speech acts betray, despite themselves, the frail outlines of a communicative *rationality*: in making an utterance a speaker implicitly claims that what she says is intelligible, true, sincere and appropriate to the discursive situation. . . . There is, in other words, a kind of 'deep' rationality built into the very structures of our language, regardless of what we actually say, and it is this which provides Habermas with the basis for a critique of our actual verbal practices. In a curious sense, the very *act* of enunciation can become a normative judgement on what is enunciated.[10]

If this claim strikes Eagleton as 'curious' – despite his broad endorsement of the Habermas position – it is no doubt because he has absorbed enough of the current post-structuralist wisdom to have problems in crediting any argument grounded in normative values beyond those inscribed within this or that 'discourse', 'language-game', narrative paradigm, signifying system or whatever. But it is precisely on the prospect of making good such a claim that Habermas stakes his entire critical enterprise, his case against the postmodernist edict that truth *just is* what we are given to believe according to the current consensus view. In fact it is a mark of the intellectual poverty of much post-structuralist theorizing that it has failed so conspicuously to address Habermas's arguments at a level anywhere near adequate to their range of philosophical and socio-political reference.

DISPUTING THE ENLIGHTENMENT: RORTY, HABERMAS, SAID

One should not underestimate the significance of these ideas in contexts of debate beyond the narrow enclave of 'advanced' cultural theory. On the one hand they offer an accurate (if depressing) indication of the drift toward conformist ways of thinking – or rationalizations of the ideological status quo – among well-placed commentors on the intellectual scene whose views have understandably received wide coverage in the US and British media. (Francis Fukuyama's celebrated article on 'The End of History', written under the auspices of a US State Department think-tank and greeted as a major contribution to Bush's 'New World Order', is perhaps the most notable recent instance of this feedback mechanism at work.)[11] On the other, they actively work to promote such a climate of willing acquiescence by providing a range of sophistical arguments (or rhetorical ruses) by which neopragmatists, postmodernists and others can justify their retreat from pressing issues of social and political justice.

Thus for Rorty it is the chief merit of a 'postmodern liberal bourgeois' society that it allows individuals to cultivate the private virtues (tolerance, compassion, moral refinement, aesthetic appreciation etc) while respecting the crucial distinction between private and public realms, and thus discouraging those same individuals from getting mixed up with political issues beyond their proper range of concern. Hence the title of his recent book *Contingency, Irony and Solidarity*, where Rorty argues the case for a scaled-down conception of the intellectual's role in public affairs which speaks directly to this current mood of *laissez-faire* liberal consensus thinking.[12] 'Irony' figures on Rorty's list since it signifies the readiness to treat one's own ideas, attitudes and values as a set of shifting and provisional beliefs, arrived at through an open-ended process of 'self-creation' that gives no right to pronounce or criticize in matters of wider socio-political debate. 'Contingency' denotes the clear-eyed recognition that those beliefs take rise within some given cultural context, or in response to a transient phase in the ongoing 'conversation of mankind', and can therefore claim nothing more in the way of ultimate validity or truth. And 'solidarity' is best served – in Rorty's view – by maintaining the liberalist-pluralist outlook, upholding the separation of private and public realms, and acknowledging (in good pragmatist fashion) that it is pointless to criticize this current consensus when it offers the only chance of conversing on relevant, socially-acceptable terms.

Thus the liberal ironist is one who has followed Rorty in abandoning all those delusive truth-claims that were once thought to distinguish 'philosophy' (or 'theory') from other, less demanding activities of thought. He or she will be readily persuaded 1) that philosophy has outlived its purpose, at least as a discipline supposedly specialized in adjudicating issues of truth, argumentative validity, ethical warrant, political justice and so forth; 2) that imaginative literature is now our main source of intellectual stimulus, not only in the form of novels and poems but also in the work of those 'post-philosophers' (Derrida among them) who set out to level such old-fashioned genre distinctions; 3) that we are mistaken – still hung up on Enlightenment beliefs about the 'political responsibility of the intellectuals' – if we seek to bridge the gap between private and public spheres; and 4) that since the only arguments that count are those with some measure of consensus appeal, therefore 'solidarity' (rather than critique) is the best – indeed the only – means of promoting the wider communal good. Any discrepancies that might arise between, for example, George Bush's vision of America's role in the 'New World Order' and the evidence of US interventionist designs in the Gulf and elsewhere would then be a matter for delicate adjustment on the part of those wise individuals who had learned not to confuse issues of moral conscience with issues of legitimacy in the public-political realm. Thus in Rorty's ideal society, as Eagleton remarks, 'the intellectuals will be ironists, practising a suitably cavalier, laid-back attitude to their own beliefs, while the masses, for whom such self-ironizing might prove too subversive a weapon, will continue to salute the flag and take life seriously'.[13]

This seems to me a fair statement of the consequences of Rorty's position when applied to the Gulf War, its coverage in the mass-media, and the attitude of many intellectuals who perceived the mendacity of 'Allied' propaganda but failed to take a stand on moral or principled grounds. But there was another, in some ways more creditable motive for this reluctance to apply the standards of 'enlightened' critique to a situation that seemed to challenge every last truth-claim, principle or value of Western ethnocentric discourse. Kevin Robins put this case in an article for *Marxism Today* that took its bearings from Edward Said's powerful indictment of the way that European and US perceptions of 'the Orient' have constructed a stereotyped image of the Arab 'mentality' – irrational, despotic, shiftless, violently unpredictable etc – as a foil to their own superior forms of self-assured 'universal' reason. This characterization of those outside the Western Enlightenment tradition as being incapable of reason and therefore inferior is a legitimate critique of that tradition in its imperialist or ethnocentric form. Scholars, diplomats, military strategists and 'experts' of every kind have colluded through the ages in producing this hegemonic discourse which can then be used – in situations like the Gulf War – to generate a whipped-up propaganda campaign of racist sentiment and anti-Arab hysteria. Thus in Robins's words,

> in this quest to appropriate the world the West learned to define its own uniqueness against *the other*, against 'non-Europe'. If the political reality has always been one of conflict and disunity, the construction of an imaginary Orient helped to give unity and coherence to the idea of the West. This Orient was, moreover, a mirror in which Europe (and subsequently America) could see reflected its own supremacy. . . . Fundamental to both its difference and its inherent superiority, it seemed, was the principle of rationality. . . . Modernity is defined against pre-modernity, reason against irrationality and superstition, and this divide is mapped on to a symbolic geography that counterposes the West and its Orient. *Its* Orient, because if 'the West' did not exist, then the Orient could not exist either. . . . And the existence and identity it has bestowed is one of constitutive inferiority and deficit.[14]

The truth of such claims will be evident to anyone who has read Said's account – in books like *Orientalism* and *Covering Islam* – of the manifold devious connections between the history of 'serious' Western scholarship in this area and the uses to which that work has regularly been put by governments, military strategists, and ideologues of various persuasion keen to exploit its handy repertoire of 'Arab' cultural and character stereotypes.[15] If further proof were needed then the Gulf War undoubtedly provided it, with examples ranging from the thinly-veiled racist overtones of Bush's anti-Saddam crusade to the usual array of media experts vying to explain how best to deal with these tricky individuals, and of course the fine frenzy of xenophobic sentiment witnessed in the right-wing popular tabloids. Few events in recent history have managed to create such an upsurge of irrational fears and phobias in the service of a Western neo-imperialist drive to reinforce the old ethnocentric values and certitudes.

Confronted with this evidence one could hardly deny the moral justice of Robins's case and the risk that must be courted by any commentator who sets out to analyze the Gulf War and its aftermath in terms of 'enlightened' critical reason *versus* the forces of ignorance, prejudice, or unexamined popular belief. For such arguments can always be suspected of trading on a version of the typecast 'us-and-them' attitude, a stance of superior knowledge or moral wisdom that all too readily perpetuates the cycle of oppression. Thus, in Robins's words,

> Oriental culture is a subaltern culture, conceived through the very process of its subjugation and subordination to the universal culture. And it is a culture defined by what it lacks (modernity, rationality, universality); its 'otherness' is defined in terms of the backwardness, the irrationality and the particularity of its values.[16]

And this attitude is given a further pathological twist when the 'subaltern' culture shows signs of producing its own secular or modernizing trends, its own high-grade weapons technology and other such modes of 'rational' adaptation to the pressures of global changes. For at this point the West finds its interests threatened by a kind of parodic self-image whose challenge can only be met by overt militarist aggression or through the various techniques of demonization deployed against figures like Saddam Hussein. Hence what Robins describes as the 'unthinkable predicament of modernity in the Orient', a situation where 'Saddam is assaulting the norms that have defined Western uniqueness and superiority . . . violating the boundaries that have differentiated rationality and irrationality'. The result is all too familiar: a sharp turnabout in strategic thinking whereby the ex-ally or protector of US interests (Saddam's perceived role during the Iraq-Iran conflict) becomes a 'menace to regional stability' and a target of massive retaliatory action. What is played out here – as Robins remarks – is a version of the Frankenstein scenario, with the creators looking on in appalled fascination at their own distorted self-image. 'The armies of Reason, the allies of the post-historical world, must then suppress this crazed unreason. They must outlaw the "mad dog". They must crush

Iraq's "monstrous military machine". What cannot be tolerated is the monster that pretends to modernity.' And any notion that the image is not so distorted – that it gives back a faithful replica of Western 'enlightened' rationality – must be warded off with the maximum degree of strenuous psychotic disavowal.

As I say, there is no denying the force of such arguments, especially when read against the background of Said's impassioned yet meticulous scholarship. But it is a different matter when these critics of Western ethnocentrism make the further (in my view mistaken) move of equating 'Enlightenment' values *tout court* with the maintenace of imperial power, the oppression of subjugated cultures, and the various pathological symptoms evinced by a discourse of hegemonic power/knowledge fixated on its own narrowly 'rational' criteria. For the upshot of this move is to deprive criticism of any grounds – any reasoned argumentative grounds – for challenging the *specific* abuses and distortions that writers like Said have so persistently brought to light. Said's purpose, after all, is not just to devise an alternative rhetoric, discourse or language-game to set against the forms of encoded racist prejudice which have so far governed Western perceptions of 'the Orient'. Rather, it is to show up the *false* – mendacious – character of much that passes for expert occidental wisdom about Arab history, politics and cultural values, and to do so, moreover, from a standpoint informed by a *better* (more profound and extensive) knowledge of the documentary sources and a *better* (more critical and unillusioned) grasp of the ideological issues involved. Such work clearly cannot rest content with producing just a kind of optional counter-narrative that happens to fit in with some existing left-liberal agenda of cultural debate. No doubt Said's argument owes something of its persuasive force to his command of large-scale narrative structures, that is to say, his gift for marshalling so much detailed evidence into a powerful indictment of Western attitudes and policies which wouldn't make the point so effectively if treated in a more dispersed or piecemeal form. And it is equally the case – as Rorty and Fish would be quick to remark – that his writings derive much of their authority from the rhetoric of moral outrage, the stance of speaking up on behalf of an oppressed and misrepresented culture, which Said can exploit to great effect against the voices of cynical US *Realpolitik*. One can readily concede these debating-points to the neopragmatists and still hold on to the crucial premise: that there is a difference between truth and falsehood in such matters, and that scholarship, criticism and reasoned argument (along with 'theory' in its more responsible or philosophically adequate forms) are the disciplines best equipped to maintain a due sense of that distinction. For otherwise there would simply be nothing to choose between the various competing narratives or rhetorical strategies, aside from their degree of suasive appeal in this or that cultural context.

At the most basic level what Said brings out are those symptoms of prejudicial thinking – manifest non-sequiturs, obsessional motifs, manipulative rhetoric, undocumented blanket assertions etc – which signal the presence of an overriding drive to construct an image of 'the Orient' in line with Western beliefs and policy interests. Beyond that, he locates a whole repertoire of stereotyped attributes, a system of exclusive binary oppositions where 'the West' connotes values of reason, enlightenment, progress, civilized conduct etc, while 'the Orient' figures in a negative or inverse relationship to those same values, that is to say, as the embodiment of everything supposedly left behind in the ascent of Western rationality and truth. Again, the Gulf War provided a showcase example of the way that these deep-laid cultural prejudices could be mobilized in the service of a moral crusade with insistent racist overtones. But to analyze the sources of this potent mythology is also, inescapably, to invoke the standards of enlightened truth-seeking discourse, even if those terms are perceived as tainted by their involvement in a history of oppressive cultural or geo-political relations which cannot be ignored by any reasonably sensitive commentator. At some point the analysis will always come down to a perception of errors, contradictions or blind-spots in the prevailing ideology, a case that can only be argued through if one accepts the basic principles of rational thought, i.e. the criteria of adequate grounds, of evidential warrant and respect for the standards of logic, consistency and truth. In default of such argument the case will amount to nothing more than a suasive rhetorical gambit, a discourse with no better claim on our moral and intellectual consciences than the narratives it seeks to displace or overturn.

Habermas makes this point most effectively in his dialogue with Hans-Georg Gadamer concerning the so-called 'hermeneutic circle' and the issues it raises for a project – like his own – aimed toward a critical recension of taken-for-granted values and beliefs. For Gadamer, such a project encounters its limits in the fact that any criticism will always be advanced within a context of tacit 'preunderstanding' – or against some existing 'horizon of intelligibility' – which alone makes it possible for dialogue to occur between text and interpreter, or between various parties to the ongoing history of interpretive debate.[17] Like Fish – and like the later Wittgenstein with his talk of 'language-games' or cultural 'forms of life' – Gadamer takes it as simply self-evident that one cannot enter into meaningful discussion on any topic of communal concern except by virtue of a shared understanding of the ideas, beliefs and inherited values which have shaped that history to date. Understanding is always already informed by a sense of what counts as a relevant or good-faith argument, a knowledge that cannot be brought to the level of conscious, articulate statement since it lies too deep – and goes too far back – for the critic or theorist who would seek to analyze its tacit presuppositions. To this extent criticism has to give way before the claims of a depth-hermeneutical approach that makes due allowance for the limits of enlightened *Ideologiekritik* or of any such method premised on notions of privileged truth-telling warrant. Thus for Gadamer, as Habermas reads him, 'any attempt to suggest that this (certainly contingent) consensus is false consciousness is meaningless since we cannot transcend the discussion in which we are engaged. From [which] Gadamer deduces the ontological priority of linguistic tradition before all possible critique'.[18] But if one adopts this position as a matter of principle – that is to say, as an *a priori* ground for rejecting all forms of critical counter-argument – then it becomes (as with Fish and Rorty) just another variant of the well-tried 'end of ideology' theme, and one with profoundly conservative implications.

For Habermas, on the contrary, criticism is not exhausted at the point where it has perforce to acknowledge its own involvement with an ongoing dialogue, a cultural tradition or background of enabling normative values which set the agenda for present debate. What this argument ignores – in his view as in Said's – is the plain fact that such values can be heavily influenced (and at times massively distorted) by the pressures of censorship, 'public-opinion' management or imposed ideological bias. Thus in Habermas's words:

> every consensus, in which the understanding of meaning terminates, stands fundamentally under suspicion of being pseudo-communicatively induced. . . . [since] the prejudgmental structure of meaning does not guarantee identification of an achieved consensus with a true one.[19]

In short, there is always the possibility that received ways of thinking will turn out to be products of a *false* (ideologically determined) consensus whose prejudicial character, whose blind-spots and motivating interests may yet be revealed through a critical treatment of the source-texts or cultural belief-systems involved. As we have seen, Habermas's later work moves away from the 'strong' (Kantian) claim that such arguments can be grounded in a direct appeal to forms of privileged epistemic access, or in an ethics of *a priori* values and principles self-evident to reason in its practical-legislative mode. Hence his turn toward a theory of 'communicative action' which incorporates many of the insights gained through speech-act philosophy, socio-linguistics, discourse analysis and other such pragmatically oriented disciplines of thought. But there is never any question, for Habermas, of collapsing the difference – the critical difference – between pragmatist thinking in the Fish-Rorty style and the interests of a 'trancendental pragmatics' that would criticize consensus-values from the standpoint of a genuine (if admittedly 'ideal') speech-situation.

For what is at stake in this debate is not only the continuance of a certain 'philosophical discourse of modernity', one whose promise has yet to be redeemed through the practice of a vigilant and socially responsive *Ideologiekritik*. Beyond that, the quarrel between Habermas and his various opponents turns on the prospect of achieving a social order which more closely resembles the current self-image of the Western liberal democracies. That is to say, it takes seriously their claim to represent the best interests of a properly informed electorate – or an enlightened 'public sphere' – where issues of truth, social conscience, evaluative priority, etc could be argued out through the maximum involvement of citizens enjoying free and equal access to the relevant information sources. Whatever his shifts of ground in response to the current anti-foundationalist trend, Habermas is still very closely aligned with that tradition of critical and social-emancipatory thought whose earliest manifesto was Kant's polemical essay 'What Is Enlightenment?'.[20] And the main point at issue in his later work – taken up with particular urgency and force in *The Philosophical Discourse of Modernity* – is the question as to whether Enlightenment values can be defended against the concerted assaults of latterday postmodernist and neopragmatist thinking.[21] To find this an absurdly utopian idea is to ignore what Habermas repeatedly asserts: that such 'ideas of reason' (in the Kantian sense) may indeed be far beyond hope of attainment in existing real-world terms, but that they none the less offer a critical yardstick – a standard of enlightened participant exchange – by which to assess the manifold shortcomings of present-day social-democratic institutions.

This kind of argument is hardly new. Three decades ago these same issues were being addressed by left intellectuals confronting the emergence of an 'end-of-ideology' creed whose claims – like those of the current postmodernists – were clearly bound up with a conservative agenda aimed toward the suppression (or the marginalization) of significant political debate. Alasdair MacIntyre's book *Against the Self-Images of the Age* (1971) was among the most impressive products of this period, chiefly for its cogent philosophical critique of the relativist outlook espoused by thinkers of the newly ascendant intellectual cast. Central to MacIntyre's argument was the distinction between *causal* and *rational* accounts of why people act and think as they do, or the difference – expressed in Habermasian terms – between beliefs brought about by some determinate set of ideological interests and beliefs arrived at through the exercise of reasoned or truth-seeking critical enquiry. Thus:

> to characterize a belief as irrational is to characterize the intellectual procedures and attitudes of those who hold it. It is to say in effect – at least in the extreme case – that the belief is invulnerable to rational argument. . . . For the explanation of rational belief terminates with an account of the appropriate intellectual norms and procedures; [whereas] the explanation of irrational belief must be in terms of causal generalizations which connect antecedent conditions specified in terms of social structures or psychological states – or both – with the genesis of beliefs.[22]

Some version of this argument is implicit in every claim to distinguish valid from invalid (or ideologically-motivated) beliefs, whether offered from a Kantian, a Marxist or – as with Habermas – a 'transcendental-pragmatic' standpoint premised on the values of communicative openness and reasoned dialogical exchange. Conversely, it is an argument rejected *a priori* by those like Baudrillard, Rorty and Fish who would level this distinction by simply conflating the orders of truthful (or truth-seeking) discourse and what is currently 'good in the way of belief'. For these latter there is nothing that could possibly count as a reason for abandoning consensus ideas just so long as they continue to fall square with the discourses, rhetorics or (in MacIntyre's prescient phrase) the prevailing 'self-images of the age'. And by the same token there is no possibility of achieving what

MacIntyre describes in the above passage, that is to say, on the one hand a critical grasp of the *causes* that operate to secure various forms of hegemonic consensus-belief, and on the other the *reasons* that can lead us to reject those beliefs whether on factual, philosophical, ethical or socio-political grounds. In which case one might as well accept the postmodern-pragmatist line and acknowledge that terms like 'truth' and 'reality' are nowadays wholly redundant, belonging as they do to an old (Enlightenment) discourse whose claims no longer make any kind of sense.

MARXISM, POSTMODERNISM AND THE ENDS OF IDEOLOGY

Eagleton's recent book *Ideology: an introduction* has a double epigraph from Rorty which points up the consequences of this doctrine when extended to matters of immediate social concern. 'Consider', Rorty invites us,

> the attitude of contemporary American liberals to the unending hopelessness and misery of the lives of young blacks in American cities. Do we say these people must be helped because they are human beings? We may, but it is much more persuasive, morally as well as politically, to describe them as our fellow-*Americans*, to say that it is outrageous that an *American* should live without hope.[23]

To which he (Eagleton) neatly appends the further, lapidary sentence of Rorty: 'On the uselessness of the notion of "ideology", see Raymond Geuss's *The Idea of a Critical Theory*'. Quite aside from the question of its fairness to Geuss – who would surely be surprised to find his book invoked in such a context – the epigraph serves as a convenient focus for the issues raised by this debate. What the longer passage amounts to is a thoroughgoing pragmatist version of the criticism that Hegel addressed to Kantian ethics, his argument that Kant had reduced morality to a matter of abstract universals, formal precepts, rule-governed prescriptive dictates etc, and thus ignored the various culture-specific factors – the aspects of Hegelian *Sittlichkeit*, or socially mediated values and beliefs – which alone provided an adequate context for the understanding of real-world ethical dilemmas.[24] On Rorty's account this criticism needs to be pushed one stage further, to the point where Hegel's dialectic survives only in a 'naturalized' form, that is to say, as an ongoing 'cultural conversation'

THE 'END OF IDEOLOGY' REVISITED

which renounces all ideas of Absolute Reason (or truth at the end of enquiry), and henceforth contents itself with whatever new language-games, rhetorics or 'final vocabularies' happen to emerge in the course of the dialogue. In this way – so Rorty argues – one can hang on to what is good about Hegel – the strong narrative line, the inventive case-histories, the wealth of imaginative metaphors and anecdotal detail – and drop all the tedious 'dialectical' talk where he tends to fall back into bad old philosophic habits of thought. Pragmatism is thus the end of the road that thinkers like Hegel have long been travelling, but whose signposts they have often misread on account of their continuing (deluded) belief in philosophy's privileged status, its access to truths beyond reach of other, less elevated forms of discourse. Had Hegel followed through more consistently with his own criticism of Kant then surely he would have seen that *Sittlichkeit* is all we need, that dialectics resolves into dialogue readily enough, and that notions like 'critique', 'ideology' and 'truth' are pretty much redundant apart from their role as a handy source of rhetorical uplift.

The irony of Eagleton's epigraph is all the more telling if one considers its implications in light of the Gulf War and subsequent events. Of course there is no reason, moral or political, to deny Rorty's basic point: that on certain issues of domestic policy and social justice the best way to move the liberal conscience is by appealing to a sense of shared cultural values, a rhetoric of 'solidarity' or communal concern which persuades fellow-citizens to think it simply 'outrageous that an *American* can live without hope'. And if this seems a somewhat selective or parochial standard – one that excludes all non-Americans from the privileged cultural fold – then Rorty can always come back with the answer that such habits of thought have an inbuilt generalizing tendency, an influence that reaches out beyond one's local habitus to take in an ever more varied range of national, political, and cultural life-forms. The main thing that is needed, from this pragmatist perspective, is a willingness to accept the inherent diversity of human values, interests and belief-systems, along with a sensible recognition that one can only start out, so to speak, from home ground, acknowledging the prior claims of one's own cultural community, and then making the imaginative effort to view other people's motives and interests in similar (liberal-pluralist) terms. In this way 'solidarity' can become something more than a narrowly American – or in Rorty's phrase, 'North Atlantic postmodern bourgeois liberal' – mutual benefit club. It can always be envisaged as moving on and out toward a sense of trans-cultural – perhaps universal – human aspirations which encompasses the widest possible range of localized community beliefs.

But this project only stands any chance of success if Western ideologues – Marxists in particular – can be got to relinquish their grandiose notions of truth, reason and *Ideologiekritik*, and persuaded to espouse the neopragmatist view that solidarity is the primary social virtue, so that any attempt to criticize consensus values from a dissenting or strong oppositional standpoint will at best be a species of chimerical delusion and at worst a form of arrogant 'Enlightenment' thinking. Much better, Rorty argues, to admit the relativity, the contingent or culture-specific character of all our most basic ethical and political beliefs, and then – as far as possible – interpret other cultures in light of those same (to 'us' inescapable) habits of deep-grained sympathetic response. For otherwise there is always the danger that we shall wind up adopting some high-toned project of emancipatory critique which ignores not only the virtues of liberal democracy, US-style, but also the benefits to be had by other cultures which we are able to interpret – and which might yet be brought to interpret themselves – in similar terms. And to Rorty it appears self-evident that the advantages of this process far outweigh any possible objections on ethical, political or (merely) theoretical grounds, since 'North Atlantic' social institutions are so obvious an improvement on the various alternatives currently on offer around the world. So the logic of his argument runs in two directions, on the one hand starting out from the home-base appeal to 'American' solidarity, fellow-feeling etc, and enjoining us to extend those compassionate virtues to cultures beyond the immediate (US or US-affiliated) pale, while on the other equating the interests of humanity at large with a view of those interests predominantly informed by the values of US liberal democracy as currently interpreted by well-placed commentators like himself. At very least one may suspect that this argument conceals an unspoken political agenda, one that falls in with Fukuyama's 'end-of-history' thesis and other such (albeit more blatant) forms of manipulative consensus ideology.

In short, Rorty's pluralism turns out to have sharp limits when it comes to conceiving that there might be alternative traditions, cultures or political 'forms of life' which sound themselves not only excluded from the ongoing (liberal-democratic) conversation, but subject to considerable pressures, economic or military, by way of enforcing its superior merits. For the pragmatist position very easily flips over from an outlook of broad-minded tolerant regard for beliefs and value-systems other than one's own to an attitude which holds – in the Fish-Rorty style – that we are all, like it or not, obliged to interpret those beliefs from a standpoint informed by deep-laid assumptions which belong to 'our' interpretive community, interest-group, cultural 'form of life' or whatever. Some years ago I made this point with reference to an argument proposed by the philosopher Hilary Putnam in response to what he saw as the covert implications of Rorty's neo-pragmatist line.

> Putnam sets the scene by imagining a cultural relativist (one 'R.R.') confronted by a foreigner, Karl, who comes out with the statement 'Schnee ist weiss' ('snow is white'). True to his lights, R.R. will set out to interpret this sentence in keeping with its own implied background of semantic and cultural norms. It will then be the case that Karl ('whether he knows it or not') can only be speaking the truth of the matter in so far as the conventions of his language allow. But, as Putnam points out, 'the sentence "Snow is white as determined by the norms of German culture) is itself one which R.R. has to *use*, not just mention, to say what Karl says. On his own account, what R.R. means by *this* sentence is: "Snow is white as determined by the norms of German culture" is true by the norms of R.R.'s culture (which we take to be American culture). This amounts to a subtle form of cultural imperialism, since it is always by his or her *own* cultural lights that the relativist decides what role might be played by other interpretative norms. 'Other cultures become, so to speak, logical constructions out of the procedures and practices of American culture.' And this holds inescapably for R.R.'s pronouncements on the problems of radical translation, 'no matter how many footnotes, glosses, commentaries on the cultural differences, or whatever, he accompanies them by'.[25]

In short, the upshot of a thoroughgoing neo-pragmatism – an ethics and a politics of Hegelian *Sittlichkeit* pushed to its logical extreme – is to cut away the grounds for any critical assessment of the prejudices, the blindspots or ideological motives that inhabit our own discourses of power/knowledge. And if the pragmatist in question just happens to speak, like Rorty, from the vantage-point of a privileged hegemonic culture with the power to impose its own values and beliefs on a well-nigh global scale, then there is reason to suspect that other interests are at work behind the liberal-pluralist rhetoric. One such motive – as Eagleton notes – is to discredit the very notion of 'ideology' (along with that of *Ideologiekritik*) as belonging to a discourse whose grounding suppositions have now been shown up as either philosophically naive or politically beside the point, since we have lately moved on into a phase of the 'cultural conversation' where such ideas count for nothing in terms of their persuasive efficacy. However one chooses to describe this phase – 'postmodern', 'post-Enlightenment', 'post-philosophical', 'anti-foundationalist', 'neo-pragmatist' or whatever – it leaves no room for the outmoded idea that criticism could come up with cogent reasons for abandoning this or that convenient item of socially-acceptable belief. In which case we should have little choice but to agree with Baudrillard's terminal prognosis, that is to say, his argument – amounting to a kind of inverted Platonist metaphysics – that 'it is no longer a question of a false representation of reality (ideology), but of concealing the fact that the real is no longer real'.[26]

Some thinkers on the left – Fredric Jameson preeminent among them – have striven to articulate a theory of this 'postmodern condition' that would treat it pretty much as a cultural given, a product of present-day (i.e. late-capitalist) socio-economic developments, while none the less maintaining that it still gives room for certain forms of localized resistance and critique.[27] It seems to me that Eagleton is nearer the mark when he attacks postmodernism as a direct reflex of the interests bound up with consumer capitalism in its latest, avowedly 'post-ideological' phase, and hence as a symptom of mere bad faith on the part of conformist intellectuals. After all, as Eagleton pointedly remarks, 'no individual life, not even Baudrillard's, can survive entirely bereft of meaning, and a society which took this nihilistic road would simply be nurturing massive social disruption'.[28] From this point of view, advanced capitalism can be seen to oscillate 'between meaning and non-meaning, pitched from moralism to cynicism and plagued by the embarrassing discrepancy between the two'.[29] In which case what really needs explaining is the readiness of so many thinkers – including Marxists and radicals of various persuasion – to regard postmodernism as anything more than a short-lived swing of intellectual fashion brought about by the widespread retreat from issues of real-world political import.

FISH, RORTY, FUKUYAMA: VARIATIONS ON A THEME

Clearly it is not an adequate argument against postmodernism or neopragmatism to simply oppose one set of beliefs with another, or to argue on suasive-rhetorical grounds that suasion and rhetoric shouldn't be regarded as the bottom line of argumentative exchange. For the way is then open for an adept like Fish to turn the tables on his earnest truth-seeking opponents by remarking that they, like himself, have no choice but to operate on the terms laid down by some existing set of cultural or speech-act conventions where certain terms (e.g. 'truth' and 'critique') just happen to enjoy a privileged rhetorical status. From which it follows, according to Fish,

> (1) that in whatever form it appears the argument for theory fails, (2) that theory is not and could not be used . . . to generate and/or guide practice, (3) that when 'theory' is in fact used it is . . . in order to justify a decision reached on other grounds, (4) that theory is essentially a rhetorical and political phenomenon whose effects are purely contingent, and (5) that these truths are the occasion neither of cynicism nor of despair.[30]

He can afford to take this relaxed line since 'theory' for Fish is an utterly *inconsequential* affair, one whose continuance or non-continuance can have not the slightest effect on our conduct of ethical, political, philosophical, literary or other kinds of debate. Whether we carry on indulging in theory-talk – as no doubt some people will – or take Fish's advice and drop the whole thing as a tedious waste of time, we shall still be in the same rhetorical position of promoting this or that pre-given agenda of beliefs, value-judgments, social priorities etc, any of which could be just as well served by a straightforward appeal to what we think or believe without benefit of theory. Quite simply, it is a 'difference which makes no difference', and which can therefore be treated as beside the point for all practical intents and purposes.

Fish has no objection to the carriers-on – the Marxists, deconstructionists, hermeneutic philosophers, defenders of enlightened *Ideologiekritik* and so forth – just so long as they acknowledge this simple fact and don't make the further (insupportable) claim that theory has 'consequences' beyond its utility as a language-game adapted to certain localized suasive or rhetorical ends. Thus:

> the distinction between theory and theory-talk is a distinction between a discourse that stands apart from all practices (and no such discourse exists) and a discourse that is itself a practice and is therefore

consequential to the extent that it is influential or respected or wide-spread.[31]

In short, one may wish to reject neo-pragmatism on various more or less persuasive grounds, among them – if one happens to see things that way – its all-purpose rhetoric of assent, its collusion with the mechanisms of ideological thought-control, or its willing embrace of a professionalized ethos that excludes any challenge to instituted values and beliefs. But one can only fall back into the old, self-deluding theoreticist trap if one thinks to mount such a case on arguments that would claim some superior vantage-point of truth, principle or reason. Still less could the theorist ever hope to arrive at a position where *his or her own* preexisting beliefs turned out – through an effort of reflective self-criticism – to be based upon taken-for-granted assumptions which merely reflected the prevailing (ideological or professional) self-image of the times. For 'such a realization could only have this effect', Fish writes,

> if it enabled the individual who was constituted by historical and cultural forces to 'see through' those forces and thus stand to the side of his own convictions and beliefs. But that is the one thing a historically conditioned consciousness cannot do – scrutinize its own beliefs, conduct a rational examination of its own convictions; for in order to begin such a scrutiny, it would first have to escape the grounds of its own possibility, and it could only do that if it were not historically conditioned and were instead an acontextual or unsituated entity of the kind that is rendered unavailable by the first principle of the interpretivist or conventionalist view.[32]

In other words, it is strictly impossible to conceive that one's ideas might be changed – or that one might come to adopt a more critical ('enlightened') viewpoint – as a result of arguments, theoretical insights, gains in self-knowledge or encounters with recalcitrant evidence which required a more or less radical re-thinking of previously held convictions and beliefs.[33] Where such changes come about they do so always in response to some wider (communal) shift in the currency of received ideas, a shift which comes about for no reason other than cultural fashion, intellectual fatigue, or boredom with the old – henceforth discredited – consensus truths.

This should make it clear how much is at stake in the current neo-pragmatist (or 'against theory') trend of which Fish and Rorty are leading protagonists, and whose appeal across the range of humanistic disciplines will be evident to anyone perusing the academic journals.[34] What these thinkers are mooting – in company with Fukuyama and other such 'end-of-ideology' ideologues – is a return to that happy condition of pre-critical consensus belief when as yet there existed no public sphere, no forum of open argumentative exchange on matters of collective social interest and responsibility, and when dissent could thus be marginalized (or simply ignored) in so far as it lacked the kind of broad-based appeal enjoyed by more populist or upbeat versions of the communal good. Such arguments trade on the self-confirming 'logic' of a consensus-theory of knowledge and human interests whose perfect circularity renders it proof against any form of reasoned critique. Rorty is the most engagingly up-front about this, urging as he does that we learn to appreciate the virtues of 'North Atlantic postmodern bourgeois liberal democracy', and give up any thought of questioning those virtues from a dissident or oppositional stand-point.[35] On the one hand this follows from Rorty's neo-pragmatist argument that we really have no choice in the matter, since – like it or not – they are the cultural air we breathe and the only means of gaining assent among a wide enough receptive audience. On the other (and here Rorty lays his cards very much on the table) they are the best set of values that have so far emerged in the 'cultural conversation of mankind', affording the opportunity for leisurely intercourse between parties who are free to maintain a wide range of social, intellectual and political views, subject only to the one condition – a welcome condition, as Rorty sees it – that they acknowledge the manifest superiority of North Atlantic liberal-pluralist social institutions. For otherwise they will be enjoying the indubitable benefits of membership in this privileged cultural community while presuming to criticize those same values from a standpoint of external (or non-participant) critique. And such a claim is not only *unintelligible* – on hermeneutic, Wittgensteinian, Foucauldian, or straightforward neo-pragmatist grounds – but involves a degree of ingratitude (not to say bad faith) on the part of intellectuals, Marxists and others, caught up in this species of unwitting performative double-bind.

Thus Rorty takes it as a fact self-evident to any but the most blinkered ideologue that North America has produced the nearest thing yet to a working system of democratic checks and balances where the vocabulary of moral concern can take its place alongside those other (albeit incommensurable) vocabularies of aesthetic self-perfection, collective well-being, economic interest, national destiny and so forth. The only rule is that one shouldn't get these vocabularies mixed up through the typical 'enlightenment' (or philosopher's) error of advising other people what to think, feel or do on the basis of one's own moral and political convictions, no matter how refined or keenly responsive to issues in the wider socio-political sphere. Thus, in Rorty's words,

> authors like Kierkegaard, Nietzsche, Baudelaire, Proust, Heidegger and Nabokov are useful as exemplars, as illustrations of what private perfection – a self-created, autonomous human life – can be like. Authors such as Marx, Mill, Dewey, Habermas, and Rawls are fellow citizens rather than exemplars. They are engaged in a shared social effort – the effort to make our institutions and practices more just and less cruel. We shall only think of these two kinds of writers as *opposed* if we think that a more comprehensive philosophical outlook would let us hold self-creation and justice, private perfection and human solidarity, in a single vision. . . . [But] there is no way in which philosophy, or any other theoretical discipline, will ever let us do that. The closest we will come to joining these two quests is to see the aim of a just and free society as letting its citizens be as privatistic, 'irrationalist', and aestheticist as they please so long as they do it on their own time – causing no harm to others and using no resources needed by those less advantaged.[36]

For the great danger here, as Rorty sees it, is that well-meaning thinkers will construct their utopian schemes – or their projects of enlightened reform – in pursuit of some privately cherished fantasy (like Habermas's 'ideal speech-situation') which seeks to transcend the limiting perspective of a given, no doubt deeply flawed social order, but which underrates the claims of social 'solidarity' with those who happen to share one's own cultural tradition. Much better – he thinks – to admit the delusory character of all such critical projects, and to engage the conversation on home ground through a rhetoric of shared American values and beliefs.

The trouble with all this – as I have suggested already – is that it offers no hold for understanding how that same communal rhetoric can give rise to the kind of populist fervour, the crusading zeal and rampant xenophobia that formed so pervasive and depressing a feature of American responses to the Gulf War. More precisely: Rorty's argument doesn't so much fail to explain such phenomena as make them appear well-nigh inevitable, given his *tout court* identification of American (or 'North Atlantic bourgeois') values with what is 'good in the way of belief' for members of the relevant cultural community. Where it *does* miss the point in a massive way is in refusing to acknowledge any possible alternative, any means of criticizing consensus-beliefs for their narrow, parochial, self-serving, exploitative, class-based, chauvinistic or downright racist character, and of doing so – moreover – in accord with those principles of justice, freedom and truth supposedly enshrined within the social institutions of Western liberal democracy. It is on this ground that thinkers like Habermas and Chomsky contest the prevailing drift toward forms of passive consensus-politics, or the way that such attitudes are readily transposed – at the level of 'advanced' cultural debate – into a postmodern-pragmatist rhetoric of assent which trades, as always, on facile notions like the 'end of ideology' or the 'end of history'. Fukuyama's made-to-measure variation on this theme was the prelude to much that has since been written about the Gulf War and its aftermath, mostly by pundits who share with Rorty the conviction that America is indeed our last, best hope for a New World Order delivered from the throes of old-world ideological conflict. And if Rorty offers a benign variant of this American dream-scenario, then we should at least recall the many instances – from McCarthy to Vietnam, Tripoli, Grenada, Panama and the Gulf War – where the rhetoric has assumed a more coercive and sinister aspect.

In his *Guardian* piece Fukuyama took the line that this war was just a wretched anachronism, an example of the way that high moral purposes – those of George Bush and his New World Order – could be dragged down into a morass of old-fashioned regional power-disputes. 'The Gulf War', he wrote,

> was a throwback to the geopolitics of the 19th century when nations could plausibly solve their economic problems through territorial conquest; but in the modern world, the creation of wealth requires peace and legitimacy. The world's real business in the future will be those economic issues that were pushed to the back of the agenda by the war: issues like competitiveness, deficits, protectionism, education, and the like. And any 'New World Order' will not be built upon abstract principles of international law, but upon the common principles of liberal democracy and market economics. . . . A large part of the world will be populated by Iraqs and Ruritanias, and will be

subject to bloody struggles and revolutions. But with the exception of
the Gulf, few regions will have an impact – for good or ill – on the
growing part of the world that is democratic and capitalist. And it is in
this part of the world that we will ultimately have to make our home.[37]

This analysis is nothing short of breathtaking in its placid acceptance of
the US state-sponsored line, its equation of 'democracy' with 'market
economics', is contempt for any 'abstract principles' that might
challenge or complicate the terms of that equation, its championing of
a 'New World Order' frankly identified with the interests of US global
supremacy, and – not least – its 'them-and-us' rhetoric where 'they'
(the surviving 'Iraqs and Ruritanias') will carry on indulging their
old-fashioned 'bloody struggles and revolutions', while 'we' happy
denizens of the promised utopia will witness their miseries with not
the least sense of past or present responsibility. It is a picture whose
sublime naivety and lack of historical perspective could only have
exerted such widespread appeal at a time when many people
(intellectuals and political analysts among them) were eager to
substitute the reassuring placebos of consensus-belief for the effort to
criticize US policy in light of its real-world consequences and effects.
And it is not hard to see how such arguments connect with the rhetoric
of communal 'solidarity' – the bottom-line appeal to shared values of
'American' ethnic and social identity – which forms a major plank in
Rorty's version of the end-of-ideology thesis. For here also there is a
built-in assumption that other cultures, other interest-groups or
political forms of life can only have a claim on 'our' moral conscience if
they measure up to the values that 'we' properly take as defining what
is good for the world at large. From this point of view the utmost
stretch of moral and political imagination can get us no further than
conceiving those 'others' as constructions out of our own (no doubt
ethnocentric but surely benevolent) self-image. And if they happen not
to see it in quite that way – as for instance by refusing to credit the
good faith, the justifying rhetoric and long-term benefits of US
strategic intervention – then we can hardly be blamed for judging their
response in a less than sympathetic light.

What is perhaps most remarkable in the above catalogue of
postmodernist *idées recues* is Fukuyama's total failure to grasp how the
Gulf War was in fact brought about by a long history of British, US
and Western involvement in the region, an involvement marked from
the outset by overnight switches of strategic alliance, by the massive

input of armaments and economic aid designed to secure short-term 'stability' for whichever dictatorial regime happened to suit the current policy line, and by a readiness always to dump old 'allies' (Saddam Hussein among them) when they threatened to become something of a regional embarrassment.[38] That Saddam and his Ba'athist party were first brought to power through a CIA-sponsored coup is a fact which few commentators saw fit to mention when offering their 'in-depth' analyses of the war and its background history. Still less could one expect them to pay much attention to other such awkward details as (for instance) the extent of US connivance at Iraq's pre-war threats against Kuwait over its oil pricing and export policy, a connivance that ceased only at the point where Saddam – supposedly 'misreading the signs' – took it as the green light for a full-scale military invasion.[39] None of these facts – however well attested as a matter of documentary record – could make the smallest dent in Fukuyama's prognosis of a 'New World Order' conceived in terms of US-style 'liberal democracy' extended to well-nigh global proportions, and of market capitalism as a universal solvent of social and political ills. That the rhetoric and the reality are lethally at odds is a notion that simply cannot enter the heads of commentators wedded to this latest variant of the *translatio imperii* theme, this vision of America as signalling the path that all nations should now wish to follow. By the same token – in Rorty's 'post-philosophical' view – pragmatists like James and Dewey represent the kind of wisdom obscurely glimpsed (but unfortunately seldom heeded) by thinkers in the mainstream Western tradition from Socrates to Kant, Hegel, Heidegger and other such earnest seekers-after-truth.[40] For the message is identical in both cases: that there is no getting outside the values and beliefs that inform one's own socio-cultural community, and that any attempt to criticize those values from an alternative (dissident) stance will either fail to make sense or lack the most basic of moral and political virtues, that of 'solidarity' with fellow members of the same cultural enterprise.

In which case Fukuyama could only be right in his assumption that henceforth nothing counts – no appeal to 'the facts', to history, 'abstract principles', discrepancies between declared and covert policy-aims, etc – when set against the emergence of a 'New World Order' where such issues are quite simply beside the point. Unless, that is, one happens to live in some other, less fortunate part of the world still 'subject to bloody struggles and revolutions' on account of its adherence to old-fashioned notions like history, ideology, 'Western imperialism' and the like. But these conflicts will have little impact, we are assured, since the agenda is now being set altogether elsewhere, in that growing geo-political sphere of influence that is 'democratic and capitalist'. And it is – one might add – very fortunate for 'us' that this sphere is steadily expanding, since after all it is 'in this part of the world that we will ultimately have to make our home'. What is not quite clear on Fukuyama's account is the extent to which recalcitrant local populations might need to be persuaded, induced or coerced to accept this vision of their own best interests, or to give up those archaic habits of thought ('the geopolitics of the nineteenth century') which have so far held out against the manifest logic of the equation 'liberal democracy = market capitalism = qualification for entry to the New World Order'. Some of them, one gathers, will be left to their own self-destructive devices, while in other regions – i.e. those (like the Gulf) where vital economic or strategic interests are at stake – it may be necessary on occasion to step in and ensure that they remain the right kind of place for 'us' to 'make our home'. But however this may be Fukuyama is in no doubt that a world safe for market capitalism is by the same token a world redeemed from the atavistic forces of regional conflict and the kinds of antagonism that diehard ideologues – Chomsky among them – still seek to explain in their old-fashioned (dissident or moralizing) terms. Thus if one thing is clear to Fukuyama from the trend of world events it is the fact that 'history', like 'ideology', belongs to that class of obsolescent language-games which nowadays lack any kind of determinate meaning or practical relevance, any power to mobilize opinion on behalf of this or that oppressed, disenfranchized, 'third-world' or other such marginal interest-group. For we have now moved on – so the argument goes – into a new dispensation where the benefits are on offer to anyone wishing to join the club, and where the only victims are those unfortunate enough to live in parts of the world (the 'Iraqs and Ruritanias') where this message hasn't yet got through.

7
CONSENSUS REALITY AND MANUFACTURED TRUTH: THE POLITICS OF POSTMODERNISM

JAMESON AND HABERMAS

According to Fredric Jameson, there is not much point in declaring oneself 'for' or 'against' postmodernism if the thing is so pervasive – such a prominent feature of the present-day social, artistic and intellectual scene – that no amount of argument either way is going to make any appreciable difference. Most discussions of the topic are bedevilled (he thinks) by a species of persistent category-mistake, a tendency to confuse the three distinct issues of 'taste (or opinion), analysis, and evaluation, . . . things I would have thought we had some interest in keeping separate'. So far as 'taste' is concerned

> I write as a relatively enthusiastic consumer of postmodernism, at least some parts of it: I like the architecture and a lot of the newer visual work, in particular the newer photography. The music is not bad to listen to, or the poetry to read; the novel is the weakest of the newer cultural areas and is considerably excelled by its narrative counterparts in film and video. . . . Food and fashion have also greatly improved, as has the life world generally. My sense is that this is essentially a visual culture, wired for sound – but one where the linguistic element . . . is slack and flabby, and not to be made interesting without ingenuity, daring, and keen motivation.[1]

I happen to differ rather sharply with Jameson's stated preferences here, finding the music (or most of it) unlistenably vapid and trivial, the poetry (Ashbery excepted) pretty undistinguished, the architecture far more interesting in the idea than the execution, and the fiction – at any rate in writers like Calvino, Pynchon, Barth and Barthelme – by far the most accomplished and distinctive body of work. But of course this is precisely Jameson's point: that in matters of 'taste' there is always room for such differences of view, and that even by coming out 'against postmodernism' in some blanket sense of the word one would only be expressing a generalized distaste for the whole cultural phenomenon. That is say, one's opinion would involve just two of Jameson's proposed terms ('taste' and 'evaluation'), without moving on to the more difficult task of 'analysis', or the business of relating these various responses to their material, historical, and socio-economic contexts of production and reception. And at this point issues of 'taste' become largely irrelevant, since we are obliged to confront postmodernism as something indisputably *there*, an aspect (so to speak) of the way we live now, and not as a 'position' that we could somehow weigh up on its merits and then decisively embrace or reject according to individual preference. To adopt such a standpoint, whether 'for' or 'against', would be much like approving or deploring the weather as it happens to affect our plans for the day. Postmodernism in this sense is a cultural climate whose progress may be charted and whose prospects forecast to more or less useful effect, but whose current disposition has nothing to do with our likings or wishes in the matter.

Thus Jameson protests against the misguided strictures on his work by critics of various persuasion who took him to be either promoting or rejecting the postmodernist line.

> Despite the trouble I took in my principal essay on the subject to explain how it was not possible intellectually or politically simply to celebrate postmodernism or to 'disavow' it (whatever that might mean), avant-garde art critics quickly identified me as a vulgar Marxist hatchet-man, while some of my more simple-hearted colleagues concluded that, following the example of so many illustrious predecessors, I had finally gone off the deep end and become a 'post-Marxist'.[2]

One can sympathize with Jameson in this unfortunate predicament and yet find something rather less than fully argued – even, at times, something shuffling and evasive – in his manner of response to such criticisms. For despite its extraordinary range of theoretical, cultural, literary, philosophical and historical reference, its brilliant displays of high-wire dialectical gymnastics and its immense ingenuity in 'reclaiming' postmodernism for a broadly Marxist diagnostic account of the 'cultural logic of late capitalism', his book none the less leaves a nagging sense that the circle remains unsquared, and that Jameson's frankly avowed 'taste' for so many of the artforms and experiences he describes sits awkwardly with his 'analysis' of the socio-economic forces that have produced such a bewildering mélange of new-found media and life-styles.

The main problem, it seems to me, is that Jameson tends at crucial points in his argument to blur the distinction between 'postmodernism' in this broad-based cultural sense and 'postmodernism' as a set of philosophical (or post-philosophical) theses concerning the eclipse of Enlightenment reason, the obsolescence of values like 'reality' and 'truth', the bankruptcy of Marxist *Ideologiekritik*, and other such items of presumptive self-evidence advanced by thinkers like Baudrillard and Lyotard. As a result he can see no way of extricating theory – or 'analysis' – from the generalized 'postmodern condition' which supposedly constitutes the very horizon of intelligibility for any thinker (like Jameson) who accepts that condition as a cultural *donnée*, and who thus seeks to interpret the signs of the times pretty much as they ask to be read, i.e. as an aspect of the present-day *Zeitgeist* informing our every last evaluative concept and category. All of which adds up to yet another version of the familiar 'hermeneutic circle', in this case a version that leaves Jameson bereft of effective counter-arguments at precisely those points where his case most urgently requires them.

The following passage is typical enough in its failure to envisage any possible alternative – any vantage-point or opening for critical resistance – to the *doxa* of current postmodernist wisdom. For if, as Jameson writes,

> postmodernism is a historical phenomenon, then the attempt to conceptualize it in terms of moral or moralizing judgements must finally be condemned as a category mistake. [This] becomes more evident when we interrogate the position of the cultural critic and moralist; the latter, along with the rest of us, is now so deeply immersed in postmodernist space, so deeply infused and inflected by its new cultural categories, that the luxury of the old-fashioned ideological critique, the indignant moral denunciation of the other, becomes unavailable.[3]

But the logic of this argument will only seem compelling if one accepts Jameson's Hegelian notion of postmodernism as an all-pervasive spirit of the times, a cultural 'condition' that extends to every aspect of our emotional, affective, intellectual, aesthetic, political and social lives, and which thus – q.e.d. – simply offers no hold for reasoned or principled resistance. In such passages Jameson comes close to reproducing the 'end-of-ideology' rhetoric that has so often resurfaced, during the past two decades, as a weapon of first resort against any form of left-oppositional critique. It is the same line of argument that enables a wholesale neo-pragmatist like Rorty to propose his 'naturalized' reading of Hegel, a reading neatly shorn of such obsolete notions as 'reason', 'criticism' or 'truth at the end of enquiry', and instead viewing Hegel as a gifted *raconteur*, one whose narrative – for all its 'dialectical' pretensions – offers just a series of strung-together episodes from the 'cultural conversation of mankind', each of them affording a glimpse of what was once 'good in the way of belief'. And of course the same applies to our present situation as 'North Atlantic postmodern liberal-bourgeois' intellectuals, having joined the conversation at a fairly late stage, and having thus come to realize that all truths are relative, that rhetoric (not reason) is the name of the game, and that there is no point criticizing consensus-beliefs since they afford the only means of conversing with members of our own interpretive community.

This is not to suggest that Jameson and thinkers like Rorty and Fish would find themselves in agreement on many – if any – of the substantive social and political points at issue. But when Jameson treats postmodernism as simply a given, inescapable fact of our cultural lives, or when he rejects as a 'category mistake' the idea that one could possibly oppose it on argued (i.e. theoretical or principled) grounds, he is yielding to the neo-pragmatist argument in exactly the way that Rorty recommends. For it then becomes strictly *unthinkable* that Marxism could muster the critical resources to analyze – let alone resist or controvert – the premises of postmodern doctrine. And the crucial point here, once again, is that one needs to distinguish the doctrinal aspects – the extreme anti-realist or inverted ontological theses of a thinker like Baudrillard – from the wider 'phenomenon' that Jameson regards as a *de facto* feature of the current cultural landscape.

In his book *The Philosophical Discourse of Modernity* Habermas pinpoints the central weakness of such thinking, namely its tendency to conflate different orders of truth-claim by levelling what he calls the 'genre-distinction' between science, morality, and art, or – expressed in more Kantian terms – between cognitive, ethical and aesthetic modes of judgment.[4] For Habermas, such confusions are one root source of that potent aesthetic ideology whose effect is to deprive thinking of its critical force, and moreover to reduce philosophy to just another 'kind of writing', history to just another 'kind of narrative', ethics and politics to so many optional 'discourses', 'language-games', rhetorical strategies or whatever. All of which leaves a way wide open for the 'neo-conservatives' – as Habermas dubs them – to renege on the 'unfinished project of modernity' and adopt various forms of counter-Enlightenment, irrationalist or straightforward consensus-based belief. For the effect of such ideas, most evident in neopragmatists like Rorty and end-of-the-line postmodernists like Baudrillard, is to remove any sense of that critical distance between rhetoric and reason which alone makes it possible to challenge false or ideologically-motivated claims to truth. And the results are nowhere more damaging – so Habermas contends – than in the current post-structuralist fashion for assimilating every kind of discourse, philosophy and history included, to a realm of generalized 'intertextuality' where judgments of a factual or ethico-political order are viewed as so many transient configurations of the omnipresent Nietzschean will-to-power. The only escape from this bad dialectic of competing truths and counter-truths is to recognize, with Foucault, that the Kantian separation of realms is nothing more than one discursive strategy among others, a strategy – in this case – designed to enforce certain preconceived juridical relations of power between the various (imaginary) 'faculties' of knowledge and judgment.[5] But in Habermas's view this attitude gives rise to a stance of ultra-relativist Nietzschean abandon, a pretext for extending aesthetic values (in their currently updated 'textualist' form) to the domains of truth-seeking rational enquiry, on the one hand, and ethico-political discourse on the other. And the result of such a move – clearly visible (he argues) on the present-day French intellectual scene – is to level those crucial 'genre-distinctions' to the point of a wholesale irrationalist mystique and a failure to engage the most urgent questions of social and political justice.

It seems to me that Habermas is right about Foucault, whose flatly Hobbesian equation of power/knowledge has various unfortunate consequences, among them the failure to draw any significant (historical, social or ethico-political) distinction between utterly diverse orders of collective existence, from the Gulag Archipelago – his favoured explanatory model – at the one extreme, to liberal democracy or socialist state-planning at the other. Commentators of various persuasion, including Michael Walzer, have likewise noted this levelling tendency in Foucault's thought, a tendency related to his sceptical view of 'enlightened' progress as just a cover for ever more refined and elaborate techniques of social surveillance and control.[6] And of course it leaves no room for what Habermas conceives as the primary task of critical social theory, that is to say, the assessment of existing institutions, power/knowledge interests and socio-political structures against a regulative standard whose criterion is that of an 'ideal speech-situation', or a public realm of free and equal access to the relevant information-sources. In relation to the Gulf War, the issue between Foucault and Habermas can be expressed in the form of a simple alternative: that the 'discourse' of hegemonic Western values was here so effectively mobilized as to render criticism wholly ineffectual, or that opponents had a duty – a moral and citizenly duty – to expose the various kinds of fraudulent rhetoric, the distortions of truth and derelictions of democratic principle that characterized the US and Allied campaign of media disinformation.[7]

On the one hand this could all be adduced in support of Foucault's argument, i.e. as further evidence that truth *just is* what we make of it according to the prevalent discourse of instituted power/knowledge. In which case – as likewise from Baudrillard's viewpoint – it could serve little purpose to invoke criteria of truth, justice or informed public debate in order to expose that sham consensus for what it was, a product of intensive propaganda techniques deployed in the absence of genuine public debate. Nor can this argument be easily dismissed, given the attitude of passive compliance evinced at every level of British involvement, from the willingness of government ministers to reproduce the Pentagon/White House line from day to day as required, to the virtual collapse of parliamentary opposition (enforced by the Labour Party's shameful attempts to muzzle dissenting voices), and the effective confinement of critical opinion to the minority newspapers and off-peak TV programme-slots. But it is also the case – as I have argued more fully above – that certain truths emerged *despite and against* this barrage of dissimulating media coverage, mainly through the efforts of investigative journalists or those with an interest (an ethical as well as a party-line political or professional interest) in exposing the falsehoods put out during the weeks of intensive Allied propaganda. Most often this involved some perceived contradiction, some manifest discrepancy or failure to cohere in the official version of events. Or again, there was the widespread sense of moral revulsion – a turning-point in public responses to the war – which resulted from the US/Allied policy of at first inciting, then effectively disowning the Kurdish and Shi'ite rebels. My point is that both kinds of judgment, factual and ethical, involve the application of certain criteria (truth, reason, consistency, good faith, openness to public debate) which Habermas provides for through his theory of 'communicative action', but which find no place in Foucault's reductive genealogies of power/knowledge.

AESTHETICIZING POLITICS

Habermas puts the case most succinctly in a passage from one of his recent books under the heading 'Relations to the World and Claims to Validity'. His argument brings out the close relationship that always exists between, on the one hand, issues of factual or veridical warrant and, on the other, issues of conscience or ethico-political accountability. Thus:

> when someone rejects what is offered in an intelligible speech-act, he [sic] denies the validity of an utterance in at least one of three respects: *truth, rightness*, or *truthfulness*. His 'no' signals that the utterance has failed to fulfil at least one of its three functions (the representation of states of affairs, the maintenace of an interpersonal relationship, or the manifestation of lived experience) because the utterance is not in accordance with either *the* world of existing states of affairs, *our* world of legitimately ordered interpersonal relations, or *each participant's own* world of subjective lived experience. These aspects are not clearly distinguished in normal everyday communication. Yet in cases of disagreement or persistent problematization, competent speakers can differentiate between the aforementioned three *relations to the world*, thematizing individual validity claims and focusing on something that confronts them, whether it be something objective, something normative, or something subjective.[8]

What emerges from the thicket of Habermas's prose-style is a set of propositions which run exactly counter to the postmodern-pragmatist arguments advanced by thinkers like Rorty, Fish, Lyotard and Baudrillard. That is to say, he provides a philosophical basis for rejecting any version of the relativist case that would assimilate truth to the currency of taken-for-granted belief, or that would treat all kinds of validity-claim – factual, ethical, or intersubjective – as entirely contingent upon this or that existing state of consensus opinion. His point, briefly stated, is that no such theory can offer an account of how beliefs can be falsified – or shown to rest upon erroneous, deceptive, or partial modes of understanding – in light of evidence turned up by subsequent enquiry, or as a result of critical reflection on the factors that make for 'systematically distorted' forms of communicative agency and grasp. To be sure, his latest way of posing these issues is one that takes account of the 'linguistic turn' and the dominant strain of anti-foundationalist thinking which has left its mark on Anglo-American analytical philosophy, as well as on the avatars of French post-structuralist fashion. But as the above passage makes clear, Habermas is still centrally preoccupied with the three major questions of Kantian critique: 'What can I know?', 'What ought I to do?', and 'What may I reasonably hope for?'.

That he now sees fit to reformulate those questions in linguistic (speech-act or communicative) terms is often assumed to signal a retreat from the 'strong' Kantian position of his earlier writings, a sign that Habermas has at last come around to acknowledging the force of current neo-pragmatist arguments. But this is to ignore his continuing stress on the difference between *false* and *authentic* modes of consensus belief, on the one hand those created by manipulative pressures, mass-media distortion, 'public opinion' management etc, and on the other those arrived at through a genuine process of uncoerced truth-seeking dialogue. It is this difference – as I have argued – that makes sense of the apparent oxymoron contained in Habermas's phrase 'transcendental pragmatics', and which sets him still very firmly apart from thinkers like Rorty and Fish. Moreover, this is the single most important question in current debates about the 'uses of theory', the politics of postmodernism, and the relevance of such seemingly specialized concerns as a matter of real-world social and ethical consequence. For what we have witnessed of late among literary theorists and commentators on the postmodern cultural scene has been a move not only to 'textualize' everything in sight – as by treating history, philosophy, jurisprudence, sociology and other disciplines as so many optional 'kinds of writing', discourses devoid of referential content or distinctive validity-claims – but also, in Walter Benjamin's prescient phrase, to 'aestheticize politics' by removing such questions as far as possible from the realm of determinate truth and falsehood.[9] It was largely in consequence of ideas like these that

Baudrillard could offer his preposterous ideas about the Gulf War and reckon to obtain a respectful hearing in at least some quarters of the *avant-garde* cultural scene. All of which suggests that Habermas is right when he takes postmodernism to task for its facile blurring of the 'genre-distinction' between judgment in its cognitive, ethical, and aesthetic modes. For most often the result of such pan-textualist excesses is to reduce everything – reason, reality, history, politics, ethics – to a dead level of suasive or performative utterance where truth (once again) is simply what counts as 'good in the way of belief'.

I have argued that this criticism is misdirected when applied to deconstruction, a project whose rhetorical (or 'textualist') aspects go along with a high degree of analytical rigour, a regard – albeit a qualified regard – for the imperatives of Kantian enlightened critique, and a keen awareness of the dangers involved in any over-extension of aesthetic values or analogues into the realm of ethical and political thought. Indeed, the later work of Paul de Man is devoted very largely to countering the influence of what he terms 'aesthetic ideology', an influence that first took hold – as he sees it – in the widepsread misreading of certain crucial passages in Kant, and which then gave rise to a whole bad history of mystified national-aestheticist themes, including (most notoriously) Heidegger's endorsement of Nazi cultural propaganda.[10] All the same it would be idle to pretend that deconstruction has not been put to other, more distracting or ideologically complicitous uses, especially when it deploys a rhetoric of the Kantian (or quasi-Kantian) sublime as a privileged trope for whatever exceeds the limits of adequate representation or the powers of reflective critical reason. I have already offered some examples of this tendency, among them that ingenious but perverse *Diacritics* article 'deconstructing' rival narrative accounts of the KAL 007 affair, to the point where any notional truth of the matter – of precisely what happened, at whose instigation, in pursuit of what (US or Soviet) strategic interests – is transfigured into a rhetoric of 'sublime' undecidability. And there are passages in Derrida's 'nuclear criticism' piece which lay themselves open to a similar charge: that they subtilize issues of real-world factual and ethical accountability to the extent of invoking the so-called 'nuclear sublime' as a species of ultimate aporia, a pseudo-referent quite beyond reach of enlightened rational debate.

That these passages are untypical of Derrida's work is a case that I have argued at considerable length, here and elsewhere.[11] But clearly there are reasons for this current revival of interest in the Kantian sublime, figuring as it does – notably for Lyotard – as an emblem of the radical 'incommensurability' that exists between factual or cognitive judgments on the one hand, and ethical or political judgments on the others.[12] And one need only look to Baudrillard's commentaries on the Gulf War to see how easily this rhetoric leans over into an attitude of downright cognitive scepticism and a flat refusal to consider such issues from a standpoint of informed and responsible truth-seeking interest. What the sublime represents – or (as these thinkers would have it) signally fails to represent – is the idea of a socio-political order that would actually achieve the wished-for condition of genuine participant democracy. For it is an article of faith among the postmodern sceptics that any such order must always remain a strictly unattainable idea, a product of 'sublime' imagining whose realization is in principle confined to the realm of abstract or utopian possibility. Thus in Lyotard's words, paraphrasing Kant,

> if humanity were progressing toward the better, it would not be because 'things are getting better' and because the reality of this betterment could be attested through procedures for establishing reality, but because humans would have become so cultivated and would have developed an ear so attuned to the Idea (which is nonetheless unpresentable) that they would feel its tension on the occasion of the most apparently impertinent, with regard to it, facts and that they would supply the very proof of progress by the sole fact of their susceptibility. This progress could therefore be compatible with the general feelings that 'things are getting worse'. In its aggravation, the gap between Ideas and observable historical-political reality would bear witness not only against that reality but also in favor of those Ideas.[13]

Lyotard's warrant for this reading of Kant is taken from the Third *Critique* where there is a close parallel between the sublime as a figure for modes of experience that exceed all our powers of cognitive or rational apprehension, and those regulative 'Ideas of Reason' (e.g. justice, freedom, democracy and perpetual peace) which likewise cannot be checked or ascertained with reference to any existing real-world state of affairs.[14] This reading is justified in so far as Kant undoubtedly proposes the sublime as an analogue, a means of insisting that such Ideas belong to the realm of 'suprasensible' values and judgments, and hence that we err in thinking to gauge their validity – their truth to experience – against standards laid down by the other tribunal of cognitive judgment or adequate representation. In this latter (epistemological) realm the requirement is always that knowledge should make good its claims by 'bringing intuitions under concepts', or by establishing a firm – critically validated – correlation between the order of phenomenal cognition and the order of conceptual understanding. Thus the main point at issue is the extent to which philosophy can underwrite the truth-claims of science by offering a worked-out explanatory account (a 'transcendental deduction', in the Kantian sense) of how such claims can be secured against the threat of epistemological scepticism. But arguments like these are wholly irrelevant when it comes to questions of aesthetic or ethico-political judgment, since here there is no possible ground of appeal to determinate (objectively validated) standards of truth and falsehood. The best that one can hope for in such matters is a measure of intersubjective agreement, brought about through the exchange of qualified opinion among suitably 'cultivated' individuals.

Nor should this be seen as in any sense a weak or regrettable conclusion, according to Kant. For it is precisely in the realm of 'suprasensible' Ideas – a realm quite apart from the determinist constraints of causal necessity, phenomenal cognition, or conceptual understanding – that thought gains access to the 'kingdom of ends', the knowledge of its ultimate freedom or autonomy with regard to matters of ethical choice (or Kantian 'practical reason'). If this were not the case – if the cognitive 'phrase-regime' (in Lyotard's parlance) applied here as elsewhere – then practical reason would itself be subject to the same inexorable causal laws, the same necessity of conforming its judgments to the dictates of phenomenal cognition. So one can see why the sublime occupies such a prominent place in Kant's thinking about ethics and politics. To this extent Lyotard is justified in treating it as the one figure of thought – not so much 'concept' or 'category' – which enables Kant to address himself to those 'great historical events' (like the French Revolution) that would otherwise exceed or baffle the powers of reflective judgment. With the sublime 'Kant advances far into heterogeneity, so much so that the solution to the aesthetic antinomy [i.e., the quest for shared evaluative standards where no rule can possibly be given] appears much more difficult in the case of the sublime than it does in the case of the beautiful'.[15] And this for the reason, as Lyotard notes, that issues of political justice and right – like issues of aesthetic taste – can never be settled by direct appeal to features manifestly or objectively 'there' in the evidence presently to hand.

But there is also, as I have argued, a serious risk that this postmodern reading of the Kantian sublime will itself push so far in the direction of radically 'heterogenous' language-games, discourses and phrase-regimes that issues of fact (or historical truth) come to seem quite irrelevant for the purposes of ethical or socio-political judgment. Certainly Kant never envisaged so drastic a split – or ontological gulf – between the interests of truth-seeking rational enquiry and the interests of speculative thought. It may well be the case, as he remarks of the French Revolution, that no appeal to 'the facts' – to the course of events as manifest in the Terror and its aftermath – can invalidate the 'enthusiasm', the mood of new-found social and political optimism, first aroused in the minds of those spectators privileged to witness the 'great event'. Such occurrences are sublime in the sense that they evoke responses in excess of the given (historical) facts, responses whose validity cannot be impugned – or whose significance called into doubt – by the subsequent record of post-revolutionary failure and defeat. Thus, in Lyotard's words, citing Kant:

> enthusiasm, for its part, sees nothing, or rather sees that what can be seen is nothing, and relates it back to the unrepresentable. Although ethically condemnable as pathological, 'aesthetically, enthusiasm is sublime, because it is a tension of forces produced by ideas, which give an impulse to the mind that operates far more powerfully and lastingly than the impulse arising from sensible representations'.[16]

As I say, this undoubtedly reflects one aspect of Kant's socio-political philosophy, namely his desire to protect the interests of progressive or emancipatory thought by distinguishing the realm of 'pure practical reason' from that of empirical self-evidence or straightforward factual-documentary appeal. But it ignores what is equally important in Kant: his belief that such 'tensions' can only be sustained through a sense of *contrast* – the manifest disparity – between things-as-they-are (or as they have been to date) and things as they might be according to the dictates of reason, justice and truth. On Lyotard's account, these two modes of thought (the cognitive and the speculative) belong to such utterly 'heterogeneous' language-games that there could be no grounds – no available criteria – for assessing present realities in light of possible future progress. In short, what results from this postmodernist reading of the Kantian sublime is an outlook of extreme cognitive scepticism, along with a politics completely cut off from questions of real-world relevance and accountability.

The following passage from *The Differend* shows how easily Lyotard's talk of incommensurable phrase-regimes leads on to something closely resembling Baudrillard's wholesale anti-realist position. 'Once the givens are established', he writes,

> a new genre of discourse is required, one whose canonical phrase is *what can we do?* This phrase is not without analogy with what Kant calls an Idea of the imagination (intuitions without a concept). . . . Today, these are called scenarios or simulations. They are narrations of the unreal, as in war games: what if they attacked our left flank? Then we would surround them by rapidly deploying our right flank. A multiplicity of possible, probable, and improbable stories are told heedless of their verisimilitude, in anticipation of what could be the case. . . . Political deliberation properly so called takes place in these scenarios. . . . Since the government of Kabul or El Salvador has asked for Moscow's or Washington's help, the presence of Soviet or American troops in the territory governed by Kabul or El Salvador is proof of the independence of those governments. . . . This is public polemics, the campaign for public opinion, propaganda: the other is wrong, therefore I'm right; he or she is unworthy of your confidence (this is aimed at the opposing orator's ethos), he or she is leading you away from your true ends (this is aimed at the listener's pathos); such is not (therefore) the case with me.[17]

As so often with Baudrillard, so here with Lyotard's argument: although valid enough as a diagnostic commentary on the way things are currently managed in the Western 'free-world' democracies, the passage goes completely over the top – in typical postmodernist style – when it equates this process with 'political deliberation properly so called', and hence implicitly endorses those 'scenarios', those 'simulations' and 'narrations of the unreal' as the nearest we shall ever get to reality and truth. Such inverted ontologies – placing rhetoric above reason, fiction above fact, or the pseudo-logic of deterrence over the interests of rational debate – are, as we have seen, the very hallmark of postmodernism in its more theoretically elaborated forms. All the more ironic that Lyotard should offer this particular passage as a gloss on what he calls – rightly enough – the 'canonical phrase' of Kantian reason in its speculative (ethico-political) aspect. For 'What can we do?' is a question that hardly makes sense in the absence of criteria for judging not only what is right in the interests of freedom, democracy and justice, but also what is wrong – demonstrably wrong – with the existing state of world political affairs.

This point can be made more directly with regard to the Gulf War by considering the way that the US/Allied powers exploited the United Nations charter and its various specific resolutions before, during and after the period of overt hostilities. For the UN could be viewed – as my colleague Simon Critchley once suggested – as a Kantian 'idea of pure practical reason' translated into the sphere of present-day geo-political interests. That is to say, it is a representative body whose principles far outrun its powers of effective practical enforcement; whose charter gives voice to enlightened ideals that have never been attained or consistently applied in real-world terms; yet whose validity is somehow attested – despite these failures – by its appeal to values that somehow transcend all the melancholy evidence to date. On the cynical view (most often backed up by comparison with the interwar League of Nations) this is just another showing of the age-old utopian dream, the deluded idea that affairs of state or international politics could ever be conducted on a basis of mutual cooperative trust and enlightened understanding. Such an outlook nowadays has few defenders among the various *au courant* schools of social and political theory. On the one hand a politics based on enlightened reason is attacked by the postmodern sceptics and disciples of Foucault, those who argue – on Hobbesian as much as on Nietzschean grounds – that all talk of 'reason', 'justice' or 'truth' is in fact just a species of dissimulating rhetoric, a cover for the workings of that ubiquitous 'power/knowledge' which leaves no room for such obsolete values. On the other it is diagnosed by theorists like Adorno and Horkheimer as a discourse fatally compromised by its association with the so-called 'dialectic of enlightenment', the process by which reason lost its critical or emancipatory force and became nothing more than a technique of oppression, a means of all-encompassing surveillance and control, an 'instrumental reason' wholly in the grip of its own will-to-power over nature and humanity.[18] To this extent they concur with Foucault's genealogies of power/knowledge, whatever the clearly-marked differences of outlook that emerge elsewhere between Frankfurt Critical Theory and Foucauldian discourse-analysis. And of course there are others – like Norman Cohn in his much-cited book *The Pursuit of the Millennium* – who argue that utopian thinking in whatever form is by far the most dangerous of political illusions, since it always gives rise to a mood of revolutionary fervour or messianic zeal, most often followed by a period of large-scale religious or political persecution.[19] From this point of view the Enlightenment values articulated by Kant could be seen as just another version – albeit a heavily secularized version – of the same self-deluding utopian impulse whose consequences can be traced down through the history of failed or betrayed revolutionary ideals. Put these arguments together and it becomes readily apparent why so many intellectuals and political commentators regard the UN either cynically, as a pawn in the power-game of US-dominated world politics, or with pitying fondness, as a splendid ideal which unfortunately lacks the least power to intervene in real-world strategic or military terms.

This is no doubt why Lyotard lays such stress on the Kantian sublime as a salutary warning that we should not confuse the two distinct realms of empirical self-evidence (or historical warrant) and 'pure practical reason' in its ethico-political mode. Thus:

> because the feeling of the sublime is an affective paradox, the paradox of feeling publicly and as a group that something which is 'formless' alludes to a beyond of experience, that feeling constitutes an 'as-if presentation' of the Idea of civil society and even of cosmopolitical society, and thus an as-if presentation of the Idea of morality, right where that Idea nevertheless cannot be presented, within experience. It is in this way that the sublime is a sign. This sign is only indicative of a free causality, but it nonetheless has the value of a proof for the phrase which affirms progress, since the spectating humanity must already have made cultural progress in order to make this signify its 'mode of thinking' about the Revolution. This sign is progress in its present state, it is as much as can be done, even though civil societies are nowhere near republican in their regime nor States anywhere near world federation (far from it!).[20]

But the trouble with all this is that it drives such a wedge between the two 'incommensurable' phrase-regimes that criticism can scarcely get a hold for comparing on the one hand what those 'Ideas of Reason' may properly be taken to signify, and on the other what is actually *performed in their name* by governments seeking some pretext or spurious justification for their policies and actions. For on Lyotard's account such criticism would have to be seen as yet another 'category-mistake', just one more instance of the confusion engendered by mixing up judgments of factual truth (or evidential warrant) with judgments of ethical and political right. The result – as in so much postmodernist thinking – is a curious combination of high speculative theory and extreme cynicism as regards the prospects for achieving anything remotely like a public sphere of informed debate or a working participant democracy. Here again, such ideas have a wider resonance in the current mood of 'post-ideological' disenchantment with any set of truth-claims, principles or values that goes against the prevailing consensus grain. And this mood found expression during the Gulf War in the widely-held view that it was pointless to hold the US/Allied coalition accountable to the terms of the UN charter or its various specific resolutions, since these – like the UN itself and the concept of 'international law' – were ideas so devoid of practical substance that their invocation was a waste of breath. My point is not so much that Lyotard's arguments lead straight to this attitude of sceptical indifference; rather that they provide no critical resources, no adequate means of resisting its untoward moral and political effects.

SOME VARIETIES OF TRUTH-CLAIM

De Man's phrase 'aesthetic ideology' is as good a way as any of describing what is wrong with this postmodern rendition of Kant. For it is only by creating such a privileged figure of the Kantian sublime – treating it not merely as *analogous* to reason in its ethico-political mode but as the very precondition for all such speculative judgments – that Lyotard can justify his talk of radically 'heteregeneous' language-games or discourses. And such talk has gained credence among many intellectuals at a time when left-oppositional thinking is at a low ebb, when consensus-doctrines occupy the high ground of fashionable 'post-Marxist' debate, and when it is easy for political commentators to ridicule any notion of judging or criticizing US actions in the Gulf by reference to those 'Ideas of Reason' embodied in a document like the UN charter. For this would involve certain presuppositions about truth, valid argument and warranted inter-pretive grounds which are rejected outright on a postmodern reading of the relevant passages in Kant. Such necessary presuppositions would include first the principle (*contra* Lyotard) that there is no ultimate disjunction between issues of fact and issues of ethical and political accountability; second, the argument (as against Baudrillard and postmodernism generally) that there are truths about the way things stand in reality – historical truths among them – which are *not* just constructions out of this or that language-game, discourse, mode of narrative representation or whatever; and third, the understanding that 'Ideas of Reason' – as embodied for instance in a communal enterprise like the United Nations – exist not merely in a realm of 'sublime' imagining devoid of any real-world pertinence and force, but can always be applied to particular situations (like the US/Allied conduct of the Gulf War) by way of establishing the rights and wrongs of the case. Of course such arguments will be open to challenge, not only as regards their justice in terms of the principles and values invoked, but also – very often – in point of historical or factual-documentary truth. Thus opinions will no doubt continue to be divided as to just what happened at crucial junctures before, during and after the period of overt hostilities in the Gulf, and as to whether various actions were justified in light of the available evidence. But it is an error – a basic philosophical error – to suppose that *just because* such claims are contested, or because any settling of the issue between pro-war and anti-war parties is unlikely to be reached yet awhile (if ever), *therefore* we should draw the obvious conclusion and acknowledge that truth in these matters is wholly unattainable. For already it is the case – as I have argued above – that certain lies have been exposed, certain propaganda ploys shown up for what they were, and certain forms of specious justifying rhetoric revealed as just a cover for the US pursuit of its regional hegemonic interests.

Sometimes this involved nothing more than a perceived mismatch or discrepancy between the way things at first appeared (as presented by the media under conditions of tight government and military censorship) and the truth as it emerged later through a process of critical-investigative enquiry. The single most striking (and appalling) case was the bombing of that civilian air-raid shelter, carried out – and defended for some days afterwards – on the pretext of its having been a key military and communications centre. Other instances that readily come to mind are the various installations (hospitals, sewage-treatment plants, water supply units, a factory producing powdered milk for baby food etc) destroyed – whether mistakenly or not – in the *Blitzkrieg* on Baghdad and other cities, and passed off as genuine 'priority' targets until the facts came out through filmed evidence of telltale remains amongst the debris. Then there was the propaganda capital made out of Iraqi television footage of shot-down Allied pilots whose injuries (we were told) had been inflicted at the hands of their 'inhuman' Iraqi captors, but which subsequent (better informed) opinion attributed to their having experienced the usual shocks and stresses of being violently ejected from a disintegrating aircraft at high speed and altitude. One could carry on multiplying examples, but the general point should be clear enough: that truth in such matters may indeed be hard to come by and subject to continuing debate, but that this is no cause – no adequate cause – to despair of ever reaching it through a process of evidential reasoning and open argumentative exchange.

In a sense this position scarcely needs defending, since it accords so readily with our everyday working assumptions about the existence of an objective world 'out there', a reality certain of whose features we may not yet (or ever) be able to cognize, yet whose sum total of objects, occurrences and events is none the less real for all that.[21] Indeed, as Thomas Nagel has argued, we cannot intelligibly claim to raise doubts as to the truth of our present – perhaps highly partial and distorted – viewpoint without at least entertaining the notion of our having got some things wrong, and thus in effect conceding the case that it is possible to get things right. 'In pursuing objectivity', Nagel writes,

> we alter our relation to the world, increasing the correctness of certain of our representations of it by compensating for the peculiarities of our point of view. But the world is in a strong sense independent of our possible representations, and may well extend beyond them. This has implications both of what objectivity achieves when it is successful and for the possible limits of what it can achieve. Its aim and sole rationale is to increase our grasp of reality, but this makes no sense unless the idea of reality is not merely the idea of what can be grasped by those methods. . . . Human objectivity may be able to grasp only part of the world, but when it is successful it should provide us with an understanding of aspects of reality whose existence is completely independent of our capacity to think about them – as independent as the existence of things we can't conceive. . . . [For] what there is, or what is the case, does not coincide necessarily with what is a possible object of thought for us. Even if through some miracle we are capable in principle of conceiving of everything there is, that is not what makes it real.[22]

Nagel's arguments are directed mainly against philosophical sceptics and idealists of various persuasion who tend to confuse ontological issues (questions of 'what there is, or what is the case') with epistemological problems (i.e., those concerning the limits of human cognitive or intellectual grasp). What these thinkers fail to recognize, he contends, is the plain *impossibility* of occupying a position from which 'truth' would figure solely as a product of our own (maybe deluded) ideas or representations, yet where nothing could count – no alternative, more critical or objectively validated standpoint – as a means whereby to establish the fact of our having thus fallen into error. In short, this is one of those 'views from nowhere' or strictly untenable positions which provide Nagel with the main topic and the memorable title of his book.

It seems to me that this argument works just as well against Baudrillard, Lyotard, Foucault and other such purveyors of the sceptical doctrine in its current (postmodern or post-structuralist) guise. That is to say, they start out from a perfectly reasonable set of premises concerning the limits of human knowledge at any given time, the essentially contested character of at least some truth-claims, and the degree to which our operative concepts and categories depend upon certain (arguably linguistic or culture-specific) norms. But they are wrong to conclude on this basis that *reality itself* – as opposed to our ideas of it – must therefore be seen as nothing more than a figment of this or that collective mind-set. For such arguments fall straight back into the error that Nagel detects behind the various forms of idealist or extreme anti-realist doctrine: namely, the tendency to confuse epistemological with ontological issues, or questions about the limits of human understanding with questions about the status or the very existence of real-world objects and events. It is on account of this confusion that postmodernists like Baudrillard – as well as neo-pragmatists like Rorty – can consider 'reality' a world well lost in exchange for the pleasures of a realm where truth is whatever we care to make of it in accordance with the latest metaphors, language-games, or 'final vocabularies'. But as Nagel makes clear this position is neither warranted on philosophical grounds nor available as a viewpoint that anyone could seriously or consistently adopt when confronted with some issue of real-world truth and falsehood. Thus:

> the idea of objectivity always points beyond mere intersubjective agreement, even though such agreement, criticism and justification are essential methods of reaching an objective view. The language that we can have because of our agreement in responses enables us to reach beyond the responses to talk about the world itself. As almost anyone would concede, it enables us to say, truly or falsely, that rain was

falling on Gibraltar exactly fifty thousand years ago, even if there is no way of reaching agreement in the application of the term to such a case. . . . Language reaches beyond itself, whether in the concept of rain or in the concept of what there is, though what it reaches can only be designated by using language or some other form of representation.[23]

Of course there are those – Baudrillard among them – who wouldn't at all concede the force of this argument, and who would maintain the (surely nonsensical) position that since truth-claims are warranted only by appeal to some preferential language-game, discourse, or 'form of representation', therefore reality drops out of the picture except as a means of rhetorical back-up, or a comforting notion for thinkers unable to shed their old 'metaphysical' realist illusions. Post-structuralism – and at least some varieties of deconstruction – have promoted this idea to a high point of sceptical doctrine. But such attitudes reduce to manifest absurdity as soon as one asks – like Nagel – how they can possibly cope with the either/or logic of certain real-world factual propositions, statements whose determinate truth (or falsehood) is an issue quite separate from that of their present undecidability. Since Kant most philosophers have managed to avoid this troublesome confusion between ontological and epistemological orders of argument. That it has now reemerged to such obfuscating effect among the followers of current postmodernist fashion is one sure sign of how retrograde this movement is, not only in philosophical but also in political terms.

For it is, as I have argued, the politics of postmodernism – along with its ethical implications – which give most grounds for disquiet when viewed in light of responses to the Gulf War and other recent events. The main issue here is once again the Kantian question: what precisely is the relation between those various inter-articulated realms of discourse – understanding, practical reason, aesthetic judgment, ethico-political speculation – which between them constitute the critical 'tribunal' of enlightened truth-seeking interests. Nagel makes the point in a different register but with much the same distinctions in mind. 'There may be some portions of discourse', he writes,

> where rock bottom is the language game and the shared responses on which it depends, with no real reference in the world outside of our responses and no objectivity except what comes from agreement.

There is a real issue about this with respect to ethics and aesthetics, and room for disagreement about where to draw the line between realism and mere intersubjectivity without external reference. But there still seems to me much of language and thought that must be interpreted in a strong sense 'realistically'.[24]

For Lyotard, conversely, the great virtue of the Kantian sublime – as opposed to the beautiful – is that it pushes far beyond the stage of 'mere' intersubjective consensus, to a point of radical 'heterogeneity' where thought is brought up against the absolute limits of adequate (sensuous or cognitive) representation. In 'the phrase of the beautiful', as envisaged by Kant, 'the community of addressors and addressees is called forth immediately, without the mediation of any concept, by feeling alone, inasmuch as this feeling can be shared *a priori* . . . The community is already there as taste, but it is not yet there as rational consensus'.[25] Whereas in the 'phrase of the sublime' there is so utter and abrupt a disjunction between concepts and sensuous intuitions as to throw the mind back upon 'Ideas of Reason' that cannot possibly discover any image of fulfilment – any adequate 'presentation' or evidential warrant – whether in the realm of phenomenal cognition or in that of real-world (historical) actions and events. From Nagel's point of view there is a problem with ethical and aesthetic judgments in so far as they invoke standards of consensual ('intersubjective') valuation which afford no grounds of objective or critical-realist assessment. However, such issues are largely irrelevant when it comes to that other, more extensive domain where objectivity is properly to be sought. Lyotard turns this argument right around by treating the beautiful – the realm of consensus values – as a half-way stage on the road to that 'extreme modality' of the Kantian sublime where there is nothing to agree upon save the utter lack of agreed-upon values and criteria. In short, he makes a high postmodernist virtue of pushing Nagel's 'problem' to the limit, renouncing any notion of intersubjective (let alone objective) validity-claims, and equating justice with maximal degree of 'dissensus' between rival phrase-regimes.

A CASE IN POINT: THE RETREAT TO BASRA

All of which brings us back – however obliquely – to the question of moral and political principles as embodied in a document like the UN charter, and the further issue of how those principles relate to matters of real-world factual understanding. To examine the relationship I shall take as an example an article that appeared on 30 May 1991 in the *New York Review of Books*. The article, by Andrew Whitley, was entitled 'Kuwait: the Last Forty-Eight Hours', and described (among other things) the carnage inflicted by US/Allied forces during the Iraqi retreat on the road northward to Basra. The article stands out from the run of 'post-war' journalistic comment, as much for its willingness to offer moral judgments as for its care in assembling the documentary evidence and establishing – from first-hand sources where possible – the truth of what actually occurred.

This is *not* to say (far from it) that Whitley lines up on the anti-war side of the argument; in fact his article devotes a good part of its space to revealing the extent of Iraqi atrocities against the civilian population of Kuwait and demanding that the perpetrators be held accountable in terms of the Geneva Conventions and other articles of international law. But Whitley also makes a point – unusually among US and British commentators on the war and its aftermath – of applying these principles with equal force to the Allied conduct of 'Operation Desert Storm' before, during and after the phase of intensive military engagement. It is for this reason that his essay merits attention as something more than just a piece of vividly evocative prose describing one individual's response to some particularly harrowing scenes. My point is that Whitley had *grounds* – both factual-documentary and principled grounds – for writing as he did and for challenging the consensus-view that any war-crimes committed were wholly on the Iraqi side, and that the 'Allies' for their part had observed all the protocols laid down by the UN, the Geneva Conventions and other such tribunals. In short, the moral issue is simply *inseparable* from the need to establish the truth of what happened from day to day of the conflict.

The following passage from his article will give some idea of Whitley's virtues as a witness of events and a commentator willing to draw the appropriate conclusions.

> I had been told about the extensive damage visible on the road, but nothing prepared me for the utter devastation a few miles ahead. . . . To judge by the intact street lamps, as well as by the heat-blasted wrecks piled crazily one on top of another, the US Navy fighters responsible for much of the slaughter must have used a combination of

fuel-air explosives and cluster bombs against the hopelessly snarled convoy of vehicles attempting to leave the city. In awesome testimony to the Allies' firepower, the trail of destruction stretches a full thirty miles along the road to the border, and fans out into the desert as far as the eye can see. . . . In the euphoria of victory, the fact that innocent civilians were killed on the night of February 25 has been passed over in silence by the Pentagon. Queasy about the implications, the Western press and television, too, have made little of it. . . . Within a mile-long section of the destroyed convoy, I counted more than a dozen ambulances and other vehicles bearing Red Crescent signs. These are entitled to absolute protection from attack under the 1949 Geneva Conventions, not to mention the Pentagon's own rules of engagement. Even if the retreating Iraqis were misusing medical vehicles, as is probable, the burden was nonetheless on the Allies to distinguish between targets, and to choose their weapons accordingly.[27]

There are three points I wish to make about this passage, quite apart from its evident qualities as a piece of impassioned yet controlled and scrupulously documented journalism. First, there is Whitley's challenge to what he perceived at the time as the virtual conspiracy of silence surrounding these events. Second, there is his strongly-held conviction – related to the arguments of Nagel summarized above – that truth in such matters is a question of what *did or didn't happen on some given occasion*, not – as the sceptics and postmodernists would have it – a product of our current, necessarily partial perceptions and habits of belief. Thus this is a case of a journalist's endeavour to get things right to the best of his ability, involving an appeal to the facts as reliably witnessed or reported, and, *pace* Rorty and Fish, a readiness to go clean against the dominant consensus-wisdom. And third, there is Whitley's principled stand on the Geneva Conventions and other such articles of agreed-upon conduct and restraint, including – as he notes – the Pentagon's own professed 'rules' of military engagement. This stands in clear contrast to the attitude of many commentators who dismissed such appeals (along with any talk of 'abiding by UN resolutions') as a species of wishful thinking on the part of well-meaning liberal types hopelessly ignorant of what goes on in the heat of battle. Whitley thus comes out in marked opposition to that cynical view of the UN and suchlike other-worldly 'Ideas of Reason' which assigns them to a realm of utopian fantasy devoid of real-life practical consequence.

As I argued above, there is a prominent strain of postmodernist thinking – notably in Lyotard – which promotes this view by insisting on the absolute 'heterogeneity' of phrase-regimes, the unbridgeable gulf that supposedly exists between judgments of fact and judgments of ethico-political justice and right. But such arguments possess neither philosophic warrant nor the merit (as Lyotard would no doubt claim) of sharpening our sense for the conflicts of principle involved in disputed cases. On the contrary, such an outlook of extreme cognitive scepticism – especially when joined to an ultra-relativist stance in matters of ethical judgment – fits in all too readily with the mood of prevailing 'post-ideological' conformist belief. Let me cite a further passage from Whitley's article by way of clarifying this point. It is of particular interest for several reasons, among them its raising of the moral issue with specific reference to Bush's talk of 'war-crimes' and the relevant provisions of international law.

> Some who have criticized the Bush administration for the level of destruction during the fighting now complain that too much of the Iraqi army was left intact, and was therefore able to turn on the Kurds and the rebellious Shi'ites. Such critics cannot have it both ways. But on one ground – launching indiscriminate attacks likely to cause civilian deaths, by destroying identifiable vehicles carrying the sick and wounded – the allies could be charged with war crimes, at least for one terrible night's work. The hundreds of civilian deaths on the night of February 13 at the Amiriyah bomb shelter in Baghdad could also be cited in making such a case. One reason why President Bush's wartime enthusiasm for seeing Saddam Hussein in the dock of an international tribunal has cooled so rapidly since the allied victory may be that the administration is aware that such charges could possibly be made.[28]

Again, this makes nonsense of any argument (postmodernist or otherwise) based on the fact/value dichotomy, the idea that it is impossible to reason one's way from an 'is' to an 'ought', or from a truth-claim concerning some real-world state of affairs to a judgment as regards the rights and wrongs of the case. As I noted above, this 'dilemma' is normally attributed to Hume, but in fact figures in his work as just one of those nagging philosophical perplexities, problems that are apt to drop out of sight as soon as one re-enters the orbit of genuine moral and practical concerns.[29] This is what emerges with particular force in the passage from Whitley's article: the way that certain statements of fact lead on *inescapably* to moral or evaluative judgments, at least in so far as the implied reader agrees upon some shared (fairly basic) standards of truth, justice and ethical accountability.[30] Of course it may be said that this begs the whole question, since such disputes typically involve disagreement – or radical 'dissensus', in Lyotard's terms – over just what constitutes a relevant 'fact', or the issue of how far ethical judgments can possibly be warranted on factual-documentary grounds. And there will always be sceptics who raise this problem into a ready-made pretext for indulging various kinds of high-flown sophistical argument. But there is really no need to be over-impressed by a strategy whose upshot – as in Lyotard's case – is to treat factual and ethical truth-claims as realms utterly apart, and hence to leave criticism stranded in a 'phrase-regime' devoid of any real-world practical import.

This is not to say that Whitley's article establishes so firm and demonstrative a link between factual and ethical orders of judgment that any counter-argument is effectively played off the field. Thus, for instance, I would reject his claim in the above passage that the critics of Bush's Gulf War policy 'cannot have it both ways', on the one hand objecting to the level of destruction visited upon Iraqi forces during the period of full-scale hostilities, while on the other complaining that 'too much of the Iraqi army was left intact, and was therefore able to turn on the Kurds and the rebellious Shi'ites'. It seems to me that this misses the crucial point: the fact that, having once launched their campaign of mass-destruction, the US/Allied forces *then* turned around – after inflicting (on current estimates) more than 150,000 military and civilian casualties – and abandoned the rebels to their own unfortunate devices. Had it not been for the scale and intensity of that offensive – as well as the expressions of US support for an internal uprising that would, in Bush's words, 'finish the job' – then of course there would have been no rebellion, no mass-exodus of Kurdish refugees, and nothing to match the extent of human misery caused by the callous pursuit of regional policy interests. In this respect, I would argue, Whitley misreads the evidence and puts forward an interpretation of events that lacks argumentative warrant. But the point is not so much that his article goes wrong on this or that specific issue as that he does nonetheless offer truth-claims – factual and principled truth-claims – which are then open to challenge and debate by those who would consider them ill-founded. One could hardly say the same of much that passed as 'informed' commentary on the Gulf War and its aftermath. For that commentary was characterized all too often by a failure of moral and intellectual nerve – a refusal to engage critically with the sources of official disinformation – whose effect was to stifle public debate, to marginalize the voices of dissent, and to smoothe the way for whatever new twist of consensus-opinion seemed 'good in the way of belief'.

REASON, TRUTH AND HISTORY

This book started out (as the reader may have guessed) in the form of a brief polemical rejoinder to Baudrillard's postmodernist musings on the Gulf War. But the more I reflected on Baudrillard's relation to other contemporary movements of thought, the more it became apparent that his was just the limit-point – the giddy extreme – of a fashionable *doxa* whose symptoms ranged from the breakdown of informed critical debate in the media to the specialized varieties of intellectual bad faith manifested by thinkers of a kindred (postmodernist or neo-pragmatist) persuasion. Some readers may feel that I have exaggerated the impact of these latter developments, confined as they are to a fairly small interest-group of critics, philosophers and cultural theorists with no great following beyond the academic or specialized intellectual sphere. It could also be said – with some justice – that an event like the Gulf War should not be treated as a pretext for airing differences of view at such a rarified level of abstract philosophical debate. But this objection ignores the extent to which issues of truth, validity and ethical warrant are always bound up with matters of real-world factual and moral accountability. That a sizable number of prominent intellectuals could be won over to a postmodern-pragmatist viewpoint – a position that negates the critical difference between truth and the currency of consensus belief – is at very least a factor worth attention when it comes to understanding how 'public opinion' was swung into accepting the US line on the Gulf War and its justifying causes. More generally, I have argued (as against thinkers like Fish) that theory has *consequences* in the strong sense of the term; that to line up (say) with Chomsky or Habermas on the question of validity-claims or truth-telling warrant is also to adopt an oppositional stance when confronted with the evidence of a false consensus brought about by techniques of manipulative mass-persuasion.[31] The idea that theoretical and substantive issues are realms utterly apart is just one more instance of the old dilemma so unfairly fathered on Hume; a pseudo-problem that postmodernism has revived for no very cogent or creditable reasons.

So there is nothing in the least irrelevant or ivory-tower about the effort to demonstrate – on philosophical grounds – how these current styles of ultra-relativist thought are on the one hand devoid of argumentative warrant and on the other complicit with the widespread drift toward habits of inert consensus-belief. And this applies even to the further reaches of speculative literary theory, as with that fashion for mystified readings of the Kantian sublime which offer a pretext for aestheticizing politics by imposing the maximum possible distance between issues of factual or historical truth and issues of ethico-political justice. On Lyotard's account, the UN as an embodiment of 'pure practical reason' would have nothing to say – no proper jurisdiction or real-world operative force – when it came to deciding upon the rights and wrongs of what actually occurred as a direct consequence of US policy decisions. Thus it would seem beside the point – a mere 'category-mistake' – to invoke those pre-war UN resolutions which required that sanctions be allowed a reasonable period in which to take effect, and then to observe that the US launched its all-out assault at a time when there existed plentiful evidence (much of it provided by Pentagon sources) that the blockade was already producing significant results, mainly by depriving the Iraqi military of access to spare parts and routine maintenance supplies.

Of course the line of argument changed overnight – and the 'relevant' facts and figures along with it – when the Bush administration opted for war and decided that sanctions had always been a hopeless (because simply 'unenforceable') strategy. Nor can one deny that there is still room for considerable differences of view as regards their likely effectiveness and the prospects that war might yet have been averted by adherence to the UN resolutions. Also there is the argument – on ethical grounds – that no matter what their military or logistical impact, sanctions were unjustified in so far as they inflicted hardship on the neediest sections of the Iraqi population, those who would be first to suffer (as always) when dwindling food and medical supplies were diverted for military consumption. But again, the point is *not* that such issues can be settled once and for all simply by establishing the facts of the case and then addressing the moral question on a basis of self-evident demonstrative truth. Rather, it is to make the more modest (but none the less crucial) claim: that we can't even begin to discuss these matters in a responsible fashion without on the one hand attempting to separate truth from falsehood, statements of fact from convenient propaganda ploys, and on the other trying to make sense of the ethical issues through a reasoned appeal to the best (most adequately documented) sources of information. And the same applies in the case of those specific UN resolutions whose content, relevance and practical bearing are very much open to debate, but which cannot be discussed to any purpose without invoking both factual and ethical criteria.[32] For otherwise we shall always wind up in the position – so eagerly embraced by Lyotard – of erecting the fact/value dichotomy into a high point of sceptical doctrine, and thus leaving criticism wholly bereft of valid argumentative grounds.

In his book *Critique of Cynical Reason* – first published in 1983 – Peter Sloterdijk offers by far the fullest and most shrewdly diagnostic account of this present-day postmodernist malaise. 'Cynicism is enlightened false consciousness', he writes. And again:

> it is that modernized, unhappy consciousness, on which enlightenment has laboured both successfully and in vain. It has learned its lessons in enlightenment, but it has not, and probably was not able to, put them into practice. Well-off and miserable at the same time, this consciousness no longer feels affected by any critique of ideology: its falseness is already reflexively buffered. . . . To act against better knowledge is today the global situation in the superstructure; it knows itself to be without illusions and yet to have been dragged down by the 'power of things'. Thus what is regarded in logic as a paradox and in literature as a joke appears in reality as the actual state of affairs. Thus emerges a new attitude of consciousness toward 'objectivity'. . . . With the passing of defiant hopes, the listlessness of egoisms pervades. In the new cynicism, a detached negativity comes through that scarcely allows itself any hope, at most a little irony and pity.[33]

The justice of these remarks is nowhere more strikingly (and depressingly) borne out than in Baudrillard's two essays on the Gulf War. And the point will not be lost on anyone who has thought about the 'politics of theory' in the context of recent (postmodern-pragmatist) developments on the intellectual scene. For there is, as I have argued, a clear continuinty between earlier 'end-of-ideology' doctrines and a movement of thought that makes a positive virtue of collapsing the truth/falsehood distinction and aestheticizing issues of ethics and politics to the point where they can only be handled by appeal to a mystified version of the Kantian sublime. Any hope of reversing this irrationalist trend must rest with those thinkers –

Habermas and Chomsky among them – who have defended the values of enlightened truth-seeking enquiry against the siren-calls of current intellectual fashion.

Of course this is not to say that the really important issues must always be engaged at an elevated level of philosophic argument where particular events (like the Gulf War and its aftermath) figure only as a source of handly illustrations with which to back up one's case. If my book can be read as in way endorsing such a topsy-turvy notion of moral and intellectual priorities then it has fallen straight back into the worst form of postmodern 'enlightened false consciousness'. For the main task ahead for historians of the Gulf War is to establish more precisely the facts of what happened, the extent of US/Allied complicity in presenting a false interpretation of events, and the long prehistory of Western endeavours to secure a balance of power in the region favourable to their own economic and policy interests. This process of critical assessment has already started and will no doubt gather pace – and accumulate evidence – as the post-war consensus begins to break down under the sheer weight of its perceived contradictions and falsehoods. Thus for instance Christopher Hitchens had a piece in *New Left Review* (March/April 1991) recounting various episodes from the squalid history of US double-dealing with Iraq, its neighbouring Gulf States, and the Kurdish and Shi'ite oppositional forces.[34] What his article brought out most vividly was the strange combination of incompetence, naivety and cynical *Realpolitik* that marked those dealings from the outset, especially in the period (the early 1970s) when Nixon and Kissinger established the pattern for subsequent bouts of interventionist plotting and high-level diplomatic intrigue. A knowledge of this background, Hitchens argued, was indispensable for reaching an informed estimate of current US strategic designs.

The following passage – one of many that might be cited – makes this case all the more pointedly by presenting the relevant (well-documented) facts and allowing the moral judgment to emerge as a scarcely controvertible upshot.

> The principal finding of the Pike Commission, in its study of US covert intervention in Iraq and Iran in the early 1970s, is a clue to a good deal of what has happened since. The committee members found, to their evident shock, the following: 'Documents clearly show that the President, Dr Kissinger and the foreign head of state [the Shah] hoped that our clients [the Kurds] would not prevail. They preferred

instead that the insurgents simply continue a level of hostilities sufficient to sap the resources of our ally's neighboring country [Iraq].' Official prose in Washington can possess a horror and immediacy of its own, as is shown by the sentence that follows: 'This policy was not imparted to our clients, who were encouraged to continue fighting'. 'Not *imparted*' to the desperate Kurdish villagers to whom Kissinger's envoys came with outstretched hands and practised grins. 'Not imparted', either, to the American public or to Congress. 'Imparted', though, to the Shah and to Saddam Hussein (then the Ba'athists' number-two man), who met and signed a treaty temporarily ending their border dispute in 1975 – thus restoring balance in the region. On that very day, all US aid to the Kurds was terminated – a decision that, of course, imparted itself to Hussein. On the next day he launched a search-and-destroy operation in Kurdistan that has been going on ever since and that, in the town of Halabja in 1988, made history by marking the first use of chemical weaponry by a state against its own citizens.[35]

In fact Hitchens' piece – or the major part of it – was written in December 1990, at a time when the outcome of US 'diplomacy' was still in some doubt, when the issue of war or negotiated settlement was as yet unresolved, and when the record of previous US interventionist designs provided at most a basis for informed conjecture. That his arguments received such a striking confirmation in light of subsequent events is a measure not only of Hitchens' critical acumen but of the way in which objective (real-world) probabilities can and should figure in the reading of relevant source-material. His postscript to the article (March 91) avoided any hint of triumphalist 'I-told-you-so' rhetoric while also – quite reasonably – making the point that the war and its aftermath might well have been predicted had commentators attended more closely to the documentary evidence. It thus offers a striking contrast with Baudrillard's attitude of high postmodernist disdain for the idea that truth has any role to play in the discourses surrounding a notional 'event' like the Gulf War. And more than anything it shows how enormous is the gap between cultural theory in its *soi-disant* 'radical' guise – the line running down from Nietzsche, via post-structuralism to a thinker like Baudrillard – and the interests of a genuinely critical discourse aimed toward exposing the sources and mechanisms of a massively distorted consensus ideology.

Perhaps Hegel was right in thinking that 'the Owl of Minerva takes wing at dusk', or that philosophers can never do more than give belated (albeit more articulate) expression to the impulses, tendencies and cultural life-forms that emerge from stage to stage in the progress of the world-historical *Zeitgeist*. Certainly this is the reading of Hegel that has found favour among the adepts of postmodern-pragmatist intellectual fashion.[36] After all, it is one fairly plausible way of construing that other Hegelian dictum which takes it as a matter of plain self-evidence that 'the real is the rational', or – as interpreted by Fish, Rorty *et al* – that any notion of truth at the end of enquiry necessarily winds up by equating 'truth' with what is 'good in the way of belief'. However, such arguments not only mistake Hegel's meaning but yield philosophy and criticism up to a style of 'post-ideological' consensus thinking which owns itself utterly without resources in the matter of distinguishing truth from falsehood, valid from invalid grounds of belief, or agreement arrived at through open argumentative debate from agreement imposed through the exercise of various (more or less coercive) rhetorical strategies. It is hardly surprising, in view of all this, that the softening-up of public opinion in preparation for war in the Gulf went along with a renewed publicity-drive on behalf of Fukuyama's 'end-of-history' thesis, his quasi-Hegelian claim that reality was now nothing other than the truth as perceived from the standpoint of a 'free-world' (US-dominated) outlook on geo-political developments. For this notion has long been the stock-in-trade of ideologues who seek to shore up support for some particularly bankrupt consensus-view by maintaining that the language of critical dissent – terms like 'history', 'truth', 'reason', 'critique' and 'ideology' itself – lacks any purchase in an epoch when the real *just is* what we make of it according to prevalent habits of thought and belief. That we have been here before (and 'the second time around as farce') is a thought that must have surely occurred to many readers struck as much by the vapid pretentiousness of Fukuyama's essay as by the quite extraordinary *succès d'estime* which it nonetheless enjoyed in US intellectual circles.

Let me end by citing another passage from Eagleton's book, one that asserts the continuing relevance of 'ideology' as a critical concept, not only in the specialized discourse of philosophy, criticism and the human sciences, but also at the point where theory comes up against the brute facticity of the thing. It is a passage whose relevance should not be lost on anyone who lived through those bad months (November 1990 to February 1991) when it became a matter of commonplace experience to attend a massive anti-war protest rally and then to be told – on the television news or in the papers next day – that the numbers were in fact fairly small, and in any case comprised very largely of 'fringe elements' with no real claim to represent any but a 'far left' dissident minority. As Eagleton remarks,

> no radical who takes a cool look at the tenacity and pervasiveness of dominant ideologies could possibly feel sanguine about what would be necessary to loosen their lethal grip. But there is one place above all where such forms of consciousness may be transformed almost literally overnight, and that is in active political struggle. This is not a Left piety but an empirical fact. When men and women engaged in quite modest, local forms of political resistance find themselves brought by the inner momentum of such conflicts into direct confrontation with the power of the state, it is possible that their political consciousness may be definitively, irreversibly altered. If a theory of ideology has value at all, it is in helping to illuminate the processes by which such liberation from death-dealing beliefs may be practically effected.[37]

Every word of this passage – from the plain-speaking idiom of 'empirical fact' to the sense of moral outrage conveyed by such phrases as 'lethal grip' and 'death-dealing beliefs' – will surely ring true to the experience of those who lived through the Gulf War and its routine extension by other (mass-media) suasive techniques. It seems to me that such events are the ultimate test of whether theory has anything useful to say, or whether it leads (as so often of late) to an attitude of downright cynical acquiescence which affords intellectuals their alternative role as purveyors of a 'post-ideological' consensus ideology.

Hence that ethos of 'enlightened false consciousness' whose advent coincided, punctually enough, with the first thoroughly 'postmodern' war and the first sustained exercise in full-scale media 'hyperreality'. But to treat these phenomena merely as signs of the times – or (on Baudrillard's account) as the truth for all that we can possibly know it – indicates a degree of intellectual and moral bad faith that cannot be redeemed by its occasional flashes of genuine diagnostic insight. If postmodernism is currently the name of the game in advanced theoretical circles then this should not be seen as somehow granting it privileged exemption from basic standards of argumentative truth and ethical accountability. As Douglas Kellner remarks, 'this view may be comforting to a "critical critic" in his Paris apartment who no longer wants to go out and do battle in the public sphere, but it will not help the millions being harmed, even killed, as a result of the domestic and foreign policies of the Reagans, Bushes, Thatchers, Bothas and Pinochets of the world'.[38] It is a harsh verdict but by no means unjustified if one considers how easily such 'radical' ideas can be enlisted as a source of argumentative back-up for current variations on the end-of-ideology thesis. Bad philosophy has often gone along with bad politics, as we should scarcely need reminding after the 'Heidegger affair' and kindred revelations. Postmodernism is bad philosophy on every count, not least – as I have argued – its uncritical adherence to a theory of language and representation whose extreme anti-realist or sceptical bias in the end gives rise to an outlook of thoroughgoing nihilism. That the Gulf War provided such a telling instance of our so-called 'postmodern condition' is reason enough to take stock of that condition on terms other than its own.

POSTSCRIPT

On 29 March 1991, shortly after the official cessation of hostilities, Baudrillard produced another essay, 'The Gulf War Has Not Taken Place', published in *Libération*. Considering what had happened in the interim it is remarkable indeed that Baudrillard found no reason to retract or significantly revise his original theses. Of course he acknowledges – albeit in passing – that this 'simulated' war has not been *entirely* a product of mass-media illusionist techniques; that large numbers of Iraqi conscripts and civilians had been killed by the Allied aerial bombardment; that massive damage had been inflicted on the country's urban infrastructure; that the so-called 'smart' or precision laser-guided bombs which figured so prominently in news coverage in fact made up a small fraction of the total Allied armoury, far outnumbered by the weapons of indiscriminate mass-destruction used against 'front-line' and other targets; that the US call for an internal insurrection that would 'finish the job' (i.e. put an end to Saddam's rule) and the subsequent failure to back that call with any measure of logistical or diplomatic support had created a catastrophe of appalling scale among the Kurdish and Shi'ite populations; that large areas of Kuwait had been laid waste by an Iraqi scorched-earth policy which the Western 'experts' had mostly discounted as an idle (because physically impossible) threat; and that US-Allied claims on a range of issues – from casualty figures to strategic interests, regional policy, aims for post-war 'reconstruction' etc – had been shown up as a propaganda package designed to head off domestic opposition.

All these points Baudrillard effectively concedes, along with several others (e.g. the extent and influence of media disinformation) which might seem to mark a decisive shift on the question of whether the war had indeed 'taken place'. But no: he sticks to his original position, declaring it a species of mass-hallucination, a 'virtual' engagement played out in the absence of anything that corresponded to a genuine 'war' as hitherto known or experienced. For this was a conflict where the massive imbalance of forces meant that the outcome was never in doubt; where the Allied and Iraqi strategies were so utterly disparate as to make comparisons (or talk of 'victory') beside the point; where the combatants occupied different worlds of time and space, different orders of 'reality' created – at least on the US side – by a hyperreal technology preventing any sense of direct, 'face-to-face' contact; where 'advance' and 'retreat' were meaningless terms, given the absence of any real terrain (as apart from the simulated war-game scenarios) by which to measure such claims; and where Saddam's 'defeat' turned out to be a mode of shrewdly timed strategic withdrawal, a move whose consequence (the deployment of his best-equipped troops against the Kurdish and Shi'ite internal opposition) amounted to a moral and political defeat for the Allies and their management of post-war public opinion. All of which Baudrillard takes as confirming his initial hypothesis: that this would be a fictive or fabulous war, a conflict of rival imaginary realms in which the stakes were unamenable to any analysis in real-world, rational, truth-seeking terms.

His essay concludes with the following remarks, aimed squarely at those readers who might be so naive as to think that his predictions had been somehow falsified by the event. 'In the case of this war', he writes,

it is a matter of the vivid illustration of an implacable logic, one that renders us incapable of envisaging any other hypothesis save that of its real occurrence. The realist logic that lives off the illusion of a final outcome. . . . [For] the final solution of an equation as complex as a war is never to be found in the evidence of the war itself. It is a matter of grasping, without prophetic illusions, the logic of subsequently unfolding events. To be 'for' or 'against' the war is idiotic if one doesn't give a moment's thought to the probability of this war, its credibility, its realist credentials. All ideological or political speculations amount to a form of mental deterrence (stupidity). Through their immediate consensus on the evidence they heighten the unreality of this war, they reinforce the bluff by their unwitting readiness to be duped.

The true belligerents are those who thrive on the ideology of the truth of this war, despite the fact that the war itself exerts its ravages on another level, through faking, through hyperreality, the simulacrum, through all those strategies of psychological deterrence that make play with facts and images, with the precession of the virtual over the real, of virtual time over real time, and the inexorable confusion between the two. If we have no practical knowledge of this war – and such knowledge is out of the question – then let us at least have the sceptical

intelligence to reject the probability of all information, of all images
whatever their source. To be more 'virtual' than the events themselves,
not to reestablish some criterion of truth – for this we lack the means.
But at least we can avoid being dupes and, to this end, reimmerse
(*replonger*) all that information and the war itself into the element of
virtuality from which they took rise. To turn deterrence back against
itself. To be metereologically sensitive to stupidity in all its forms.[2]

One could scarcely wish for a clearer statement of the moral and
political nihilism that follows from Baudrillard's far-out sceptical
stance on matters of truth and falsehood. Of course there is a need to
question immediate appearances, to doubt what is proferred in the way
of 'on-the-spot' evidence, and always to allow that the unfolding of
subsequent events – like those in Kurdistan – may necessitate a
large-scale adjustment in our view of what actually occurred (or was
envisaged all along) behind the smokescreen of propaganda coverage.
But we can only be in a position to make such judgments if we
continue to seek out the best available sources of information, and
moreover to interpret that evidence according to the standards of
veridical utterance, of enlightened participant debate, and of
ethico-political accountability. On Baudrillard's view these ideas are
just a species of intellectual and moral 'stupidity', a failure to grasp that
the Gulf War was unreal (or 'virtual') through and through, and that
anyone thinking to discuss it in terms of truth *versus* falsehood – or
reality *versus* 'ideological' illusion – is committing the greatest
stupidity of all, one that plays straight into the hands of those with an
interest in maintaining such delusive ontological distinctions. If there is
any effective power of resistance then it will only come about – as he
argues in *Fatal Strategies* – when 'the masses' evince such a total
indifference to issues of media truth and falsehood that the whole
apparatus of public-opinion management collapses into manifest
nonsense.[3]

At this point notions like 'truth', 'ideology' and 'critique' will have
lost their old power to hold the intellectuals in thrall, as well as their
other, socially legitimizing function: that of convincing the populace at
large that there *is* (must be) some ultimate reality behind appearances,
and that truth will surely come to light in the long run, whatever the
extent of current mass-media disinformation. For it is this belief – as
Baudrillard sees it – that prevents 'the masses' (i.e. the captive TV
viewers, tabloid readers, opinion-poll respondents etc) from

perceiving the enormous confidence-trick that has been practised in the name of a liberal democracy where 'truth' is defined purely and simply according to current consensual norms. To this extent the Gulf War was merely an extravagant example of what has long been the case with regard to our reliance on information-sources with not the least semblance of 'authentic' truth-telling warrant. So the best – indeed the only – lesson to be learned from it is the need to exercise a 'sceptical intelligence' that refuses to be taken in *not* by 'appearances' (since appearances are all we have), but by the thought that there exists a truth 'behind' appearances, a level of rock-bottom factual appeal and ethical responsibility which may yet be invoked by investigative journalists, critical intellectuals, and others with a principled interest in exposing the extent of mass-media complicity. Such ideas made sense – as Baudrillard implicitly concedes – during that period when wars were conducted in the 'real' time and space of a battlefield encounter where talk of 'victory', of advance and retreat, of tactical superiority and so forth could at least be gauged against the evidence supplied by first-hand (or front-line) sources. But in the Gulf War no such standards could possibly apply since combatants, strategists, politicians, commentators, readers and viewers alike were all locked into a gigantic simulation-machine which programmed their every last thought and perception.

The result, in Baudrillard's sublimely offensive simile, is much like that of the air-burst bombs which the Americans deployed to such appalling effect against large concentrations of Iraqi soldiers and other (unspecified) targets. For the saturation coverage through channels like CNN had this much in common with the saturation bombing: that it produced, in his words,

> an unbearable atmosphere of deception and stupidity. . . . And if people were vaguely aware of having been caught up in this surfeit (*assouvissement*) and this illusory yet undeluding play of images, still they revelled in this deception and remained fascinated by the evident staging of this war, an effect with which [or to which] we were innoculated by every means, through our eyes, through our senses, through discourse. . . . In the Gulf, no matter what (*rien de tel*), it was as if the outcome had been devoured in advance by a parasitic virus, the retro-virus of history. This is why one could offer the hypothesis that this war would not have taken place. And now that it is over, one can finally take account of its non-occurrence (*on peut enfin se rendre compte qu'elle n'a pas eu lieu*).[4]

One is tempted to treat all this – in Dr. Johnson's phrase – as a piece of 'unresisting imbecility' to which it would be wasted effort to return any kind of rational rejoinder. But whatever their provocative or mischievous intent, Baudrillard's 'arguments' have generated widespread discussion and have been taken seriously by a sufficient number of commentators to require something more than a knock-down commonsensical riposte, like Johnson's celebrated kicking of the stone to 'refute' the claims of Berkeleian transcendental idealism. In fact this analogy is very much to the point since Berkeley's position has a good deal in common with Baudrillard's stance of thoroughgoing cognitive and epistemological scepticism. In both cases the most effective response is one that goes by way of that critical tradition whose first major spokesman was Kant, and whose later representatives (from Marx to Habermas) have sustained the project of enlightened *Ideologiekritik*, whatever their undoubted differences of view as regards the best means of so doing. One measure of postmodernism's retrograde stance – its intellectual and political bankruptcy – is the way that its proponents have either (like Lyotard) misread certain crucial passages in Kant, especially those concerning the sublime, or otherwise (like Baudrillard) consigned the whole legacy of critical-emancipatory thought to the dustbin of outworn 'Enlightenment' ideas. His Gulf War articles should be enough to settle any remaining doubts on that score.

REFERENCES

1 Baudrillard and the War that Never Happened

1. Jean Baudrillard, 'The Reality Gulf', *The Guardian*, 11 January 1991.
2. See for instance Mark Poster (ed), *Jean Baudrillard: selected writings* (Cambridge: Polity Press, 1989); also Baudrillard, *America* (London: Verso, 1988), *Fatal Strategies* (London: Pluto Press, 1989), *On Seduction* (London: Macmillan, 1990), *Revenge of the Crystal: a Baudrillard Reader* (London: Pluto Press, 1990).
3. Christopher Norris, 'Lost in the Funhouse: Baudrillard and the politics of postmodernism', in *What's Wrong with Postmodernism: critical theory and the ends of philosophy* (Hemel Hempstead: Harvester-Wheatsheaf and Baltimore: Johns Hopkins University Press, 1990), pp. 164-93. See also Alex Callinicos, *Against Postmodernism: a Marxist critique* (Cambridge: Polity Press, 1989); David Harvey, *The Condition of Postmodernity: an enquiry into the origins of cultural change* (Oxford: Basil Blackwell, 1989); Hilary Lawson and Lisa Appignanesi (eds), *Dismantling Truth: reality in the postmodern world* (London: Weidenfeld and Nicolson, 1989); Douglas Kellner, *Jean Baudrillard: from Marxism to Postmodernism and beyond* (Cambridge: Polity Press, 1989) and John McGowan, *Postmodernism and its Critics* (Ithaca, NY.: Cornell University Press, 1991).
4. See especially Richard Rorty, *Consequences of Pragmatism* (Minneapolis: University of Minnesota Press, 1982) and *Contingency, Irony, and Solidarity* (Cambridge: Cambridge University Press, 1989); also Stanley Fish, *Doing What Comes Naturally: change, rhetoric, and the practice of theory in literary and legal studies* (Oxford: Clarendon Press, 1989).
5. For further discussion of these ideas from a range of more-or-less critical viewpoints, see Derek Attridge, Geoff Bennington and Robert Young (eds), *Post-Structuralism and the Question of History* (Cambridge: Cambridge University Press, 1987); also Perry Anderson, *In the Tracks of Historical Materialism* (London: Verso, 1983); Catherine Belsey, *Critical Practice* (London: Methuen, 1980); Tony Bennett, *Outside Literature* (London: Routledge, 1991); Terry Eagleton, *Ideology: an introduction* (London: Verso, 1991); John Frow, *Marxism and Literary History* (Cambridge, Mass.: Harvard University Press, 1986); Ernesto Laclau and Chantal Mouffe, *Hegemony and Socialist Strategy: towards a radical democratic politics* (London: Verso, 1985); Christopher Norris, *Deconstruction and the Interests of Theory* (London: Pinter Publishers, 1988); and Michael Ryan,

Marxism and Deconstruction: a critical articulation (Baltimore: Johns Hopkins University Press, 1982).

6. See for instance Michel Foucault, *Power/Knowledge: selected interviews and other writings* (Hemel Hempstead: Harvester-Wheatsheaf, 1980) and D.F. Bouchard and S. Simon (eds) *Language, Counter-Memory, Practice*, (Oxford: Basil Blackwell, 1977); also H. Aram Veeser (ed), *The New Historicism* (London: Routledge, 1989) and Stephen Greenblatt, *Shakespearean Negotiations: the circulation of social energy in Renaissance England* (Berkeley and Los Angeles: University of California Press, 1988).

7. See particularly Norris, *Derrida* (London: Fontana, 1987) and *Deconstruction and the Interests of Theory (op cit)*.

8. These points are made most emphatically in Derrida's 'Afterword: toward an ethic of discussion', *Limited Inc* (Evanston, Ill.: Northwestern University Press, 1989), pp. 111-60.

9. Jacques Derrida, *Of Grammatology* (Baltimore: Johns Hopkins University Press, 1976), p. 158.

10. See Norris, 'Limited Think: how *not* to read Derrida', in *What's Wrong with Postmodernism (op cit)*, pp. 134-63.

11. See for instance John R. Searle, 'Reiterating the Differences', *Glyph*, Vol. I (Baltimore: Johns Hopkins University Press, 1977) and Jürgen Habermas, *The Philosophical Discourse of Modernity: twelve lectures* (Cambridge: Polity Press, 1987).

12. Richard Rorty, 'Philosophy as a Kind of Writing', in *Consequences of Pragmatism (op cit)*, pp. 90-109. See also Norris, 'Philosophy as *Not* just a "Kind of Writing": Derrida and the claim of reason', in Reed Way Dasenbrock (ed), *Re-Drawing the Lines: analytic philosophy, deconstruction, and literary theory* (Minneapolis: University of Minnesota Press, 1989), pp. 189-203 and Rorty, 'Two Meanings of "Logocentrism": a reply to Norris', *Ibid*, pp. 204-16.

13. See Norris, 'Limited Think' *(op cit)*.

14. See references to Foucault and the New Historicism above; also Hayden White, *Tropics of Discourse* (Baltimore: Johns Hopkins University Press, 1978) and *The Content of the Form* (Johns Hopkins, 1988).

15. Tony Bennett, *Outside Literature (op cit)*, p. 280.

16. See Norris, 'Postmodernizing History: right-wing revisionism and the uses of theory', *Southern Review* (Adelaide), Vol. XXI, No. 2 (July 1988), pp. 123-40; also Norris, 'Introduction: criticism, history and the politics of theory', in *What's Wrong with Postmodernism (op cit)*, pp. 1-48.

17. Baudrillard, *America (op cit)*.

18. Judith Williamson, 'It's mad bad Saddam vs the Scudbusters', *The Guardian*, 31 January 1991, p. 21.

19. See Raymond Tallis, *Not Saussure* (London: Macmillan, 1988) and *In Defence of Realism* (London: Edward Arnold, 1988) for a cogently argued

critique of these ideas; also Terry Eagleton, *Ideology: an introduction (op cit)* and Raman Selden, *Criticism and Objectivity* (London: Allen & Unwin, 1984).

20. Anderson, *In the Tracks of Historical Materialism (op cit)*; see also Norris, *The Contest of Faculties: philosophy and theory after deconstruction* (London: Methuen, 1985).
21. See Ferdinand de Saussure, *Course in General Linguistics* (London: Fontana, 1974).
22. Gottlob Frege, 'On Sense and Reference', in Max Black and P.T. Geach (eds), *Translations from the Philosophical Writings of Gottlob Frege* (Oxford: Basil Blackwell, 1952), pp. 56-78; see also Norris, 'Sense, Reference and Logic', in *The Contest of Faculties (op cit)*, pp. 47-69.
23. See my discussion of this work in *The Contest of Faculties* and *Deconstruction and the Interests of Theory (op cit)*.
24. See for instance Stephen Bann, *The Clothing of Clio: a study of the representation of history in nineteenth-century Britain and France* (Cambridge: Cambridge University Press, 1984); Arthur C. Danto, *Analytical Philosophy of History* (Cambridge: Cambridge University Press, 1965); W.B. Gallie, *Philosophy and Historical Understanding* (London: Chatto and Windus, 1964); Peter Gay, *Style in History* (London: Chatto and Windus, 1975).
25. Roy Bhaskar, *Scientific Realism and Human Emancipation* (London: Verso, 1986) and *Reclaiming Reality: a critical introduction to modern philosophy* (London: Verso, 1989). See also Bhaskar's book-length critique of Richard Rorty in *Philosophy and the Idea of Freedom* (Oxford: Basil Blackwell, 1991).
26. See especially Jürgen Habermas, *The Philosophical Discourse of Modernity (op cit)*; also Peter Dews, *Logics of Disintegration: post-structuralist thought and the claims of theory* (London: Verso, 1987) and – from a somewhat different but related viewpoint – Gillian Rose, *Dialectic of Nihilism: post-structuralism and law* (Oxford: Basil Blackwell, 1980).
27. For a powerfully-argued critique of this tendency among Derrida's 'literary' disciples, see Rodolphe Gasché, *The Tain of the Mirror: Derrida and the philosophy of reflection* (Cambridge, Mass.: Harvard University Press, 1986).
28. See especially the essays collected in Derrida, *Margins of Philosophy* (Chicago: University of Chicago Press, 1982).
29. For an example of such arguments pushed to their absurdist (post-everything) extreme, see Gilles Deleuze and Félix Guattari, *Anti-Oedipus* (New York: Viking, 1977) and *A Thousand Plateaus* (Minneapolis: University of Minnesota Press, 1987).
30. See Foucault, *Power/Knowledge (op cit)*.
31. See especially Edward Said, *Orientalism* (New York: Pantheon Books,

1978) and *The World, the Text, and the Critic* (Cambridge, Mass.: Harvard University Press, 1983).

2 Deconstruction versus Postmodernism

1. See Norris, *Derrida* (London: Fontana, 1987) for a reading that situates his work in relation to this broadly Kantian tradition of thought.
2. For a detailed bibliography of writings on Derrida, see Norris, *Deconstruction: theory and practice* (2nd edn., London: Routledge, 1991); also Geoffrey Bennington, *Jacques Derrida* (Paris: Seuil, 1991) and Peggy Kamuf (ed), *A Derrida Reader: between the blinds* (Hemel Hempstead: Harvester-Wheatsheaf, 1991).
3. Rorty, 'Nineteenth-Century Idealism and Twentieth-Century Textualism', in *Consequences of Pragmatism (op cit)*, pp. 139-59.
4. See Rorty, 'Philosophy as a Kind of Writing', in *Consequences of Pragmatism* (Minneapolis: University of Minnesota Press, 1982), pp. 90-109.
5. Rorty, 'Deconstruction and Circumvention', *Critical Inquiry*, Vol. XI (1987), pp. 1-23.
6. Peggy Kamuf's *A Derrida Reader (op cit)* contains a good representative selection of these later writings.
7. Derrida, *Limited Inc* (2nd edn., Evanston, Ill.: Northwestern University Press, 1989).
8. Derrida, 'The Principle of Reason: the university in the eyes of its pupils', *Diacritics*, Vol. XIII, No. 3 (1983), pp. 3-20.
9. Derrida, *Limited Inc (op cit)*, p. 146.
10. *Ibid*, p. 146.
11. *Ibid*, p. 122.
12. *Ibid*, p. 153.
13. Jürgen Habermas, *The Philosophical Discourse of Modernity* (Cambridge: Polity Press, 1987)
14. Derrida, *Limited Inc (op cit)*, p. 141.
15. Derrida, 'White Mythology: metaphor in the text of philosophy', in *Margins of Philosophy* (Chicago: University of Chicago Press, 1982), pp. 207-71; also 'The *retrait* of metaphor', *Enclitic*, Vol. II, No 2 (Fall 1978).
16. Derrida, *Limited Inc (op cit)*, p. 134.
17. *Ibid*, p. 150.
18. J. Fisher Solomon, *Discourse and Reference in the Nuclear Age* (Norman, Okl.: University of Oklahoma Pres, 1988).
19. Derrida, 'No Apocalypse, Not Now (full speed ahead, seven missiles, seven missives)', *Diacritics*, Vol. XIV, No. 2 (Summer 1984), pp. 20-31.
20. *Ibid*, p. 22.
21. *Ibid*, p. 24.

22. *Ibid*, p. 24.
23. See my discussion of these various kindred developments in Norris, 'On Not Going Relativist (where it counts): deconstruction and "Convention T" ', in *The Contest of Faculties* (London: Methuen, 1985), pp. 193-217.
24. For arguments against this conventionalist or anti-realist position, see for instance Anthony Appiah, *For Truth in Semantics* (Oxford: Basil Blackwell, 1986); Hilary Putnam, *Reason, Truth and History* (Cambridge: Cambridge University Press, 1981); Gerald Vision, *Modern Anti-Realism and Manufactured Truth* (London: Routledge, 1988); and Crispin Wright, *Realism, Meaning and Truth* (Oxford: Blackwell, 1987).
25. Solomon, *Discourse and Reference (op cit)*, p. 29.
26. *Ibid*, p. 104.
27. Aristotle, *De Interpretatione* (Oxford: Clarendon Press, 1928). Passage cited in Solomon, *op cit*, p. 28.
28. Solomon, *op cit*, p. 28
29. *Ibid*, p. 31.
30. *Ibid*, p. 31.
31. Derrida, 'No Apocalypse, Not Now' *(op cit)*, p. 23.
32. *Ibid*, p. 27
33. *Ibid*, p. 27
34. See the special number of *Diacritics* (Vol. XIV, No 2: Summer 1984) which contained Derrida's essay and other pieces on the topic of 'nuclear criticism'.
35. Derrida, 'The Principle of Reason' *(op cit)*, p. 20.
36. Derrida, 'No Apocalypse, Not Now' *(op cit)*, p. 30.
37. *Ibid*, p. 29.
38. *Ibid*, p. 29.
39. *Ibid*, p. 26.
40. For a latterday defence of these Kantian principles, see Jürgen Habermas, *Knowledge and Human Interests* (London: Heinemann, 1972); also Peter Uwe Hohendahl, *The Institution of Criticism* (Ithaca, NY: Cornell University Press, 1982) and Terry Eagleton, *The Function of Criticism* (London: Verso, 1984).
41. See Jean-Francois Lyotard, *The Differend: phrases in dispute* (Manchester: Manchester University Press, 1988).
42. See Immanuel Kant, *Critique of Judgement* (London: Oxford University Press, repr. 1978).
43. See especially Derrida, 'Parergon', in *The Truth in Painting* (Chicago: University of Chicago Press, 1987), pp. 15-147; also 'Economimesis' *Diacritics*, Vol. XI, No 2 (1981), pp. 3-25.
44. Derrida, 'No Apocalypse, Not Now' *(op. cit)*, p. 23
45. *Ibid*, p. 24.

3 How the Real World Became a Fable

1. Tony Bennett, *Outside Literature* (London: Routledge, 1991), p. 54.
2. See especially Pierre Macherey, *A Theory of Literary Production* (London: Routledge, 1978) and Terry Eagleton, *Criticism and Ideology* (London: New Left Books, 1976).
3. See my references to Baudrillard's more recent works in the Notes to Chapter One, above.
4. See for instance Gregory Currie, *The Nature of Fiction* (Cambridge: Cambridge University Press, 1990).
5. See especially Thomas Pavel, *Fictional Worlds* (Harvard, Mass.: Harvard University Press, 1987); also David Lewis, *On the Plurality of Worlds* (Oxford: Basil Blackwell, 1986) and – from a different angle – Michael Riffaterre, *Fictional Truth* (Baltimore: Johns Hopkins University Press, 1990).
6. Currie, *op cit*, pp. 47-8.
7. *Ibid*, p. 47
8. *Ibid*, p. 48
9. *Ibid*, p. 46
10. Thucydides, *The Peloponnesian War*, T.E. Wick (ed) (New York: Modern Library, 1982), p. 13.
11. *Ibid*, p. 14. Cited by Solomon, *Discourse and Reference in the Nuclear Age* (Norman, Okl.: University of Oklahoma Press, 1988), p. 43.
12. Solomon, *op cit*, pp. 46-7
13. See *War and Peace News* (Milton Keynes: Open University Press/ Glasgow University Media Group, 1985) for analysis of press and television bias in the coverage of war and anti-war protest campaigns; also John Pilger, 'Alternative Reality: why don't we hear about what is happening in the Gulf?', *New Statesman*, 29 May 1991, pp. 8-9.
14. For an attempt to sift the truth from these conflicting accounts, see John Simpson, *From the House of War: John Simpson in the Gulf* (London: Arrow Books, 1991), pp. 328-31. Despite its scrupulous even-handedness, Simpson's book leaves no doubt of the lies that were told – with varying degrees of media compliance – in order to conceal the true scale and horrific detail of Iraqi casualties.
15. See Andrew Whitley, 'Kuwait: the last forty-eight hours', *New York Review of Books*, Vol. XXXVIII, No 10 (30 May 1991), pp. 17-8.
16. Lyotard, *The Differend (op cit)*.
17. Michael Ignatieff, 'Back to Reality on the Home Front', *The Observer*, 3 March 1991, p. 21. See also his subsequent *Observer* articles (e.g. 'Triumphalists Take Sweet Revenge', 10 March 1991, p. 27) for signs of Ignatieff's (entirely creditable) willingness to shift ground in response to the unfolding catastrophe in Iraq and Kuwait.

18. See especially Richard Rorty, *Contingency, Irony, and Solidarity* (Cambridge: Cambridge University Press, 1989) and Stanley Fish, *Doing What Comes Naturally: change, rhetoric, and the practice of theory in literary and legal studies* (Oxford: Clarendon Press, 1989).
19. See Rorty, 'Dewey's Metaphysics', in *Consequences of Pragmatism* (Minneapolis: University of Minnesota Press, 1982), pp. 72-89.
20. For details of this episode, see Alan B. Spitzer, 'John Dewey, the "Trial" of Leon Trotsky, and the Search for Historical Truth', in *History and Theory*, Vol. XXIX (1990), pp. 16-37.
21. See William James, 'Remarks at the Peace Banquet' and 'The Moral Equivalent of War' (excerpts), in Margaret Knight, *William James* (Harmondsworth: Penguin, 1950), pp. 240-8; also Frank Lentricchia, *Ariel and the Police: William James, Wallace Stevens, Michel Foucault* (Hemel Hempstead: Harvester-Wheatsheaf, 1988).
22. Tony Bennett, *Outside Literature (op cit)*, pp. 280-1
23. See Rorty, *Contingency, Irony, and Solidarity (op cit)*.
24. Daniel Bell, *The End of Ideology* (Glencoe, Ill., 1960); see also Robert E. Lane, *Political Ideology: why the American believes what he does* (New York: Free Press, 1962).
25. See for instance Francis Fukuyama, 'The End of History', *The National Interest*, Summer 1989; also – on the Gulf War and its consequences – Fukuyama, 'Changed Days for Ruritania's Dictator', *The Guardian*, 8 April 1991, p. 19.
26. On this topic see David Hoy, *The Critical Circle: literature and history in contemporary hermeneutics* (Berkeley and Los Angeles: University of California Press, 1978) and Richard E. Palmer, *Hermeneutics* (Evanston, Ill.: Northwestern University Press, 1980).
27. This point is made most effectively in Jürgen Habermas, *Moral Consciousness and Communicative Action* (Cambridge: Polity Press, 1990).

4 From the Sublime to the Absurd

1. As I write *The Guardian* carries details of a Greenpeace report which estimates total casualties in the Gulf War at over 150,000. Of these, between 5 and 15,000 are thought to have been Iraqi civilians killed by the aerial bombardment; 2-5,000 Kuwaitis killed either under Iraqi occupation or as a result of the war; between 15 and 30,000 'Kurds and other displaced persons [who] have died in refugee camps and on the road'; 4 to 16,000 Iraqis who have 'died of disease or starvation since the war ended'; and by far the greatest number (up to 120,000) Iraqi troops – mostly conscripts – killed during the US-Allied offensive. There were also, according to this report, some 20,000 Iraqis who died 'in the month-long civil war set off by

the Kurdish and Shi'ite rebellions against President Saddam Hussein' [encouraged, one should add, by George Bush and John Major, then abandoned to their fate with the subsequent switch of US strategic priorities]. For the rest: '343 allied troops died in combat and accidents, among them 266 Americans, of whom 145 were killed in action'.

The article ends by noting some additional points of detail: that '30,000 more refugees and Iraqis are estimated to have died of disease, lack of medical care, and malnutrition since the [Greenpeace] report was compiled', and that 'the ratio of Iraqi deaths to allied explosives was the most "efficient" in modern history – an average of more than one Iraqi killed for every ton of explosives dropped by allied planes'. (*The Guardian*, 30 May 1991, p. 9). None of which prevented the staging in Washington and New York of a massive victory parade – officially an 'act of commemoration' – where the few protestors were subject to police harrassment and violent abuse from outraged flag-waving citizens. These events took place in early June 1991, at a time when the above facts and figures were available to anyone who wanted to know, and when even the popular press and TV channels had for weeks been presenting graphic evidence of the catastrophe visited on the Kurdish and Shi'ite populations. The obscenity of this spectacle was hardly diminished by the close-up shots of President Bush choking back the tears as he thanked God and America for the triumph of right over might.

2. See Lyotard, *The Differend (op cit)*, p. 3 and *passim*.
3. *Ibid*, p. 9.
4. Geoffrey Bennington, *Lyotard: writing the event* (Manchester: Manchester University Press, 1988), p. 148.
5. Lyotard, *The Differend (op cit)*, p. 19.
6. Immanuel Kant, *Critique of Judgement* (London: Oxford University Press, repr. 1978).
7. Lyotard, *The Differend*, p. 13.
8. *Ibid*, p. 168.
9. *Ibid*, p. 18.
10. *Ibid*, p. 19.
11. *Ibid*, p. 179.
12. *Ibid*, p. 168.
13. *Ibid*, p. 169.
14. See Norris, *What's Wrong with Postmodernism* (Hemel Hempstead: Harvester-Wheatsheaf and Baltimore: Johns Hopkins University Press, 1990) for further commentary on this postmodern reading of the Kantian sublime.
15. Lyotard, *The Differend (op cit)*, p. 169.
16. *Ibid*, p. 13.
17. *Ibid*, p. 19.

18. *Ibid*, p. 48.
19. *Ibid*, p. 49.
20. *Ibid*, p. 50.
21. *Ibid*, p. 46.
22. See Walter Benjamin, 'The Work of Art in the Age of Mechanical Reproduction', in Hannah Arendt (ed) *Illuminations*, (London: Fontana, 1973), pp. 219-53, p. 244; also Paul de Man, *The Resistance to Theory* (Minneapolis: University of Minnesota Press, 1986).
23. See Immanuel Kant, *Critique of Practical Reason* (Indianapolis: Bobbs Merrill, 1975).
24. See for instance Alasdair MacIntyre, *After Virtue: a study in moral theory* (London: Duckworth, 1981) and Bernard Williams, *Ethics and the Limits of Philosophy* (London: Fontana, 1985).
25. Habermas, *Moral Consciousness and Communicative Action (op cit)*, p. 204.
26. See particularly Lyotard, *The Postmodern Condition: a report on knowledge* (Minneapolis: University of Minnesota Press, 1983).
27. Lyotard, *The Differend*, (*op cit*), p. 158.
28. *Ibid*, p. 159.
29. *Ibid*, p. 18-19.
30. *Ibid*, p. 19.

5 Alternative Resources: against postmodernism

1. See for instance some of the essays in *Diacritics*, Vol. XIV, No 2 (1984), a special issue devoted to the topic of 'nuclear criticism'. (See also my discussion in Chapter One, above.)
2. Ferdinand de Saussure, *Course in General Linguistics* (London: Fontana, 1974).
3. Roland Barthes, *S/Z* (London: Jonathan Cape, 1975); see also Catherine Belsey, *Critical Practice* (London: Methuen, 1980) and Colin MacCabe, *James Joyce and the 'Revolution of the Word'* (London: Macmillan, 1978).
4. Roland Barthes, 'The Reality Effect', in Tzvetan Todorov (ed), *French Literary Theory Today* and 'The Discourse of History', in Michael Lane (ed), *Structuralism: a reader* (London: Jonathan Cape, 1970); also Hayden White, *Tropics of Discourse* (Baltimore: Johns Hopkins University Press, 1978) and *The Content of the Form* (Johns Hopkins, 1988).
5. See for instance Robert H. Canary and Henry Rozicki (eds), *The Writing of History: literary form and historical understanding* (Madison, Wisc.: University of Wisconsin Press, 1978). See also my notes to Chapter One (above) for further relevant material.
6. Tony Bennett, *Outside Literature (op cit)*, p. 55.
7. *Ibid*, pp. 54-5.

8. *Ibid*, pp. 56-7.

9. J. Fisher Solomon, *Discourse and Reference in the Nuclear Age* (Norman, Okl.: University of Oklahoma Press, 1988).

10. *Ibid*, p. 46.

11. See J. Hillis Miller, *The Ethics of Reading* (New York: Columbia University Press, 1987); also Miller, *Theory Now and Then* (Hemel Hempstead: Harvester-Wheatsheaf, 1991), pp. 295-393.

12. Michel Foucault, *The Order of Things: an archaeology of the human sciences* (London: Tavistock, 1970).

13. See also Richard Rorty, 'Nineteenth-Century Idealism and Twentieth-Century Textualism', in *Consequences of Pragmatism* (Minneapolis: University of Minnesota Press, 1982), pp. 139-59.

14. Miller, *The Ethics of Reading (op cit)*, p. 24.

15. *Ibid*, p. 4.

16. *Ibid*, p. 4.

17. Richard Klein and William B. Warner, 'Nuclear Coincidence and the Korean Airline Disaster', *Diacritics*, Vol. XVI, No 1 (Spring 1986), pp. 2-21. See also Oliver Chubb, *KAL Flight 007: the hidden story* (Sag Harbor, New York: The Permanent Press, 1985); Alexander Dallin, *Black Box: KAL 007 and the superpowers* (Berkeley and Los Angeles: University of California Press, 1985); and Murray Sayle, 'KAL 007: a conspiracy of coincidences', *New York Review of Books*, 25 April 1985.

18. See W.V.O Quine, *Word and Object* (Cambridge, Mass.: M.I.T. Press, 1960) and *'Ontological Relativity' and Other Essays* (New York: Columbia University Press, 1969). As applied to literary texts, Roland Barthes' *S/Z (op cit)* remains the most brilliant (and most likely unrepeatable) achievement in this curious genre.

19. Gregory Currie, *The Nature of Fiction* (Cambridge: Cambridge University Press, 1990), pp. 4-5.

20. See for instance Noam Chomsky, *American Power and the New Mandarins* (Harmondsworth: Penguin, 1969); *At War with Asia* (New York: Pantheon Books, 1970); *For Reasons of State* (New York: Pantheon, 1973); *The Fateful Triangle: the United States, Israel and the Palestinians* (Boston: South End Press, 1983); *On Power and Ideology* (Boston: South End Press, 1987); *Language and Politics* (Montreal: Black Rose Books, 1988); with Edward S. Herman, *The Political Economy of Human Rights* (Boston: South End Press, 1979); and *Manufacturing Consent: the political economy of the mass media* (New York: Pantheon Books, 1988). For his view of the Gulf War and its aftermath in relation to Bush's 'New World Order', see Chomsky, 'The Weak Shall Inherit Nothing', *The Guardian*, 25 March 1991, p. 19.

21. Chomsky, *Cartesian Linguistics* (New York: Harper and Row, 1966).

22. Chomsky, *Problems of Knowledge and Freedom* (New York: Pantheon,

1971); *Language and Mind* (New York: Harcourt, 1972); *Reflections on Language* (New York, Pantheon, 1975); *Language and Responsibility* (New York: Pantheon, 1979); *Language and Problems of Knowledge* (Cambridge, Mass.: M.I.T. Press, 1988).

23. See especially the essays and interviews collected in Chomsky, *Language and Politics (op cit)*; also Joshua Cohen and Joel Rogers, 'Knowledge, Morality and Hope: the social thought of Noam Chomsky', *New Left Review*, No. 187 (May/June 1991), pp. 5-27.

24. 'Noam Chomsky and Michel Foucault: Human Nature, Justice *versus* Power', in Fons Elders (ed), *Reflexive Waters: the basic concerns of mankind* (London: Souvenir Press, 1974), pp. 133-97.

25. See especially Michel Foucault, *Power/Knowledge: selected interviews and other writings* (Brighton: Harvester, 1980).

26. Chomsky, *Manufacturing Consent (op cit)*, p. xi.

27. *Ibid*, pp. xiv-xv.

28. *Ibid*, p. 300.

29. See Foucault, *Power/Knowledge (op cit)*.

30. Foucault, *The Order of Things (op cit)*.

31. Chomsky, *Manufacturing Consent (op cit)*, p. 304.

32. *Ibid*, pp. 304-5.

33. *Ibid*, p. xii.

34. *Ibid*, p. 305.

35. *Ibid*, p. 298.

36. *Ibid*, p. 298.

37. Dick Hebdige, 'Bombing Logic', *Marxism Today*, March 1991, p. 46.

6   The 'End of Ideology' Revisited

1. See Rorty, *Contingency, Irony, and Solidarity* and Fish, *Doing What Comes Naturally (op cit)*.

2. On this shift of political ground between the 'old' and 'new' varieties of pragmatist thought, see Frank Lentricchia, *Ariel and the Police: William James, Wallace Stevens, Michel Foucault* (Hemel Hempstead: Harvester-Wheatsheaf, 1988).

3. See Marcy Darnovsky, L.A. Kauffman and Billy Robinson, 'Warring Stories: reading and contesting the New World Order', *Socialist Review* (San Francisco), Vol. XXI, No 1 (January-March 1991), pp. 11-26; pp. 20-21.

4. Terry Eagleton, *Ideology: an introduction* (London: Verso, 1991).

5. *Ibid*, p. 202.

6. *Ibid*, p. 38.

7. Some of the most useful work in this area over the past decade has been

contained in a series of volumes published by the Glasgow University Media Group. See especially *War and Peace News* (Milton Keynes: Open University Press, 1975). A further volume on the Gulf War and its aftermath is currently under preparation.

8. See Jürgen Habermas, *Communication and the Evolution of Society* (London: Heinemann, 1979) and *The Theory of Communicative Action*, 2 vols. (Boston: Beacon Press, 1984 and 1989).

9. See Habermas, *Knowledge and Human Interests* (London: Heinemann, 1972).

10. Eagleton, *Ideology: an introduction (op cit)*, p. 130.

11. Francis Fukuyama, 'The End of History', *The National Interest* (Summer 1989). See also Jonathan Steele, Edward Mortimer and Gareth Stedman Jones, 'The End of History?' (a discussion of Fukuyama's essay), *Marxism Today*, November 1989, pp. 26-33.

12. See also Rorty, *Objectivity, Relativism, and Truth* and *Essays on Heidegger and Others* (Cambridge: Cambridge University Press, 1991).

13. Eagleton, *Ideology: an introduction (op cit)*, p. 11.

14. Kevin Robins, 'The Mirror of Unreason', *Marxism Today*. March 1991, pp. 42-4; p. 43.

15. Edward Said, *Orientalism* (New York: Pantheon, 1978) and *Covering Islam* (New York: Pantheon, 1981).

16. Robins, 'The Mirror of Unreason' *(op cit)*, p. 43.

17. See Hans-Georg Gadamer, *Truth and Method* (London: Sheed and Ward, 1975) and *Philosophical Hermeneutics* (Berkeley and Los Angeles: University of California Press, 1977).

18. Habermas, 'Summation and Response', cited in David Held, *Introduction to Critical Theory: Horkheimer to Habermas* (London: Hutchinson, 1980), p. 314.

19. *Ibid*, p. 315.

20. See the discussion of Kant's essay by Habermas, 'Taking Aim at the Heart of the Present', in David Couzens Hoy (ed), *Foucault: a critical reader* (Oxford: Basil Blackwell, 1986), pp. 103-8; also Hubert L. Dreyfus and Paul Rabinow, 'What Is Maturity? Habermas and Foucault on "What Is Enlightenment?" ', *ibid*, pp. 109-121.

21. Habermas, *The Philosophical Discourse of Modernity: twelve lectures* (Cambridge: Polity Press, 1987).

22. Alasdair MacIntyre, *Against the Self-Images of the Age* (London: Duckworth, 1971), p. 247.

23. Cited by Eagleton in *Ideology: an introduction (op cit)*, p. ix.

24. See G.W.F. Hegel, *Philosophy of Right* (London: Oxford University Press, 1952).

25. See Hilary Putnam, *Realism and Reason* (Cambridge: Cambridge University Press, 1983), p. 237; also Norris, *The Contest of Faculties* (London:

Methuen, 1985), pp. 195-6.

26. Mark Poster (ed), *Baudrillard: selected writings* (Cambridge: Polity Press, 1988), p. 172.

27. See Fredric Jameson, *Postmodernism, or, the Cultural Logic of Late Capitalism* (London: Verso, 1991).

28. Eagleton, *Ideology: an introduction (op cit)*, p. 39.

29. *Ibid*, p. 39.

30. Fish, *Doing What Comes Naturally* (Oxford: Clarendon Press, 1989), p. 380.

31. *Ibid*, p. 14.

32. *Ibid*, p. 245.

33. For further discussion of this topic, see Peter Muntz, *Our Knowledge of the Growth of Knowledge* (London: Routledge and Kegan Paul, 1985).

34. See for instance the essays by Fish and others collected in W.J.T. Mitchell (ed), *Against Theory: literary theory and the new pragmatism* (Chicago: University of Chicago Press, 1985).

35. See especially Rorty, 'The Priority of Democracy to Philosophy', 'Postmodernist Bourgeois Liberalism' and 'Cosmopolitanism Without Emancipation: a response to Jean-Francois Lyotard', in *Objectivity, Relativism, and Truth* (Cambridge: Cambridge University Press, 1991), pp. 175-96, 197-202 and 211-222. For some pointedly relevant discussion of these issues in the present context of argument, see Peter Gowan, 'The Gulf War, Iraq and Western Liberalism', *New Left Review* No. 187 (May/June 1991), pp. 29-70.

36. Rorty, *Contingency, Irony, and Solidarity (op cit)*, p. 29.

37. Francis Fukuyama, 'Changed Days for Ruritania's Dictator', *The Guardian*, 8 April 1991, p. 19.

38. For some of the relevant background history, see Efraim Karsh (ed), *The Iran-Iraq War: impact and implications* (London: Macmillan, 1989) and Dilip Hiro, *The Longest War* (London: Grafton Books, 1989); also Daniel Yergin, *The Prize: the epic quest for oil, money and power* (New York: Simon and Schuster, 1991).

39. Among the best-informed commentators before, during and after the Gulf War period were Edward Pearce and John Pilger, writing for *The Guardian* and the *New Statesman* respectively. See also Edward Greer, 'The Hidden History of the Gulf War', *Monthly Review* (New York), Vol. 43, No. 1 (May 1991), pp. 1-14 and Christopher Hitchens, 'Realpolitik in the Gulf', *New Left Review*, No 186 (March/April 1991), pp. 89-101. More generally, there is much information to be gleaned from John Simpson, *From the House of War: John Simpson in the Gulf* (London: Arrow Books, 1991) and J. Bullough and H. Morris, *Saddam's War* (London: Faber, 1991).

40. See Rorty, *Consequences of Pragmatism* (Minneapolis: University of Minnesota Press, 1982).

7 Consensus Reality and Manufactured Truth

1. Fredric Jameson, *Postmodernism, or, the Cultural Logic of Late Capitalism* (London: Verso, 1991), pp. 298-9.
2. *Ibid*, pp. 297-8.
3. *Ibid*, p. 46.
4. Habermas, *The Philosophical Discourse of Modernity* (Cambridge: Polity Press, 1987).
5. See particularly Foucault *Language, Counter-Memory, Practice* (Oxford: Basil Blackwell, 1977).
6. Michael Walzer, 'The Politics of Michel Foucault', in David Couzens Hoy (ed), *Foucault: a critical reader* (Oxford: Blackwell, 1986), pp. 51-68; also Charles Taylor, 'Foucault on Freedom and Truth', *ibid*, pp. 69-102 and Barry Smart, 'The Politics of Truth and the Problem of Hegemony', *ibid*, pp. 157-74.
7. See for instance John Pilger, 'Alternative Reality: why don't we hear about what is happening in the Gulf?', *New Statesman*, 29 May 1991, pp. 8-9.
8. Habermas, *Moral Consciousness and Communicative Action* (Cambridge: Polity Press, 1990), p. 137.
9. Walter Benjamin, 'The Work of Art in the Age of Mechanical Reproduction', in Hannah Arendt (ed) *Illuminations*, (London: Fontana, 1970), pp. 219-53; p. 244.
10. See especially the essays collected in Paul de Man, *The Rhetoric of Romanticism* (New York: Columbia University Press, 1984) and *The Resistance to Theory* (Minneapolis: University of Minnesota Pres, 1986).
11. Norris, *Derrida* (London: Fontana, 1987), *Deconstruction and the Interests of Theory* (London: Pinter Publishers, 1988) and *What's Wrong with Postmodernism* (Hemel Hempstead: Harvester-Wheatsheaf and Baltimore: Johns Hopkins University Press, 1990).
12. See for instance Peter de Bolla, *The Discourse of the Sublime: readings in history, aesthetics and the subject* (Oxford: Basil Blackwell, 1989); Meaghan Morris, *The Pirate's Fiancée: feminism, reading, postmodernism* (London: Verso, 1988); Slavoj Zizek, *The Sublime Object of Ideology* (London: Verso, 1989).
13. Jean-Francois Lyotard, *The Differend: phrases in dispute* (Minneapolis: University of Minnesota Press, 1988), p. 180.
14. Kant, *Critique of Judgement* (London: Oxford University Press, repr. 1978); also Kant, *Political Writings*, Hans Reiss (ed) (Cambridge: Cambridge University Press, 1973) and *On History*, L.W. Beck (ed) (Indianapolis: Bobbs-Merrill, 1963).
15. Lyotard, *The Differend (op cit)*, p. 169.
16. *Ibid*, p. 168.
17. *Ibid*, pp. 148-9.

18. See Max Horkheimer and Theodor W. Adorno, *Dialectic of Enlightenment* (London: Verso, 1979).

19. Norman Cohn, *The Pursuit of the Millennium: revolutionary millennarians and mystical anarchists of the middle ages* (London: Paladin, 1970).

20. Lyotard, *The Differend (op cit)*, p. 166.

21. For recent philosophical defences of this position from a range of argumentative viewpoints, see Roy Bhaskar, *Reclaiming Reality: a critical introduction to contemporary philosophy* (London: Verso: 1989); Bhaskar, *Philosophy and the Idea of Freedom* (Oxford: Basil Blackwell, 1991): Andrew Collier, *Scientific Realism and Socialist Thought* (Hemel Hempstead: Harvester-Wheatsheaf, 1989); Michael Devitt, *Realism and Truth* (Oxford: Basil Blackwell, 1984); Rom Harré, *Varieties of Realism: a rationale for the natural sciences* (Oxford: Blackwell, 1986); Hilary Putnam, *Representation and Reality* (Cambridge, Mass.: Harvard University Press, 1988); Sean Sayers, *Reality and Reason* (Oxford: Blackwell, 1985); Roger Trigg, *Reality at Risk: a defence of realism in philosophy and the sciences* (Brighton: Harvester, 1980); J.J.C. Smart, *Philosophy and Scientific Realism* (London: Routledge and Kegan Paul, 1963); Gerald Vision, *Modern Anti-Realism and Manufactured Truth* (London: Routledge, 1988); and Crispin Wright, *Realism, Meaning and Truth* (Oxford: Blackwell, 1987).

22. Thomas Nagel, *The View From Nowhere* (New York and London: Oxford University Press, 1986), p. 91.

23. *Ibid*, p. 108.

24. *Ibid*, p. 109.

25. Lyotard, *The Differend (op cit)*, p. 169.

26. Andrew Whitley, 'Kuwait: the last forty-eight hours', *New York Review of Books*, 30 May 1991, pp. 17-18.

27. *Ibid*, p. 17.

28. *Ibid*, p. 18.

29. For a recent challenge to the orthodox view on this and other points of interpretive detail, see Galen Strawson, *The Secret Connexion: causation, realism and David Hume* (Oxford: Clarendon Press, 1989).

30. This question has of course been much discussed by philosophers and ethical theorists, among them Sabina Lovibond, *Realism and Imagination in Ethics* (Oxford: Basil Blackwell, 1983).

31. For some cogent arguments to this effect, see Trevor Pateman, *Language, Truth and Politics* (Lewes, Sussex: Jean Stroud Publications, 1980).

32. See for instance J.J.C. Smart, *Ethics, Persuasion and Truth* (London: Routledge and Kegan Paul, 1984).

33. Peter Sloterdijk, *Critique of Cynical Reason* (London: Verso, 1988), pp. 5-6.

34. Christopher Hitchens, 'Realpolitik in the Gulf', *New Left Review*, No.

186 (March/April 1991), pp. 89-101; also Jon Wiener, 'Domestic Political Incentives for the Gulf War', *New Left Review*, No. 187 (May/June 1991), pp. 72-8 and R. Woodward, *The Commanders* (New York: Simon and Schuster, 1991).

35. *Ibid*, p. 92.
36. See for instance Rorty's 'naturalized' (i.e. neo-pragmatist) reading of Hegel, developed at various points in *Consequences of Pragmatism (op cit)*. The relevant passages can best be tracked down via the index.
37. Eagleton, *Ideology: an introduction* (London: Verso, 1991), p. 223-4.
38. Douglas Kellner, *Jean Baudrillard: from Marxism to postmodernism and beyond* (Cambridge: Polity Press, 1989), p. 113.

Postscript

1. Baudrillard, 'La guerre du Golfe n'a pas eu lieu', *Liberation*, 29 March 1991.
2. *Ibid* (my translation).
3. Baudrillard, *Fatal Strategies* (London: Pluto Press, 1989).
4. Baudrillard, 'Le guerre du golfe n'a pas eu lieu' (*op cit*).

INDEX

new formations

A multi-disciplinary journal reflecting and engendering debates in contemporary cultural theory, **New Formations** explores issues in the critical analysis of cultural forms across the visual and literary spectrum.

'New Formations *is an indispensable source of information about new thinking on a wide range of cultural issues.'* Robert Hewison

'New Formations *is essential reading for those who want to understand politics in the light of the most important trends of contemporary theory.'* Chantal Mouffe

COMPETING GLANCES
NUMBER 16, SPRING 1992

A special issue of **New Formations** featuring a critical reappraisal of the work of the late Robert Mapplethorpe, celebrated and controversial photographer. Jane Gaines and Kobena Mercer reassess Mapplethorpe, questioning the previous criticisms that he represented black people as the exotic Other, and discussing how this argument lines up with attacks from the New Rights and the 'moral majority'. They come around to the view that the pictures can be viewed from the opposite angle – that they deconstruct certain forms of racism and racist stereotyping.

   This issue also includes essays on modernism and masculinity, Christa Wolf, rap music, Jacques Derrida, and techno-orientalism.

Contributors: Warren Buckland, Graham Dawson, Simon Frith, Jane Gaines, Sandra Kemp, Jean Jacques Lecercle, Kobena Mercer, David Morley, Kevin Robins, Daglind Sonolet, Gregory Stephens and Elizabeth Wilson.

ISBN 0 85315 757 X   192pp   April 1992   Single issue price **£12.99**

Subscriptions: UK – Institutions £45, Individuals £28
                        North America – Institutions $74, Individuals $50
                        Rest of World – Institutions £46, Individuals £30

Send cheque of money order to:
Lawrence & Wishart, 144a Old South Lambeth Road, London SW8 1XX.
Back Issues available price £12.99.

The Critical Image
Essays on Contemporary Photography
Edited by Carol Squiers

The Critical Image is an exciting collection of essays on the multitudinous uses and abuses of photography in contemporary cultural life. Photographs are all around us – in newspapers and magazines, on advertising hoardings and postcards, as well as in galleries – yet we take them for granted. We rarely examine how they shape our perceptions, manipulate our feelings and influence our ideas. In this collection, celebrated theorists join forces with famous practitioners to cover the whole range of photography's roles: from digital modification in photojournalism to surrealism, and from 'green' advertising to pornography. This is the most challenging exploration of the subject since Susan Sontag's *On Photography*.

'recent photographic criticism at its best'
Alan Trachtenberg

'a valuable contribution to contemporary debate on the role of theory' Homi Bhabha

Contributors: Victor Burgin, Rosalyn Deutsche, Abigail Solomon-Godeau, Andy Grundberg, Silvia Kolbowski, Rosalind Krauss, Joanne Lukitsh, Christian Metz, Kathy Myers, Griselda Pollock, Fred Ritchin, Carol Squiers, John Tagg, Carole Vance and Simon Watney.

ISBN 0 85315 737 5   Paperback **£12.99**   240pp   38 b/w photos